CONTESTED AND DANGEROUS SEAS

CONTESTED AND DANGEROUS SEAS

North Atlantic Fishermen, Their Wives, Unions, and the Politics of Exclusion

COLIN J. DAVIS

University of Massachusetts Press
Amherst and Boston

Printed in the United States of America

ISBN 978-1-62534-436-6 (paper); 435-9 (hardcover)

Designed by Sally Nichols
Set in Arno Pro
Printed and bound by Maple Press, Inc.

Cover design by Frank Gutbrod
Cover photo: *The Headscarf Revolutionaries led by Lillian Bilocca,* August 1968. Courtesy of *Hull Daily Mail.*

Library of Congress Cataloging-in-Publication Data

Names: Davis, Colin J. (Colin John), 1954– author.
Title: Contested and dangerous seas : north Atlantic fishermen, their wives, unions, and the politics of exclusion / Colin J. Davis.
Identifiers: LCCN 2019019866 | ISBN 9781625344359 (hardcover) | ISBN 9781625344366 (paper) | ISBN 9781613766866 (ebook) | ISBN 9781613766873 (ebook)
Subjects: LCSH: Big game fishing—Atlantic Ocean—History—20th century. | Big game fishing—Atlantic Ocean—History—21st century.
Classification: LCC SH457.5 .D38 2019 | DDC 799.1609163—dc23
LC record available at https://lccn.loc.gov/2019019866

British Library Cataloguing-in-Publication Data
A catalog record for this book is available from the British Library

CONTENTS

PREFACE

As a young boy I regularly visited my grandparents in the fishing port of Lowestoft in the east of England. I lived only ten miles away but the bus or train trip was always an adventure. When arriving in Lowestoft, a visitor was always hit with the strong smell of fish. The town was a major fishing port and shipbuilding center. I grew up in the world of fish, constantly aware of the danger that men faced and of the wives and children who waited for their return; indeed, my grandmother had lost two husbands to the sea.

Because historians pride themselves on their objectivity, for many years I steered away from a focus on the larger issues of this industry I knew so well personally. But during a visiting professorship at Georgetown University as I was searching at the Library of Congress for a topic for a book-length study, I kept veering toward the sea. Since then, the historian Sir George Clark's reassurance that, "there is no 'objective' historical truth" has sustained me in my quest to further understand North Atlantic fishermen, their wives, and their unions. At the same time, as I delved into this world, I began to see that details of their history were generally missing from the record. The situation reminded me of the extraordinary words of another prominent historian, Lytton Strachey: "ignorance is the first requisite of the historian."[1] Thus to a certain extent, my initial research was an attempt to address the insightful statements of Clark and Strachey.

As I read through the congressional records of the 1960s and 1970s, I could see that New England fishermen and their wives had a vital say in the status of their industry, and clearly they believed that their fisheries were in dire need of protection from the modern integrated approaches of foreign fishing fleets. In their testimony they urged political leaders to stop those fleets from pillaging fish. Their basic argument was that industrial methods were destroying the fisheries.

When I looked across the Atlantic Ocean toward Britain I discovered the opposite phenomenon. British fishermen were demanding open access to Atlantic waters. Unlike their New England counterparts, they still regarded the ocean as a "commons"—one that was open to all who wanted to fish. What explained these different attitudes? Why did the New Englanders want exclusion? What drove the British to emphasize inclusion? More importantly, how did these opposing stances play out in national and international politics?

I am deeply grateful to the institutions and people on both sides of the Atlantic who helped me begin to answer such questions. On the United States side, the staff at the Library of Congress was particularly helpful as I began investigating the working and household worlds of New England fishermen. Thanks also to the librarians at the Gloucester Lyceum and Sawyer Free Library and to those in the historical collections of the New Bedford Public Library. I am grateful to the archivists at the Arthur and Elizabeth Schlesinger Library at Harvard University, home to the papers of the Gloucester Fishermen's Wives Association. The Schlesinger Library also provided critical funding support for my research trips and for the time spent collecting oral histories of Gloucester women. I offer special thanks to those Gloucester women, especially Angela Sanfilippo, who educated me about the political activism of the Gloucester Fishermen's Wives Association. Thanks also to Simone Early and Mac Bell for graciously hosting my family and me during our visit to the city. I am grateful to the special collections staff at the Harvard Law School Library, where I examined the papers of Henry Wise, the legal counsel for the Atlantic Fishermen's Union. The staff at the G. W. Blunt White Library at the Mystic Seaport Museum provided critical access to the oral histories of fishermen and their wives. Thanks also to the University of Alabama at Birmingham, which provided research funding. I am particularly grateful to that university's librarian, Brooke Becker.

Many colleagues on the American side of the pond were generous with their time and expertise. Among the most important was Matt

McKenzie, whom I first met at a conference of the North Atlantic Fisheries History Association in Bergen, Norway. His thoughtful and insightful comments on my conference papers and this book have been invaluable. I am equally grateful to my friend Joe McCartin who read the entire manuscript. Thanks also go to Ingo Heidbrink, an organizer of the North Atlantic Fisheries History Association, who paved the way for me to introduce myself to European and American fishery historians.

On the European side, I thank my colleagues at the Maritime Historical Studies Center at the University of Hull. David Starkey is a giant in maritime history but has also been a welcoming ally. He graciously gave me office space at the center, where I was able to conduct interviews with fishermen's wives and focus on other related research. Thanks to Robb Robinson for his incredible tour of Hull, particularly the Hessle Road area. Thanks also go to Richard Gorski and Paul Wilcox at the Maritime Historical Studies Center.

I am enormously grateful to the staff at the National Archives in London. The voluminous material available about the fishing life was daunting, but your quiet confidence did much to smooth my way. Thanks also to the Modern Records Center at the University of Warwick, which holds the trade union records of the fishermen's section of the Transport and General Workers' Union. I send a special thanks to Astrid Ogilvie and Guðni Jóhannesson for helping me present my work to maritime historians at the University of Iceland in Reykjavík.

A number of graduate students contributed research to this project or read chapters with a critical eye. I'm especially grateful to Joshua Hodge, Forrest McDonald, Stephanie Womack, and Zoe Zaslawsky. For their support and encouragement over the years, I thank Eric Arnesen, Robert Cassanelo, Melvyn Dubofsky, David Brundage, Julie Greene, Leon Fink, Alice Kessler-Harris, Shelton Stromquist, and the late Ray Mohl. Thanks also to my colleagues, John Van Sant and Brian Steele, who read portions of the manuscript; and thanks to Alisa Dick for her help with formatting and other critical issues. Thanks to the anonymous readers at the University of Massachusetts Press. Their suggested changes were at times uncomfortable but never unwarranted. Thanks also to Matt Becker and Dawn Potter at the press. Finally, a big thanks to my family for providing all the thrills and spills of domestic life.

CONTESTED AND DANGEROUS SEAS

INTRODUCTION

On a fishing trip to the north coast of Russia during the 1950s, the writer Hugh Popham noted: "The ship shudders as the first big sea buffets her. . . . She recovers, her bows buoyant and lifting, up the long slopes that intercept the horizon; pause, tilt, fall away in a sharp downward arc, then climb again, shaking off the smother of white water. . . . And on the bridge, the man at the wheel watches each wave like an enemy, nursing her up to meet it, warding every blow. In an hour the ship is fighting for her life."[1]

Every fishing boat that has sailed in the open Atlantic Ocean, hundreds of miles from land, has experienced such conditions. The Atlantic Ocean is a tempestuous place. Huge waves and swells, freezing rain and snow, gale force winds all contributed to the dangerous job of fishing. Yet from the late 1950s to the early 1970s, another danger was arising in the working worlds of New England and British fishermen. These trawlermen, as some were called, were undergoing a painful transition, creating new fights for them. Fear of foreign competition was rampant, and workers were increasingly dissatisfied with shipboard safety. For those, like the British, who fished throughout the Atlantic, access to prime fishing grounds was paramount to their survival. But the North Atlantic was rapidly becoming a contested space with increasing competition for common fish stocks. Beginning in the 1950s, on a daily basis fishing vessels from Europe, Japan, the Soviet Union, Canada, and the United States began to share the same work spaces. This increased international competition for fish, and coupled with improvement in fishing technologies, it created new stresses for Atlantic fisheries, threatening the sustainability of their stocks. Amid these rapid developments, both New England and British fishermen experienced dramatic changes in their work. New Englanders responded by seeking to protect their traditional fisheries, calling for exclusion of foreign fishing fleets off the New England coast. The British, in contrast, sought to maintain the right to fish anywhere throughout the Atlantic Ocean, and thus called for inclusion. This book seeks to understand the reasons for these differing strategies of exclusion and inclusion.

Despite their shared occupational identities, the economic and political interests could at times diverge. For New England fishermen, foreign competition highlighted their already weakened position. By 1960 their fishing fleet had aged: with 50 percent of their largest fishing boats, known as trawlers, more than twenty years old. As modern foreign fishing fleets began to exploit haddock and cod off the coast, the local fishermen found themselves outnumbered and outmuscled as these larger vessels could easily outfish their smaller fishing boats. Correspondingly, fish stocks began to face relentless pressure as foreign fleets scooped more and more fish from the banks surrounding the coastline. New England fishermen, along with their familial allies and union officials, looked to political authorities to drive foreign fleets out of their traditional fishing areas and demand that the federal government extend the territorial limit from a mere three miles to two hundred miles. For this group, then, extending the limit and thereby excluding foreign fishing boats was seen as the solution to their problems.

The British, on the other hand, possessed one of the world's largest fishing fleets and sought to maintain access throughout the North Atlantic. But other maritime nations challenged this open access by demanding that British fishermen be excluded from fishing in parts of the region. Iceland became the catalyst for this movement when it tried to extend its fishing limits, starting in 1958 and again in 1972–73, and in 1975–76. In a series of what became known as "cod wars" between Britain and Iceland, British fishermen discovered that even with naval support, they could not necessarily hold their ground. While they wanted open access to the fish of the seas (inclusion), other nations were looking to protect their fish stocks (exclusion). The international momentum was thus tipping toward protecting declining fish stocks from foreign fleets. Compounding these problems for the British fishermen was a series of disasters at sea during the 1960s when fishing boats were lost with all hands. The dramatic loss of trawlers highlighted the precarious nature of fishing when boats were hundreds and thousands of miles from their home ports. Fishing had, of course, always been fraught with peril, but now fishermen at this time began to protest their working conditions. Supported by their familial allies and trade unions, British fishermen demanded a change in how fishing was undertaken during bad weather and insisted that safety measures should be seriously applied and adopted.

On both sides of the Atlantic, the fishermen looked to their respective governments for solutions. As this book will detail, while British fishermen received government support to help in the creation of more inclusionary policies, that assistance was not always successful. In the New England case, the federal government was initially reluctant to get involved in protecting domestic fisheries from foreign incursion and exploitation, thus ensuring years of uncertainty for the fishermen and their supporters who wanted to see exclusionary policies implemented. In their efforts both British and New England fishermen were bolstered by trade union and familial supporters back on shore. How and why the New England fishermen and their familial supporters were ultimately successful in fulfilling their demands reflects the power of movement culture in influencing government behavior.

A study of transatlantic fishermen and their union organizations and familial allies fills a void in the historical literature. For the most part, histories of fishing in the northwestern region of the Atlantic are dominated by political, ecological and environmental studies.[2] These approaches focus on how human impact affects fisheries, but they tend to ignore the men who sustained a living catching fish. While there is a wealth of studies of maritime communities, examination of the skill of fishing and the role of fishermen as political actors are generally missing from these works.[3] There are some earlier studies that tried to address the problems fishermen experienced during the 1970s when fishing intensified beyond the ability of fish stocks to sustain their numbers, but these studies were written at the height of the fishing crises. Thus, while useful in detailing the emerging environmental destruction of New England fisheries, they lacked historical analysis. Additionally, in most studies the focus is on political leaders and marine scientists rather than the fishermen.[4] By focusing on the actions and voices of the fishermen and their supporters, this book details the crucial roles these actors played in how the issues were framed and fought, and ultimately won or lost.

Another key issue covered particularly in British studies is how fisheries developed over time.[5] There is also a smaller literature that addresses issues of community and migration, and most of these studies have been heavily influenced by Jeremy Tunstall's groundbreaking work on the fishing industry in Hull. In *The Fishermen* Tunstall highlights an industry dominated by boat owners, whose mindset was one of almost total control over their fishing crews. These overbearing owners would not countenance any push back from fishing crews, leaving in their wake a dejected and fractured work force that was left foundering in the face of this intransigence.[6] Most other studies that examine work lives onboard fishing boats and trawlers fall short of a sustained historical analysis.[7] Moreover, in most examinations of work routines onboard British fishing boats, trade union action and affiliation are generally ignored. This lack of scholarly focus on unions is replicated in work on fishermen in the United States. Indeed, only in Canada have historians examined trade union action and strikes by fishermen.[8] This book, however, documents and explains trade union development for both New England and British fishers.

Increasingly, American historians are moving away from nation-centered history to one that encompasses a comparative view. Spurred by the theoretical debates of historians such as Ian Tyrrell, David Thelen, and Thomas Bender, comparative (sometimes known as transnational history) is enjoying a resurgence.[9] Of course, the turn toward comparative history has a long pedigree. Theda Skocpol and George Frederickson have long furnished historians with a template for the comparative approach.[10] In particular, American and British historians of Atlantic history have embraced the comparative turn, led by studies of slavery in the New World by scholars such as Paul Gilroy that have tracked the movement of Africans to the New World and their impact on American culture and economies.[11]

Labor historians, however, for the most part, have not embraced the comparative approach, although there are some pioneers. Notably, Marcus Rediker (in his work on the Atlantic world of seafarers and pirates), Leon Fink, and Shelton Stromquist have driven the approach forward. My research on New York City and London dockworkers also attempted to address this issue of connectedness, by demonstrating that while these dockworkers rebelled against rigid and corrupt union hierarchies, their proposed remedies were markedly different. Such differences highlight how union cultures and government authorities can play critical roles in job security and union strength.[12] This comparative study of British and American fishermen is, in part, intended as a template for further comparative studies of labor. As the historical profession shifts toward an appreciation of global history, labor history needs to join the movement.

To explicate the challenges that fishermen in New England and Britain faced during this period of occupational change, I will profile who they were, their familial origins, and their work lives. I will examine their ages and accident records to not only illuminate an aging workforce, but also to highlight their unpredictable and hazardous job duties. Each group confronted obstacles to their livelihoods, and how they coped with these barriers says much about the strength and vitality of their respective trade unions. Furthermore, because of the casual nature of the work, trade union agitation was difficult but not inconsequential. I will therefore detail the development and stature of the New England and British fishing trade unions to understand their power to influence economics and politics. Importantly, the actions and development trajectories of these unions underline the difficulties in unifying a workforce that was fluid and at times apathetic to organizational efforts.

Like the unions, women were also vital to the work lives of the fishermen. With their men away for weeks at a time wives, daughters, sisters, and sweethearts routinely had to step into the vacuum and became the heads of the family. Thus, women, and particularly the wives, held a unique position in the maritime household, one that would often increase in power. In the political realm, however, their role was less clear. They were welcomed as allies only at certain junctures, when either the fishermen agreed to their political agency or when they occasionally grasped it themselves. From the late 1950s through the early 1970s, there were numerous junctures in which women allied with New England and British fishermen to agitate for political solutions to the economic hardships and the grievous threats of the fishing industry.

As with research of family and community structures, anthropologists and sociologists tend to dominate the study of gender in the fishing industry. Canadian scholars have led the way in studying the multiple roles that fishermen's wives have played in Northwestern Atlantic communities.[13] Some studies go beyond examining women solely within the household, investigating how and why at certain moments they stepped out of their conventional roles as wives and mothers.[14] Additionally, there is also abundant research on European fishermen's wives, but like their Canadian and American counterparts, most of these studies focus on women as economic partners who serve as temporary heads of the family during the episodic absences of their husbands.[15] This book goes beyond the narrative of familial support in the home, to one that encompasses a detailed examination of fishermen's wives as political actors at the national level.

Also rarely studied are the roles of fishermen as guardians or stewards of the sea. Generally, they and their supporters are seen as exploiters of the sea. They spend their working lives hunting for fish for profit and, at times, are in direct conflict with fishery scientists who are urging for stricter controls of equipment and the installation of fish quotas. In the New England case, though, the fishermen and their allies were confronted with plummeting fish stocks because of foreign competition. Being dependent on this renewable but exhaustible resource, they began to act as stewards to protect the threatened fisheries.[16] In the process, as this study shows, they also began to perceive themselves as guardians of these resources. How and why they responded in this way says much about a workforce with a vested interest in maintaining the health of the resource on which it depends.[17]

In both the New England and British cases, fishermen, along with their trade unions and familial allies, attempted to influence the political and economic discussions in their favor. Rather than being passive bystanders, they confronted their precarious positions by actively pushing for protections of their jobs and the fish they endeavored to capture. The point of this study is to bring these people from the shallows to the surface of history and highlight how they were determined actors who in many ways succeeded in making governments respond to their demands. This study thus challenges established narratives that posit scientists, politicians, and government officials as the leaders in confronting the increased exploitation of North Atlantic fish stocks. It does so by placing fishermen and their familial and union supporters at the center of this unfolding story.

The study begins by identifying the fish and the men who hunted them. Chapters 1 and 2 highlight the Atlantic workforces of the British and New England fishermen and how their respective fishing industries were undergoing enormous changes. Chapter 3 examines the trade union power these men exercised. What is clear is that each workforce had a unique trade union trajectory, framed by government and employer support. Chapter 4 focuses on the distinct perils of fishing in the North Atlantic, particularly for the British, and shows how the horrifying loss of three British trawlers in 1968 prompted fishermen's wives to protest the poor safety records of fishing boats. During this period, British fishermen also had to contend with other Atlantic nations that were beginning to protect their fisheries by extending their territorial limits. Chapter 5 explores how Iceland became a key player in this theater of exclusion and conflict on the high seas. Chapters 6 and 7 return to the western Atlantic, where New England fishermen and their wives were attempting to rid their traditional fishing grounds of foreign fishing fleets. This familial alliance became a potent weapon in the battle to convince the U.S. government to declare a two-hundred-mile territorial limit. Like Iceland, the American government was forced to confront the increased depletion of fish stocks by excluding foreign fishing boats. Chapter 8 examines the final attempt by the British to maintain a fishing presence off the coast of Iceland, which culminated in another cod war. Eventually, the British were forced to admit defeat and accept the notion of national sovereignty over fish stocks.

CHAPTER 1

OF FISH AND MEN

During the 1960s the North Atlantic fisheries were experiencing rapid change. For New England fishermen, foreign competition highlighted their already weakened position. Fifty percent of the large trawlers fishing out of New England ports were more than twenty years old, and their numbers had been steadily declining from 117 in 1947 to 57 in 1968, leading to a concomitant decline in fish landings.[1] Moreover, the age of the fleet matched the age of its workforce; fewer younger men were choosing to work on the sea.

On the other side of the Atlantic, the British fishing workforce was also aging, and those who did enter the industry were often migratory workers not necessarily connected to the industry by familial relations. As my profiles show, it is clear that both British and New England workers confronted obstacles to their livelihoods, and each had to come to terms with different threats to their existence.

The New England fishermen who were working at sea during these years saw foreign fishing fleets as a distinct threat. Yet for centuries they had shared the bounty of the outer banks with other nations. As early as the sixteenth century, French and Portuguese boats were fishing on the Grand Banks off the Newfoundland coast. By the seventeenth century, settlers were fishing in the coastal waters, mostly by hand-lining, a simple method that involved attaching baited hooks to lines dropped into the ocean. Men ships or in dories (two-person rowing boats) then gathered up the lines with (they hoped) their attached fish. By the 1890s, schooners were fishing on the Georges and Browns Banks.[2]

For cod (*Gadus morhua*), which are found throughout the North Atlantic, these banks, or shoals, are perfect breeding and feeding grounds. For years cod was the fishing industry's principal quarry, and their huge numbers and relatively large size made them a prize catch. Some were giants, such as a cod caught off the Massachusetts coast in 1895, which weighed as much as 211 pounds and were more than six feet long. Even by the 1960s, large cod from "30–40 inches long and weighing 10 to 25 pounds each [were] caught each year." Another advantage was that cod could be salted easily for the market. Haddock, on the other hand, did not salt well, as fishery official Lorenzo Sabine noted in 1853: "The haddock, when fresh, suits the taste of some; but when dried, it is without reputation even in the hut of the [poorest man], who is doomed to be its principal consumer."[3]

Cod are groundfish (that is, they feed on the sea floor) and generally eat small shellfish animals such as clams, mussels, and crabs. They are also aggressive hunters of smaller finned fish and squid. There is no one particular season for catching cod, but the industry does slow down in December. At that time females release up to nine million eggs each, and fishermen have observed that the surface of the water turns a milky color during this period.[4]

Various technological innovations have had a dramatic impact on the fishing catch. For instance, the availability of large-scale icemaking beginning in the 1890s changed the haddock industry. Now fishermen at sea could catch and dress (gut) the haddock, chill them in ice, and sell them fresh in the local port. Around the same time filleting facilities were being established in New England ports, such as Boston and Gloucester, and by the 1920s wholesalers were distributing haddock to retailers as fillets.[5]

Just as important as icemaking were changes in how fish were caught. Because long-lining was a slow and laborious process, the advent of the beam trawl in the late nineteenth century changed everything. The beam trawl was basically an enclosed net with a wide mouth held open with a long wooden beam. Dragged behind a steam vessel, it collected fish along the bottom of the banks. A problem, however, was that fishermen using the new method caught large numbers of unwanted fish, particularly dogfish, which they had to toss overboard. In fact, the trawls could gather so many fish that the winches often could not cope with the burden, resulting in broken twine and lost catches.[6]

The arrival of the otter trawl in the early twentieth century increased ease and efficiency. In this version of the trawl, the beam is replaced by two boards known as otter doors. Fishermen release the trawl on the windward side of a dragger (small trawler) or full-sized trawler. The cod end (the rear of the net) goes into the water first, followed by the net belly. Then the trawl is let out by a series of winches and pulleys, and the skipper and the winchman (or bosun, in the British fleet) must work together to avoid snaring it in shipboard gear or in the propeller below the waterline. Once the trawl is set and the correct length is gauged, the winchman informs the skipper, who slightly increases the boat's speed, allowing the lines to tighten but not strain before proceeding full steam ahead. Engine power is key to the operation because such trawls can be extremely heavy and difficult to manage in poor weather conditions.[7]

With these new nets and trawlers, haddock (*Melanogrammus aeglefinus*) became a target for increased fishing on Georges Bank. Closely related to cod, haddock is distinguished by a black shoulder spot and black lateral line. It tends to be a smaller fish than the cod, averaging sixteen inches long and rarely reaching more than thirty-three inches. (The world record is a forty-three inch haddock caught in Icelandic waters). Like cod, haddock feed on small shellfish and are found on banks throughout the North Atlantic, but their spawning takes place in April and May. As the fertilized eggs reach the surface, they float with the current, transform into larvae, and continue to drift until they are about four months old, when they descend to the ocean floor. They become sexually active as full-sized adults, after about three years. Their market category is based on size: fish labelled scrod weigh 1.5–2.5 pounds and fish labelled haddock weigh more than 2.5 pounds.[8]

Georges Bank, located 150 miles from Boston and Gloucester, was a haven for vast numbers of groundfish. Including Browns Bank, it covers an area about 150 miles long and 62 miles wide, though at places it is only a few meters deep. The "region . . . [is a] complex inter-action of three water masses: Atlantic, Gulf of Maine and slope waters," and the resulting turbulence constantly stirs up the shallow waters, allowing cod and haddock to thrive. Much of the haddock stock on Georges

Bank originates on Browns Bank, and this interconnectedness has long ensured a steady annual supply of fish. Interestingly, some marine scientists speculate that Georges Bank cod larvae is lost off the continental shelf bordering the bank. The Georges Banks is also home to large numbers of red fish, yellowtail flounder, hake, and herring.[9]

Georges Bank's relative proximity to the Massachusetts ports made it an ideal local fishing ground. But until the advent of steam and then diesel engines, its turbulent seas made it difficult for fishermen to work. Without power, they could not maintain their bearings among the swirling waters and currents. Large schooners might manage a degree of stability, but a change in the wind or damage to the sails could have serious consequences. Eventually, however, steam and diesel engines helped fishermen solve these problems, and different Massachusetts ports began specializing in different kinds of fish. While the Boston otter trawlers (each carrying about ten men) concentrated on haddock and cod, the Gloucester and New Bedford draggers (with crews of three to five men) broadened their focus to include yellowtail flounder, whiting, ocean perch, and sea scallops.[10]

In contrast, British trawlermen sailed vast distances to catch fish. Each boat worked in one of three fleets, near, middle or distant water fleet, and each fishing port focused on particular fishing grounds. Like the New England ports, the British ones were relatively specialized depending upon what they fished for and where. As table 1.1 shows, the fleets were concentrated in certain ports. The ports of Hull, Grimsby, and, to a certain extent, Fleetwood were home to distant water fleets, which fished as far west as Newfoundland, the eastern and western coasts of Greenland, the Barents Sea, Spitsbergen Island, Bear Island, the Lofoten Islands, Norway, and Iceland. The distances they sailed were impressive. A round trip from the home port to the western coast of Iceland covered more than two thousand miles and the Newfoundland round trip was an astounding five thousand miles.[11] To cope with extreme cold and giant seas, the trawlers tended to be large (more than 140 feet long), and they were manned by twenty men, including the fishing engine crews. Each voyage lasted for two to three weeks. In contrast the near and middle fleets typically spent seven to ten days at sea, and they limited their travel to the North Sea, the Irish Sea, and the Faroe Islands. Their smaller trawlers held crews of five to ten men.[12]

Table 1.1. Distribution of Deep-Sea Trawlers, 1967

PORT		FLEET	TOTAL BOATS FROM PORT	
	Near	Middle	Distant	Total
Hull			104 (15)	104
Grimsby	22	57	60 (7)	139
Fleetwood	14	36	11 (1)	61
Lowestoft	93	15	1	109
Milford Haven	20			20
North Shields	1	4	3 (3)	8
Aberdeen	42	61	2	105
Leith	11	8		19
Other Ports	7		1 (1)	8
Total	210	181	182 (27)	573 (27)

Note: Freezer and factory vessels are in parentheses.

Source: "Table 1-Distribution of Deep-Sea Trawlers, December 31, 1967," Board of Trade 149/1, British National Archives.

British trawlermen were at sea for most of the year, and the greatest number of them worked in the North Sea, on the western coast of Scotland, and near the Faroes. In other words, the near and middle fleets took more trips than their distant fleet counterparts did, even though the distant fleet caught more fish. In addition, different voyages were linked to different seasons. Fishing in the Barents Sea and off the Norwegian coast increased during the winter months (October through April), while fishing in Icelandic waters increased during the summer months. Fishing closer to shore, particularly in the English and Bristol Channels, and the Irish Sea, remained relatively constant throughout the year. However, records show that in 1968 only a few British trawlers made the trip to Georges Bank.[13]

Fishing seasons are directly related to spawning, when fish move down from colder waters to the relative warmth of the banks; and while most cod stocks spend their lives close to their birthplace, some do migrate over long distances. Greenland cod, for example, are related to cod stocks in Iceland, which suggests that they migrate across deep open seas to spawn. Fluctuations in length and quality also vary by region, and growth patterns differ between codling from the Grand Banks, the

Barents Sea, and Norway and those from Iceland and Greenland. Temperatures also play a huge role in the size and appearance of fish and fish stocks. Thus, cod stocks that do not migrate and live in relatively constant temperatures tend to have indistinct rings around their bodies, whereas those that fluctuate between winter and summer temperatures, (such as cod from Lofoten and Iceland) invariably have more distinct rings.[14]

Fish size can vary by diet. Greenland cod, for example, feast on capelin fish, which they pursue into fjords and bays during spawning time. They also feed on small lance fish, and when caught and taken onboard often "vomit small and big lances, many of them still alive."[15] As a result of this gorging, Greenland cod can be huge. Off the coasts of Newfoundland, New England, Iceland, and in the Barents Sea, large herring stocks attract huge numbers of cod, but here and elsewhere larger cod also exhibited cannibalistic activity. In studies off the coasts of Lofoten and southwest Iceland, researchers found smaller cod in the stomachs of large cod, among them, a four-foot long Greenland cod that had recently consumed five other cod, each about sixteen inches long.[16]

As I have noted, the New England fleet was made up of smaller trawlers and draggers that traveled fewer miles in search of fish and were generally away from their home ports for shorter periods of time. Their more localized fishing ensured that these fishermen were away from their home ports for shorter periods of time. In this way, they bore some resemblance to the British near and middle distance fleets. However, the New Englanders had nothing that paralleled the British distant fleet, and this difference ensured that each nation's workforce regarded its access to fishing grounds differently. The New Englanders saw their regional fisheries as their own, while the British fleets saw fishing as an international proposition. As competition increased during the 1960s, these preexisting beliefs had a dramatic effect on the reactions of both workforces.

Understanding the era's global fishery is key to understanding this competition, for the British and New Englanders were engaged in an industry that was rapidly expanding and changing. Catch levels throughout the world were rising and stiff competition among nations was a constant. In 1968, the industry reached a new world record with a total catch of 64 million metric tons, beating the previous year's catch of 60.7 million metric tons. Table 1.2 highlights the haul by nation.

Table 1.2. Fishing Catch by Nation, 1968

COUNTRY	METRIC TONS OF FISH
Peru	10,520,000
Japan	8,669,800
Soviet Union	6,082,100
China	5,800,000
Norway	2,800,1000
United States	2,442,000
South Africa	2,000,000
Denmark	1,633,000
India	1,526,000
Spain	1,503,000
Canada	1,490,000
Chile	1,376,000
Indonesia	1,175,000
Thailand	1,088,000
United Kingdom	1,040,000
Iceland	600,700

Source: "World Fishing in 1968-Set Record," *Commercial Fisheries Review* 32 (January 1970): 65.

The total national catch did not necessarily reflect technological or market dominance. In the case of the United States, most of the tonnage was the immense anchovy catch by west coast fishermen. A better indicator was the size of trawler fleets. Large national fleets tended to have more sophisticated technology for locating large shoals of fish. Rather than fishing as single boats, they fished in groups and often spent long periods of time at sea. The Soviet Union had the largest trawler fleets (2,604), followed by Japan (2,067), Spain (1,289), and Great Britain (578).[17]

Although the 1960s-era technology was changing how fish were hunted down and captured, the job itself remained remarkably the same. Brute strength and long hours were the norm for both British and American fishermen. As one British trawlerman explained, "Once you got down there [to the fishing grounds] it was all hell for leather then. You used to start your 18 hours a day working, hauling, and shooting it was never ending."[18] By shooting, the trawlerman meant pushing the large net over the side of the boat until it began to submerge into the water. Following the net were the giant wooden otter doors that kept the front of the net open. Holding the whole apparatus together were warps, or steel cables, that connected to a winch. Earlier in this chapter, I describe the way in which a boat's engine was necessary to maintaining the correct position and operation of the net assembly. Equally important was the bosun, who was in charge of the deckhands who pulled in the catch. Once the net reached the required depth, the boat moved forward, straining the warps as they pulled the net behind the trawler. After a short period of time, and under the supervision of the bosun, the winch would raise the net close to the boat, and deckhands would reach over with their hands or hooks and begin to haul in. Once the net was brought in and hung over the deck, the bosun would release the knot at the cod-end emptying the fish onto the deck. Immediately, the crew would sort the fish by type (cod, haddock, and so on) and begin the arduous task of gutting them. Meanwhile, the net would be lowered into the sea and fishing would recommence. On deck, the gutted fish would be dropped into a washer machine and then the mate, with assistance from a deckie learner (generally a teenage boy), would begin the job of storing the fish in bays in the hold.[19]

The pattern of fishing was shooting, hauling, gutting, and storing, and each operation had its own routine. Hauling was by far the most strenuous and the most dangerous. As the huge net came alongside, the deckhands hung onto it waiting for the roll of the boat to help them pull it in. Sometimes waves washed over the men leaving them waist deep in water. These fishermen would have recognized Hugh Popham's observations in his chronicle of shipboard life off the Russian coast: "Every shift of wind and tide, all bear upon us, altering the stance and motion of the deck beneath our feet, demanding attention of nerves and muscles, stinging our skin; while every change in the unbroken arch of the sky flaunts itself before our eyes."[20] Some trawlermen wore rubber gloves, woolen mittens, or oilskins. Others wore few clothes because they interfered with their work routine. As Harry Colby, a trawlerman fishing out of the British port of Fleetwood, explained, even in the frigid Arctic waters, the work was so hard that sweating made clothing uncomfortable: "Cor, that used t' be wicked up there sometimes, workin' in the cold. An' yit the more clo's you hed on, the worse orf you were. You used t' sweat, an' then when you took you oily an' that orf you used t'gid cold. I never used 't wear hardly anything."[21]

Gutting fish was also an arduous task, though the job itself was relatively simple: a deckhand "dexterously split the fish from gills to anus, flick[ed] the two lobes of liver into baskets, wrench[ed] out the intestines, and sen[t] the evacuated corpses spinning into the washer." What made it so difficult was that it was performed for hours at a time between catches. Just as difficult, it involved working hunched over the fish in frigid wet air, constantly contending with the rolling motion of the boat as it navigated the swells. Deckie learners as young as sixteen helped with the gutting, but their youth and relative lack of strength tended to slow them down over time, which angered the older deckhands. Popham observed this situation, "On the deck he [the boy] gutted fish, getting slower and slower until he was virtually asleep on his feet. . . . This particular boy was continually cursed and shoved, and . . . during slack fishing he was unmercifully bullied."[22]

After the fish were washed, they were sent down a chute into the hold of the ship. Storing the fish correctly was critical. The key was laying the fish side by side on a bed of ice, building up the stack from the bottom toward the ceiling. But the job had to be done carefully and precisely. The holding pens had to be full, but not so full as to bruise the fish, which would destroy their market value. Because of the importance of this job, the mate would usually supervise the operation, with the assistance of a deckhand or a deckie learner. Once the hold had been filled with fish, the boat could return to its home port.[23]

While the mate, bosun, and deckhands were engaged in fishing operations, the engineer and his assistant (commonly called a fireman), were managing and maintaining the diesel engine to guarantee its smooth running. This was crucial, for if the engine failed, then the boat was at the mercy of the sea. The engine rooms on trawlers were relatively small, and engineers and firemen worked in a hot, loud environment. Burns and bruises were almost guaranteed, given the constant rolling of the boat and the heat kept the men lightly dressed. Popham remarked, that any "under-clothed" worker on the boat in the Barents Sea "was unmistakably an engineer."[24]

Engineers recalled that the odor of diesel fumes made work in the engine room very uncomfortable, and often dangerous. As one engineer explained, "you would be breathing, drinking and eating the fumes." In bad weather, the fumes were worse because the hatches had to be closed, thus trapping the foul air inside the engine room.[25] But despite these hardships, the engineers regarded their workspace as a special sanctum, and other crew members were not welcome there. Even skippers accepted that the engine room was off-limits. As one skipper explained, "How would they like it . . . if I was always down in their engine-rooms, poking my nose in their drip-feeds and gauges, eh? They wouldn't like it; and I don't like them on my bridge."[26]

Skippers and captains across the Atlantic were lonely lords of the bridge. The job was isolated, yet the skipper was solely responsible for deciding where and when to fish. Using his past experience he choose areas that tended to harbor large shoals of fish. His skill at finding fish was his chief preoccupation. He continually gauged the weather, studied the electronic fish finders, and followed actions of other trawlers and draggers, and even noted the behavior of fish-hunting sea birds as indicators of the presence of fish. After deciding to begin fishing, the skipper rarely left the bridge. Only the ship's mate could spell him on the bridge.[27]

Although the skipper's job did not involve hard physical labor, his long hours (up to twenty-two hours a day when fishing) were exhausting. He had the ultimate responsibility for a successful trip; and if he failed, an unemployed skipper or a confident mate might replace him. The stress of the job could trigger disease and heart attacks, and anxiety about the catch often pushed skippers, especially younger ones, to take risks with the boat. Pressured to fill their holds with fish, some would continue to fish even in stormy weather. As one skipper explained, "You used to know on seamanship, on common sense, and humanity, you were doing wrong, but I had to do it, all skippers did because of the pressure." Yet skippers endured this pressure alone. A deckhand recalled, "the skipper was all-powerful, almost like a God, but he was alone—on his own—always like. One bad trip and he was out of a job."[28]

Other than the mate, the only other person who could enter the bridge was the cook or galley boy. Like the engineer, the cook worked in a hot, cramped environment, where he prepared three meals a day. When fishing, he also had to be prepared to feed the deckhands in short breaks between shooting the net and gutting. Though pots and pans were secured to offset the constant motion of the boat, cooks were still often burned and scalded. And like the rest of the crew's, their working hours were long and, at times, hazardous.[29]

Whether on a British or American trawler, the job hierarchy was very similar. Deckie learners and deckhands were at the bottom of the ladder. To become a mate (second in command to the skipper) fishermen had to pass a certification test, which would make them eligible for promotion to skipper, should the opportunity arise. This hierarchy had been set in both custom and law, yet by the 1960s the industry was struggling with labor recruitment problems, and an aging workforce indicated that the future of fishing was in serious trouble.

While data for the 1960s clearly show that workforces on both sides of the Atlantic Ocean were getting older, the British fishermen were comparatively younger than New Englanders. Table 1.3 illustrates a wide variety of ages among Grimsby trawlermen.

Table 1.3. Estimated Population of Grimsby Trawlermen in 1963, by Age and Occupation

AGE GROUP	SKIPPERS/ MATES	BOSUN/ DECK HAND	ENGINEERS	COOKS
Under 20	0	19	0	37
21–30	9	32	13	19
31–40	27	22	26	13
41–50	33	15	31	13
51–60	22	8	24	11
61–70	9	4	6	7

Source: "Appendix Nine—Evidence from the British Trawlers Federation," Board of Trade 149/66, British National Archives.

As the table shows, a large percentage of the younger members of the Grimsby work-force were engaged as cooks with more than a third of them under the age of twenty. These high numbers partially reflect the fact that many apprentices and deckie learners served as galley helpers. Likewise, more than 50 percent of deck hands were under the age of thirty. Skippers, mates, and engineers were evenly split between the 31 to 40 and 41 to 50 ranges, and their relatively older ages, especially the engineers' concerned both the owners and the unions. As noted above, the engine room on a trawler could be a miserable and dangerous place to work, and by the 1960s engineers were able to find related employment in other sectors of the British economy, a shift that was severely curtailing recruitment in the fishing industry.

One reason for fishing's overall the recruitment problem was the disappearance of established or traditional communities. In 1968, Charles I. Meek of the British White Fish Authority predicted that "recruitment of fishermen would be an increasing problem in the future as the traditional fishing communities were tending to dissolve."[30] The dissolution of fishing communities appeared to be a common phenomenon. In the same year the Hull and District Council of Churches released a report titled "The Trawling Industry" that highlighted the gradual destruction of Hull's Hessle Road fishing community, which, it said, "is now being increasingly dispersed." Adding to the problem was that "skippers seldom now live[d] among the crews" but were moving out to Hull's surrounding suburbs.[31]

Owners recognized that turnover rates were increasing dramatically among some workforce segments but not others. In Grimsby, for example, the turnover rate among crew members grew from 18.7 percent to 47.6 percent in 1962–67, while skippers maintained a stable turnover rate of 14.7 percent to 16.3 percent in the same period.[32] Clearly, as employment prospects expanded in British port cities and towns, young men, whether married or single, became harder to retain. The Lowestoft Trawler Owners Association reported that the turnover rate (what it called "*wastage*") was "particularly heavy in the age-group 25–30." According to the association, such men often felt the "pressure" of "a wife who naturally wants to see her husband each day. The power of this particular pull grows strongly and appears to reach a maximum between the ages of 25 and 30." Owners discussed bonus payments to retain these men but never implemented them. Yet they continued to worry as young workers drifted away from fishing to shore jobs. Most had initially turned to fishing because they were attracted to relatively high pay, but after three years the wage differential between fishing and shore work "tended to narrow." The association noted that as a result, "shore employment becomes . . . relatively much more attractive when a deckhand reaches the age of 21, particularly if he does not see himself being promoted above deckhand."[33]

Even more problematic was young men's reluctance to join the industry in the first place. As the association reported, owners were finding it difficult to attract young men from the "middle stream of secondary schools." The association blamed the situation on a "general decline in interest in a sea-going career amongst school leavers" and, secondly, "the unattractiveness of casual employment in the fishing industry."[34] But owners also had to contend with growing sentiments against recruiting and hiring fifteen-year-olds directly from school. Industry critics decried the practice of exposing these youngsters to dangerous seas and gales, not to mention the heavy labor and long hours. In response, the British Trawlers' Federation argued if they waited until the young men were seventeen years old, as reformers recommended, "the industry would find it difficult to recruit sufficient labor." In a telling remark, the federation insisted that "few young people would join if they had to spend two years in another occupation before going to sea." Clearly, the owners had to snatch these young men while they were still at a very young and impressionable age.[35]

During this period, the New England fishing industry was also trying to cope with the problems of an aging workforce and the difficulty in recruiting young men. But as table 1.4 shows, a different pattern was emerging.

Table 1.4. Ages and Occupations (%) of Boston Trawlermen, 1966

AGE	CAPT/MATES	DECKHANDS	ENGINEERS	COOKS
Under 25	0	2	2	0
25–44	11	22	9	9
45–54	16	17	20	17
55–64	58	38	52	29
65 and Over	15	21	17	45

Source: Virgil J. Norton and Morton M. Miller, *An Economic Study of the Boston Large-Trawler Labor Force,* Circular 248 (Washington, D.C.: U.S. Department of the Interior, 1966), 8.

In the cook category, there was a pronounced difference between the British and New England workforces. Only 9 percent of the Boston cooks were younger than the age of forty-four, and 74 percent were age fifty-five and up. The difference was related to local customs: in New England aging fishermen reserved the right to move into the easier job of cook. There was a similar age differential among segments of the workforce. In Grimsby more than 50 percent of the deckhands were under the age of thirty, whereas in Boston only 2 percent were under the age of twenty-five. In the captain/mate category, only 31 percent of Grimsby fishermen were older than fifty-one, but in Boston a remarkable 73 percent were older than age fifty-five. Skippers tended to retire earlier than deckhands did: only 5 percent of them were older than age sixty-five, in contrast to 18 percent of mates, and 20 percent of deckhands.

As table 1.5 demonstrates, the Boston age ranges were inconsistent with the American labor force as a whole. This discrepancy concerned both fishing industry and government officials. In a May 21, 1969, report to President Richard Nixon, the secretary of the interior, Walter J. Hickel, pointed out that while "83% of [the] U.S. labor force was under 55 years; only 38% of Boston's fishermen was under 55." Accentuating the problem, according to Hickel, was that the numbers of fishers in the Atlantic groundfish fleet had fallen dramatically. In 1957, there were 3,316 fishers in the fleet, but by 1966 it had dropped to 2,912, a 12 percent drop.[36] Local bankers believed that the aging workforce would have dire consequences for the industry's future. Allen P. Keith, a waterfront loan officer for the National Bank of New Bedford, explained, "It's too bad that more young men are not following in their dad's footsteps, because once a man goes into fishing, he rarely leaves it."[37]

Table 1.5. Age Distribution of U.S. Male Civilian Labor Force and Boston Offshore Trawler Labor Force (%), 1964

AGE GROUP	MALE LABOR FORCE	BOSTON FISHERMEN
Under 25	20	2
25–34	21	10
35–44	22	9
45–54	20	17
55–64	13	41
65 and Over	4	21

Source: Virgil J. Norton and Morton M. Miller, *Economic Study of Boston Large-Trawler Labor Force,* Circular 248 (Washington D.C.: U.S. Department of the Interior), 6.

Most Boston fishers had not finished high school, and of those that did, very few had attended college. Many, however, had military experience: 21 percent of skippers, 36 percent of deckhands, 26 percent of engineers, and 13 percent of cooks. Most of the skippers had served in the U. S. navy, and their relatively advanced ages suggest that most were World War II veterans rather than Korean War veterans.[38]

The Boston fishermen had another unique characteristic: most were foreign born, and the vast majority were from the Canadian maritime provinces. In addition, 79 percent had a relative who was or had been a fisherman, 68 percent had fisherman-fathers, and 59 percent had fishermen-brothers.[39] As in other areas of the world, familial recruitment was a traditional route into the labor force. In New England, young men entering the fishing industry generally began by working on family-owned boats. Retired fisherman Frank Tringale recalled that he began fishing on his father's boat at the age of ten. Early on "it was only child's play," but as he got older "I had to do more important things." Tringale's family was Sicilian, a common ethnic background among fishermen in the Gloucester fleet. His uncles and cousins all worked on draggers, fishing out of Gloucester and, at times, Boston. Tringale first noticed the shift away from fishing during the 1950s, when returning veterans chose not to follow family members into the industry. Even small changes such as road improvements had the effect of luring young men away from fishing. For instance, as Tringale explained, Route 495 opened near Gloucester, "people started driving and they were able to get jobs in other cities and stuff like that."[40]

As established Sicilian families began to drift away from fishing, they were initially replaced by Sicilian immigrants. After the end of World War II, Tringale observed, "there were a lot of people coming from overseas, you know, the most of them were Sicilians that came in and they kept this here [fishing] industry going." Margaret Favazza, a fisherman's wife, also testified to this post-war migration. Her husband, who had been born in Boston's North End, began fishing in that city and then moved to Gloucester. "He had a [dragger] crew you wouldn't believe. . . . They were so dedicated and there were all young foreign boys. They had just come from Italy. And they all wanted to go fishing. They were fishermen anyway, and my husband said 'sure.'"[41]

In addition to contending with the increasing age of its workforce, the New England fishing industry was struggling with dilapidated boats. To many, the fleet was a laughing stock of whose disintegration had been fueled by government indifference and long-term legislative inertia. As far back as 1792, lawmakers had made it illegal for an American skipper to land fish using a foreign-made vessel, and that law was still on the books in the 1960s. Thus because New Englanders were unable to buy cheaper foreign-manufactured fishing boats, they were forced to make do with what they had. As Manuel Lewis, the executive secretary of the Gloucester Fisheries Commission, stated during congressional testimony, "It has been said that a man with his hands tied cannot defend himself. And that just about sums up the predicament of the domestic fishing industry in regard to vessel construction." His contentions were supported by Donald L. McKernan of the Bureau of Commercial Fisheries, who told the U.S. Senate that the American fleet was "the most obsolete in the world."[42]

The New England fishermen's trade unions echoed this concern. Two unions represented the fishermen in the region's fleet. Those who fished out of Boston and Gloucester were represented by the Atlantic Fishermen's Union, while those from New Bedford were represented by the New Bedford Fishermen's Union. The two unions lobbied hard to modernize the fleet but were hampered by the 1792 law. In congressional testimony in 1963, Howard Nickerson, secretary-treasurer of the New Bedford Fishermen's Union, argued that allowing the owners to buy boats on the free market would solve the problem: "It is strange, but only in America are fishing vessels as aged as ours allowed to go to sea." In most other countries, he said, "they would be condemned."[43]

As table 1.6 shows, the U.S. fishing fleet was one of the smallest and oldest in the world. Among the world's fourteen largest fishing fleets, the Americans were dead last.

Table 1.6. World's Largest Fishing Fleets, 1970

NATION	NUMBER OF TRAWLERS	COMBINED TONNAGE
Soviet Union	2,604	3,405,148
Japan	2,067	719,097
Spain	1,289	397,755
United Kingdom	578	240,212
France	663	192,876
Norway	623	178,156
Poland	168	176,275
West Germany	215	161,886
Canada	458	124,134
East Germany	161	107,111
Portugal	154	105,523
Italy	158	71,617
Iceland	228	62,310

Note: There is no information on size of U.S. fleet in this review.
Source: "Three Nations Own Half World's Fishing Vessels," *Commercial Fisheries Review* (March 1970): 48.

U.S. fishing vessels could not compete with these foreign fleets, especially as their number of seaworthy boats steadily declined. Up to 250 vessels were fishing out of Gloucester in 1950, but by 1963 that number had dropped to 125. The majority of the vessels were draggers or small trawlers with three to five man crews. Only forty-three of these vessels were considered large (more than ninety-feet long). The boats of the Gloucester fleet were divided into two distinct groups that gradually dwindled in number as vessels and workers aged. Fishermen of Italian descent dominated the larger group of draggers, which tended to pursue fish close to shore or during weeklong trips to Georges Bank. The remaining group was dominated by men of Portuguese descent, who fished in deeper waters for red fish or ocean perch. The fleet's draggers were primarily fishermen-owned, and both husbands and wives contributed to running the enterprise.[44]

Boston trawlers were also aging. During congressional testimony, Frank P. Briggs, assistant secretary of the U.S. Fish and Wildlife Service, noted that half of the port's trawlers were more than twenty years old. In his view, the central problem was the high cost of American-made trawlers, which were 50 percent more expensive than their foreign counterparts. He also pointed out that governments such as the Soviet Union, Canada, and East and West Germany heavily subsidized the construction of new fishing vessels, but U.S. vessel owners were forced to shoulder the extra cost of domestically produced ships.[45]

All three principal New England ports were grappling with the problem of aging and decreasing fleets. Of New Bedford's boats, 177 out of a total of 217 were more than 15 years old. The same was true of 77 of Boston's 91 vessels, and 117 of Gloucester's 136. The governor of Massachusetts, Endicott Peabody, declared that the "useful life of the average vessel is between 12–20 years;" thus the New England fleet was groaning with old age. Manuel Lewis shared data showing that 83 of Gloucester's 136 vessels (that is, 61 percent) were more than 20 years old. The problem went beyond simple decrepitude because the older a vessel was the more expensive it was to maintain and insure. While deferring maintenance could save money, the safety ramifications could be dire. The older the ship the more likely structural weakness could occur resulting in a catastrophic loss. As Lewis asked, "Can we in good conscience ask our men who seek a living from the sea to risk their lives in outmoded and obsolete fishing vessels? Doesn't our Government bear some responsibility for the condition that the fishermen and vessel owners find themselves in?"[46]

James Ackert, the president of the Atlantic Fishermen's Union, charged that the antiquated equipment on New England trawlers resulted in frequent breakdowns and dangerous situations. He pointed out that the twenty-one of the twenty-four large trawlers fishing out of Boston, were more than fifteen years old and noted that the German authorities were "scrapping German trawlers that are much younger than our vessels." The Canadian government was also subsidizing new construction that covered 50 percent of the cost. For Ackert, the situation was spiraling out of control. With a rapidly aging fishing fleet and a corresponding decline in fishing efficiency, the nation's "fishing industry cannot survive."[47]

There was widespread concern among New England's local politicians, seafood processors, boat owners, and fishermen that the industry was being left behind. Not only were they dealing with a decaying fleet and an aging work force, but they also recognized that America's share of the fisheries was plummeting. In the past, U.S. fleets had enjoyed almost unfettered access to its coastal fishing grounds and had led the way in fish landings, but by mid-century this access was under foreign threat. In the northwestern region of the Atlantic Ocean (which includes New England), the total landings by all countries increased from 1.98 million tons in 1935 to 3.63 million tons in 1967. Yet simultaneously, the U.S. catch declined from 0.55 million tons to 0.33 million tons that is, from 27 percent of all landings to a mere 9 percent.[48] In terms of world catch, the United States was also declining. In 1957 it was ranked second in total catch (behind Japan), but by 1968 the U.S. had fallen to sixth (see table 1.2).

The New England fishery, in particular, was feeling the effects of declining U.S. catches. Table 1.7 illustrates the precipitous decline in the region's haddock landings. Much of this decline can be attributed to substandard vessels and equipment, but as I discuss in chapter 6, foreign competition was also taking a toll. As bigger and more powerful foreign fleets and vessels plied their trade on Georges and Browns Banks, fish stocks—especially haddock—began to suffer. By the late 1960s the trend was clearly downward and would continue that way for years to come.

Table 1.7. New England Haddock Landings of Haddock (in million pounds), 1955–1968

YEAR	BOSTON	GLOUCESTER	NEW BEDFORD	MAINE PORTS
1955	96.3	7.6	7.7	4.0
1956	106.6	8.7	11.0	4.3
1957	93.6	8.9	8.5	4.1
1957	81.5	9.8	8.2	3.5
1959	72.4	12.1	9.4	3.0
1960	76.7	12.1	9.2	3.4
1961	84.1	15.0	12.0	2.6
1962	83.1	16.0	12.3	2.2
1963	75.1	17.2	10.2	2.5
1964	76.3	22.9	12.1	2.6
1965	75.7	24.4	11.8	1.7
1966	65.5	27.1	15.7	1.8
1967	51.0	19.3	10.9	1.5
1968	35.6	15.1	7.4	2.7

Source: *Food and Fish Outlook*, May 1967, U.S. Bureau of Commercial Fisheries, 24; *Food and Fish Outlook*, May 1969, U.S. Bureau of Commercial Fisheries, 22.

On Georges Bank, the Boston trawler fleet was competing with trawlers and draggers from Gloucester and New Bedford as well as boats from Chatham, Massachusetts; Stony Point, Connecticut; and Point Judith, Rhode Island. Despite their age and condition, these bedraggled fleets were managing to survive in large part because they were so close to the fishing grounds. But when large foreign fleets appeared on Georges Bank in the early 1960s, the picture changed dramatically. Intense foreign competition eventually shattered governmental indifference, and the age of the New England fleet and its fishermen became a cause for concern.

The British fleet was also suffering, if by a lesser degree, from a lack of sustained investment in new boats. Stern trawler deliveries were lagging behind the Norwegians, Soviets, and East and West Germans. However, their concerns about the safety of these aging trawlers were over shadowed by the conflicts with efforts of Iceland and other nations that were closing their fishing grounds to British trawlers.

Meanwhile, on both sides of the Atlantic, men continued to work and die fishing for cod and haddock. Awaiting them outside their home ports was an unforgiving ocean, and the men who challenged it often paid the price with their lives.

CHAPTER 2

THE HAZARDS OF FISHING

Commercial fishing has always been a hazardous occupation, as residents of every fishing port in the world can testify. But for many American and British fishermen during the years between 1960 and 1974 there was the added danger of working in giant seas that were hundreds or thousands of miles from the coast. Their lives were filled with strenuous labor, peril, and fear—not least because they were working on an open platform on a volatile vehicle as it traversed an unpredictable realm. At sea for days and weeks at a time, the vessel served as both a work site and a floating home. Thus fishermen shared a unique sense of workplace as living space.

While seafarers and dockworkers have enjoyed widespread scholarly attention, most labor historians have ignored the work of British and American fishermen during this period.[1] The literature that does exist has been produced primarily by anthropologists, political scientists, sociologists, economists, and journalists.[2] The absence of historical inquiry is surprising given the dynamic nature of the industry and the widespread impact of the fishing communities that dot the thousands of miles of coastline fringing the United States and Great Britain. Perhaps historians' disinterest has been influenced by the perceived stoicism or fatalism of the fishing workforce. Certainly many labor historians have made assumptions about the lack of sustained trade union and political activity. Moreover, because most North Atlantic fishermen during these years were white men, their history has not attracted labor historians in the post-1960s era, many of whom have been concerned with recovering the experiences of women and workers of color.

Yet the history of fishermen is a vital one. During the 1960s, they traveled and worked the world's oceans and seas. Every day they saw the trawlers and fleets of other nations. The seas were international hunting grounds where the world's fishing vessels plied their trade. Despite the industry's cosmopolitan character, all of these men shared similar work lives and dangers.

For the purposes of clarity and consistency, I label these fishers as trawlermen. The U.S. spotlight is on New England trawlermen who fished out of Boston, Gloucester, and New Bedford. They fished on Georges and Browns Banks, and in the Gulf of Maine. In the British case, my focus is on the distant, middle, and near fleets. The distant water fleet (generally from the ports of Hull and Grimsby) fished the Russian White Sea, Iceland, and Greenland. The middle and near water fleets generally confined themselves to the North and Irish Seas, the Faroes, and Norway. Their ports were Milford Haven, Fleetwood, Aberdeen, North Shields, and Lowestoft. The routine of trawling had not fundamentally changed since the nineteenth century. Both U.S. and British workforces labored in trawlers that dragged their nets (trawls) over the surfaces of shoals and banks that contained large numbers of groundfish—notably cod, haddock, and plaice.

This chapter highlights the connections and differences between the British and New England fleets by examining the hazardous nature of the work, disciplinary problems, heavy drinking patterns, and fatigue factors. While there are variations on either side of the Atlantic, all of the men knew that the job involved playing the odds. The goal was to earn a living and survive each fishing trip.

Most people had a grudging respect for Atlantic trawlermen and the extreme conditions in which they worked, yet this respect did not lead to useful governmental intervention. For instance, neither the U.S. nor British agencies were responding to the industry's high accident rates with any significant regulatory action. The two countries were not alone in their apathy. In a 1962 study, the United Nations' International Labor Office had highlighted widespread governmental indifference to fishing safety, despite the extreme dangers of the job. It reported that only a few nations enforced safety regulations for fishermen, though regulations regarding the seaworthiness of fishing vessels were pervasive. Only Canada, West Germany, Ireland, Japan, and Norway had extensive rules and regulations pertaining specifically to fishermen's occupational safety and health. And even in those cases, their workplace safety conditions were rarely monitored.[3]

Most trawlermen survived their ordeals at sea, but the cost was high. Just being out in deep water was treacherous. Even during decent weather, rough seas could create problems for draggers and other small boats, and storms could be dire. Another North Atlantic problem was ice buildup, which increased a ship's weight and could even capsize it. Men risked their lives to chip away at the ice building up around the ship.

Accident rates, especially on deck, were appalling throughout the world. Between 1958–64 the British fishing industry recorded 5,283 injuries on deck, a shocking 71 percent of all injuries. A trawler's constant movement made standing difficult, especially when a worker was engaged in hard physical labor while simultaneously trying to maintain his balance on a surface slick with water, fish, blood, and entrails. During the 1960s, few winches had safety guards, which meant the machinery could easily crush a man's hand or even mangle his entire body. But the greatest threat was the sea, waves plucked or washed their prey off the deck. Men lost overboard comprised a significant number of the industry's fatalities.

Although deck hands generally believed that engineers had a soft job, the engine room was in fact a perilous workplace. Between 1958–64, there were 1,024 engine-room injuries on British trawlers, 14 percent of all onboard injuries reported during that period.[4] As I discuss in chapter 1, the excessive noise of the diesel engines made work unpleasant and the engine room was extremely hot. Moreover, unlike deck-hands, who could occasionally take a break during bad weather, the engine-room members were continually at work during their twelve-hour shifts. With only six hours off between shifts, the men were constantly "pale and exhausted." Machinery in the engine room could also be deadly. On one vessel, chief engineer Harold Fryer was killed instantly when his clothing got caught in an "auxiliary engine clutch drive." His death was somewhat unusual because his ship, the *Rewga,* was docked in Fleetwood Harbor at the time of the accident.[5]

Even more dangerous was the threat of fire—a risk in both the engine room and the galley. On Christmas Day 1966, a fire started in a cabin on the *St. Finbarr* out of Hull, fishing off the Labrador coast. Soon fierce flames were shooting up to the bridge, and the skipper, Thomas Sawyers, sent out a Mayday call for help. Luckily the trawler *Orsino* was close by and steamed to the rescue. As the fire spread, two of the life rafts on the port side were "damaged" and became unusable. Ten of the crew members were overcome by smoke and fumes and died in their cabins. Two more were killed when transferring from a life raft to the *Orsino*. Sawyers, his first mate, and chief engineer remained onboard trying to fight the fire, but eventually the three were carried, exhausted, to the *Orsino*. Although the *Orsino* tried to tow the stricken vessel, it sank.[6]

The location of the fire on the *St. Finbarr* suggests that human error was the cause. This was certainly the case when a New England trawler, skippered by Hubert Cluett, caught fire. The fire began in the galley after the cook put two pounds of bacon into the oven and then returned to his bunk. As the fire spread the crew were forced to "cut up the bulkhead" to get to the fire. Once the fire had been contained, Cluett gave his cook a "good talking to," but, as he told an interviewer, "neglect" caused no end of problems on ships, particularly in the engine room when the "engineers are not there, fire gets ahead of them."[7] In the New England fleet, fire was a major problem during this period. For instance, on May 27, 1969, the *Wild Duck* out of Gloucester caught fire off the coast of Montauk, Long Island. Luckily for the crew, two other Gloucester fishing vessels were close by and rescued them. Another Gloucester vessel, the *Villanova*, caught fire off the Canadian coast on January 26, 1971. Again, a nearby fishing vessel rescued the crew.[8]

Table 2.1 details onboard accidents in the British trawler fleet in 1969.

Table 2.1. Onboard Accidents in the British Trawler Fleet, 1958–64

	NUMBER	PERCENTAGE OF TOTAL ACCIDENTS
DECK ACCIDENTS	5,283	71
ENGINE ROOM ACCIDENTS	1,024	14
FALLS ONBOARD	77	0.7
FALLS OVERBOARD	30	0.3
OTHER CAUSES	1,053	14
Total	7,467	100

Source: "Appendix B-Statistics on Accidents and Casualties-Table 3 (a&b)," Board of Trade 149/9, British National Archives.

When examining how British trawlermen were injured, deck work is again the main culprit. When combining the categories of "slipped," "struck by ship's equipment," and "caught or wedged in ship's equipment," the total reaches 57 percent.[9] Working on deck had fatality potential too. When combining fatal accidents on deck and falling overboard or being washed overboard, it is clear the deck was a dangerous location.

Table 2.2. Deaths Registered as Having Been Caused by Accidents

YEAR	DEATHS RELATED TO VESSEL CASUALTY	KILLED ON DECK	LOST OVERBOARD	SUICIDE	TOTAL
1962	8	2	14	0	24
1963	0	3	7	0	10
1964	3	3	7	1	14
1965	23	4	7	4	38
Total	34	12	35	5	

Source: "Appendix B-Statistics on Deaths at Sea, Table 1 (a&b)," Board of Trade 149/9, British National Archives.

Many of the deck deaths were caused by winches and warp lines. These warps pulled the net through the sea. In a ten-year report focusing on Lowestoft trawlermen, three deaths were attributed to "winch accidents." In one case the cause was detailed as "caught in Gilson Wire on winch whipping drum." Stepping over warp lines could have devastating effects. One Hull trawlerman had "climbed over a moving warp to reach his knife" but was "caught" and "taken bodily through" the warp casing. A deckie learner who was resting his head on a crankshaft guard while trying to recover a shackle died after his "head went through the opening and was crushed by the moving machinery." Another deckie learner caught a finger in the Gilson wire and was literally "taken around the whipping drum" and flayed to death.[10]

As table 2.2 shows, many men were killed in everyday work incidents. In other words, while disasters at sea caused widespread alarm, the daily grind took an even greater toll. The table also highlights the constant danger of being washed or thrown overboard. Earlier in this chapter I note that the deck was invariably wet, even when not threatened by waves, so it is not surprising that many trawlermen ended up in the sea. There were also cases in which accidents on deck pitched men overboard. In 1961, for example, the deck crew of a Lowestoft trawler, the *Suffolk Kinsman*, were trying to haul a full net during a "Force 5 wind [21 miles per hour] with a heavy swell." Without warning, the winch line attached to the cod end snapped, sending the trawl overboard. The skipper noticed the problem and went down to the deck to help out. Unfortunately a wave smashed into the side of the trawler, and the skipper and a deckhand Ernest Locke were washed into the sea. Both men were wearing heavy boots and oilskins. Nonetheless, the skipper managed to get hold of the trawl and climb back onboard. Locke, however, felt himself being swept away. As he later testified, "I cannot swim and I found myself drifting away from the ship. I struggled to keep afloat but I could feel myself being pulled down by the water in my boots." A nineteen-year-old deckhand—Barry Measures, who had been operating the winch—was observing the unfolding drama. He immediately threw off his boots and dove into the sea, where he grabbed Locke with one hand while holding onto a lifebelt with the other. The two were hauled back onboard, and a grateful Locke later testified: "I am firmly of the opinion that Barry Measures saved my life. . . . I feel certain that I could not have kept afloat much longer . . . as I was drifting further away from it [ship] all the time."[11]

Not all such incidents ended so well. While fishing in the White Sea, a sixteen-year-old deckie learner named John Sinclair was swept off the trawler *Thuringia* on October 26, 1962. The crew were hauling during particularly bad weather—a force 8 gale (winds at 42 miles per hour) when a massive wave "laid over" the ship. While the crew scrambled for the handrail, the ship "took another sea and wrenched the Deckie Learner away." Peter Garner, a deck hand, threw Sinclair a lifebelt, but it fell short, and "he was taken away from the ship very quickly." By the time the rest of the crew had been alerted Sinclair had "disappeared." Although the *Thuringia* searched for two and a half hours after the accident, they could find no trace of the unfortunate Sinclair.[12]

Sinclair's fate was especially tragic because of his youth, yet all fishermen knew that luck played a huge role in their survival. Sometimes there were even fatalities during rescues. In one such case a Gloucester fisherman, Jose Pinho Vinagre, was pulled overboard by the net and "fell forward into the water." According to the skipper, Tony Parisi, "The man must've gone into shock [because] he passed out." The crew managed to hook "[Vinagre's] jacket and pulled him close enough to the boat to haul him on deck," but despite immediate mouth-to-mouth resuscitation he failed to respond.[13]

Fishermen were particularly worried about being thrown overboard as they were hauling nets. One of the most common fatalities listed in the reports about Hull trawlermen is that a crewmember was "taken over the side by [the] trawl when gear was being got inboard." Though stern trawlers were somewhat safer, accidents occurred there as well. In one incident on a stern trawler, the "warp pulled out, caught the man's clothing and took him over the port side." In another, a mate was drowned when the derrick he was releasing dropped and hit him, and he "was knocked overboard and drowned." Lowestoft deckhand, C. W. Edwards, was smashed overboard after a "tub shifted and hit him below the knees." Another deck hand, N. J. Hart, was "dragged overboard with gear when unclipping the 'G' link on trawl door" of the stern trawler, *Universal Star*.[14]

Rough weather could play a role in any accident at sea. After their "ship took [a] heavy sea starboard side," two Hull trawlermen were "washed against lifelines," and when the "lashing parted, both men washed overboard." Another Hull trawlerman was trying to chip ice off a radar scanner when he "lost balance or was blown off [the] bridge top in very bad weather."[15] The records often include little evidence of how such accidents happened. The Lowestoft report, for instance, listed the general categories "disappeared," "lost," and "swept" overboard. The "disappeared" category included cases such as this one, involving a mate named Nigel Bailey. While the crew of the *Ethel Mary* were hauling in a catch, Bailey, "complained of feeling sick and went to lie down." That was the last the crew saw of him. In another case, the skipper J. Quiton of the *Frederick Spashett* "disappeared whilst steaming" and was "presumed drowned."[16]

Fishing in severe weather was relatively common. Indeed, trade union officials and fishery experts often complained that some skippers were prone to taking such risks. Rear Admiral G. C. Leslie, who had served as a captain in the fishery protection squadron during the 1958–59 cod war told the 1968 Holland-Martin Committee of Inquiry into Trawler Safety, that, if "catches were poor," the skippers "might be willing to take serious risks mainly by fishing in bad weather." He blamed such pressures on company owners' "ruthless . . . treatment of skippers." Any skipper who failed to bring in good catches did not last long on the job.[17]

Incentive payments influenced decision-making during rough weather. Both the skipper and the crew members were paid according to poundage (the weight of fish caught and delivered to market). While the crew also received a small basic wage, skippers relied more on the poundage or share system, which could lead them to test the limits of their fishing vessels and their men. The job security of skippers was tenuous at best. As one reporter pointed out "the skipper's job is chronically insecure," out-of-work skippers often ended up serving in the deck crew. Thus, a skipper in command had to keep a watchful eye on both mates and former skippers who might be potential competitors for his job. The "savage strain of a trawler command" meant that skippers got little sleep during fishing trips: they invariably remained at their posts longer than any other crewman did. They were constantly monitoring the trawling gear, the radar, the echo sounders and the weather. If the fishing was not going well, they had to decide whether to shift to new ground or maintain their bearings.[18] Navigating swells and storms took skill, courage, luck, and extreme focus, and skippers' need for sleep was chronic. Because near- and middle-fleet skippers might keep up this pace for ten days at a time, they often made errors. The seas can be unforgiving and cruel.

New England trawlermen faced the same dangers that the British fishermen did, although there are few available records about their deaths at work or about the site of their accidents and the fatalities. Nonetheless, available data suggest that the deck was the most hazardous area.

Table 2.3. Onboard Accidents in the New England Trawler Fleet, 1960–64

	NUMBER	PERCENTAGE OF TOTAL ACCIDENTS
FALLS ON DECK	96	23
FALLS ELSEWHERE	19	7
HIT BY OBJECTS	86	20
HIT BY SEA	29	8
WINCH INJURIES	22	8
HAND INJURIES	16	4
Other Injuries (e.g., knife wounds)	117	32

Source: John J. Murray, "Safety for the Commercial Fishing Vessel and Crew," *Commercial Fisheries Review* 30 (June 1968): 47.

Working on the deck was by far the most dangerous job. The combined total of falls on deck, hit by objects, hit by the sea, and winch injuries, reaches 59 percent. This figure corresponds well with the British data of 57 percent. Even shore workers who filleted fish suffered knife cuts, but gutting fish on a rolling and dipping vessel was significantly more treacherous. Hunched over an unstable table the deck crew had to gut the fish quickly and cleanly, and at any moment another net of fish could be added to the pile. No wonder the knives slipped and cut hands and fingers; the constant pitch and roll could handicap the most skilled deckhand. In addition, knife injuries often led to skin or wound infection. Dermatitis was one of the common results of such an injury. Cuts and abrasions were breeding grounds for bacteria and quickly became inflamed. Infection on a hand tended to travel along the fingers, giving them a "distinct purplish hue," that New England fishermen called it the "run around." Also problematic were fish bites, particularly from dogfish. It was no wonder that trawlermen hated dogfish. Chafing from oilskins could cause wrist dermatitis, and British trawlermen nicknamed these lesions "pigeons."[19]

Table 2.4 shows that fishermen's workplace injuries surpassed those of most other occupations. If we consider the frequency rate of injuries and the average number of income-earning days lost to injury, we can conclude that trawlermen were clearly handicapped by their work conditions.

Table 2.4. Workplace Injuries in Major American Industries, 1964

INDUSTRY	FREQUENCY RATE OF INJURY (%)	AVERAGE NUMBER OF DAYS LOST
Coal Mining	43.5	NA
Boston Fishermen	40.3	47
Transportation and Warehousing	31.3	17
Construction	28.6	18
Metal Mining	23.8	NA
Wholesale and Retail Trade	12.2	14
Manufacturing	11.9	18

Source: Virgil J. Norton and Morton M. Miller, *Economic Study of Boston Large-Trawler Labor Force,* Circular 248 (Washington D.C.: U.S. Department of the Interior), 21.

While the fishery workforces on both sides of the Atlantic had much in common, they also had distinct differences. One key difference was in how they signed on for their fishing trips.[20] British trawlermen had to follow a more formalized institutional path, one that had been codified by the 1894 Merchant Shipping Act. For each trip they needed to sign what were known as "Articles of Agreement," which covered a range of responsibilities for the trawlermen. The disciplinary section spelled out rules and penalties for neglect of duty, desertion, and disobedience of lawful commands. The fisherman had to pledge to arrive for the trip on time and in a sober condition. If, after signing the "articles," he did not sail, he could be fined and/or suspended. Port committees were responsible for overseeing these disciplinary regulations and an examination of the list of offences brought before these port committees reveals that many trawlermen were ignoring the terms of the contracts (see table 2.5). In five ports (Fleetwood, Grimsby, Aberdeen, Hull, and North Shields), most of the offences involved the failure or refusal to sail.

Table 2.5. Offences Brought before Port Disciplinary Committees, 1974

	FLEETWOOD	GRIMSBY	ABERDEEN	HULL	NORTH SHIELDS
FAILED TO REPORT	70%	37%	16%	25%	26%
REFUSED TO SAIL	22%	37%	32%	14%	11%
Others	8%	26%	54%	61%	63%

Source: "Parliamentary Report of the Working Group on Discipline in the Fishing Industry, November 1975" (HMSA, London).

According to the 1975 parliamentary Working Group on Discipline in the Fishing Industry, alcohol abuse was often linked to "failure to report" offences. In Aberdeen, for example, 9 percent of offences were categorized as "reporting drunk." This percentage is almost certainly too small. Indeed, the working group declared: "It seemed clear to us that drink did in fact play a major part in offences that were reported." Obviously there was a culture of acceptance around alcohol abuse. In Hull, fishermen's "cheer parties" were traditional drinking events before and after sailing, and skippers everywhere tended to turn a blind eye when a drunken trawlermen turned up for duty, generally assuming that he could sleep it off on the outward voyage. Acceptance of such behavior was predicated on the notion that some of the "heaviest drinkers" were "some of the best fishermen" and would "prove [to be] perfectly sober and reliable" by the time the boat reached the fishing grounds. While this approach may have worked for Hull's distant water fleet (who were usually outbound for days at a time), it could be a disaster for near fleet trawlermen who might begin fishing within hours of leaving port.[21]

Observers understood the reasons behind such behavior, for the prospect of returning to sea and all its attendant dangers made men hesitant and fearful of what awaited them. Even though some safety and communication equipment had improved by the 1960s and 1970s, the vessels were still subject to the vagaries of wind and sea, and anticipating these conditions could daunt even the bravest man. Thus to boost their courage to make a new trip often entailed the consumption of alcohol. As the working group reported, some fishermen "are psychologically incapable of facing the prospects of a new trip without first dulling their senses by over-indulgence in alcohol."[22] The crew were not alone in their drunkenness. According to the British Transport and General Workers' Union, which represented the deck crews, "drink was abused more by skippers than by crews." James Gurley, the cook on the *Navena* testified in court that when he went to the bridge to serve tea, "The captain, mate and bosun were drinking spirits and beer and I might [as well] have spoken to a wall. The mate was the only one sober." Workers on the trawler the *Northern Chief* complained to the union that their skipper, E. Favell, "was heavily intoxicated for a period of six days to such an extent that he was not fully capable of carrying out his duties or responsibilities." When the attorney representing Favell denounced the charges as "thoroughly unfounded," a deckhand Harry Smith caustically responded, "It is always the drunken deckhand, but never a drunken skipper."[23]

During the late 1950s and early 1960s, the sociologist Jeremy Tunstall traveled out to sea with a number of Hull trawlermen. He noted that the stress of trying to find fish in rough waters had an unsettling effect on many skippers, and "to calm their jittery nerves some . . . resort[ed] to drink." They also had easier access to alcohol than the crew did: a skipper could "bring on board a suitcase full of bottles if he wants." Skippers were aware that they were risking their jobs by such behavior, especially if word got back to owners about their problematic drinking. But they could not fight their alcoholism. In Tunstall's words, "He cannot keep going without the drink and yet if he drinks he may get discovered and fired." Thus "his loneliness feeds his obsessions."[24]

New England trawlermen were also heavy drinkers, but unlike their British counterparts, they were not institutionalized by anything similar to the "Articles of Agreement." They merely had to turn up on a timely fashion for the next trip. Evidence does suggest that drinking took place onboard, though for many Gloucester and Boston fishermen—particularly onboard boats owned by people of Italian descent—this primarily meant drinking wine with dinner. On vessels without such ethnic traditions, there was a greater likelihood of drunkenness. Skipper Hubert Cluett, who fished out of Gloucester, described drinking before the trip as "false courage." He also recalled cases of men drinking while on watch or in charge of the ship. For instance, he recounted noticing that his boat "was not going on a true course," and when he reached the bridge, he saw that the it "was going around in circles." The man in charge was found "asleep on the floor" with an empty bottle of whiskey nearby.[25] While there were no statutory provisions for penalizing such behavior, the fisherman "knew enough to take his bag and go" once the ship returned to port. In many cases, men routinely got drunk on every return to port. Harry Eustis, who also fished out of Gloucester, explained that after a particularly severe storm you'd "swear to yourself you'll never to do that again . . . [but then I would] have a few drinks, it's a great medicine." Then, once he was inebriated, Eustis would tell himself, "Oh this may never happen again," and he would go back out to sea.[26]

While trawlermen on both sides of the Atlantic Ocean had reputations as hard drinkers, most of the available evidence suggests that the majority of the heaviest consumers were younger men. In 1975 the parliamentary working group reported "that the hardcore [drinkers] consisted of younger men between the ages of 18 and 35." The pattern in New England was similar. As Cluett confirmed, "young men were more apt to give you trouble" with their drinking.[27] Several fishermen's advocacy groups testified to the widespread abuse of alcohol. In evidence before the 1968 Holland-Martin inquiry, officials from the Royal National Mission to Deep Sea Fishermen argued that "short periods ashore between trips colored . . . [the trawlermen's] basic attitudes and helped explain many of the problems of excessive drinking." They also denounced owners' willingness to allow drunken crewmen aboard ship, arguing that "owners [instead] should be willing to support skippers in refusing to take trawlers to sea with illicit drink or drunken men on board." The reverend Leslie Yelland, a spokesman of the Gloucester Fisherman's Institute, in 1978 declared he had "seen drunkenness decline." Yet just as he was explaining to a visitor to the institute that fishermen were "more sensible" than they had been, a drunken New Bedford fisherman knocked on the institute's door. According to Yelland, the fisherman "couldn't stand up, . . . [and] it took two or three of us to get him downstairs."[28]

As I have discussed, heavy drinking was, to a large degree, grounded in the fears that accompanied fishing in the North Atlantic. As one British fisherman explained, "Of course fishermen get drunk. Anybody who does what we do has to get drunk to stay sane." But Tunstall identified another important influence, status deprivation. In working class backgrounds, heavy drinking was a masculine rite of passage. Thus, according to Tunstall, a drunken trawlerman was "trying not only to shut out the thought of another trip to the Arctic, but also . . . to forget his lowly position in society." He believed that such fear and loathing also explained why young working-class men were more likely to engage in this behavior.[29]

Alcohol was a problem, but fatigue was a worse one. R. S. Schilling, an industry safety expert, frankly stated: "Lack of sleep is the curse of this occupation." In the course of his research, Schilling made numerous trips on British trawlers and witnessed firsthand the rigors of the job and fishermen's excessive working hours. He compared their fatigue to that of retreating British soldiers during World War II: "an ashen grey pallor of the face, slower movements, irritability, chain smoking. It reminded me very much of what I saw among soldiers during the retreat to Dunkirk in 1940."[30] Schilling was not alone in his concerns about fatigue. Oliver G. Edholm, a physiologist with the Medical Research Council, testified during the 1968 Holland-Martin inquiry that "fatigue-induced accidents would be very likely" in the fishing industry. Short stays back in port did not solve these problems. Many fishermen spent no more than forty-eight to sixty hours on land before they went out to sea again. Such short rest spans were "inadequate and could cause fatigue to develop cumulative effects."[31] In other words, the more trips a trawlerman took, the more fatigued he became. This is why fishermen avoided sailing when they could. R. S. W. Moore, a former deputy medical officer in Hull, testified to having "observed signs [onboard] of fatigue amongst the crew (slow reactions, pallor, irritability, etc)" and recommended more rest time. He also explained that only a few workplace accidents were ever reported, noting that "over half the cases treated by the Grimsby Medical Officer had not been logged [as injuries]." In many cases the injured trawlermen received rudimentary treatment onboard. "The first priority," he believed, was "to improve training of officers and men in *first aid*; standards at present were too low and in particular no attempt was made to instruct skippers in the use of the Ships Captain's Medical Guide."[32]

According to the Transport and General Workers' Union (TGWU), fatigue was key to understanding and appreciating the fishermen's difficult occupational conditions. They were not overwhelmed by hard work per se but by excessive hours and little time to rest on ship or in port. The near- and middle-water fleets, which worked mostly in the North Sea, were particularly affected. During a boat's ten days at sea, the crewmembers would labor for up to eighteen hours a day, and their relatively short return trip (usually a single day) did not give them enough time to rest and recuperate.[33] In contrast, trawlermen in the distant-water fleet had much longer return trips, which gave them some extra time to recover.

Employees in other industries, including steelworkers and truckers, also struggled with excessive working hours. The accident rates in those jobs made the hazards of long hours clear. Yet among fishermen, working long hours without a break and under perilous circumstances was often seen as a sign of manliness. They perceived any sign of fatigue as weakness and corresponding loss of masculinity. To endure the long hours and the accompanying fatigue was regarded as part of the job, and ultimately was a measure of their value as strong and fearless men. As the current television program *The Deadliest Catch* reminds us, long hours continue to be viewed as part of the job's ritualized performance.[34]

Fatigue, excessive drinking, and bad weather were major safety issues, but so were unskilled deckhands. Often owners scrambled to fill crews with last-minute additions and replacements. This irritated trawlermen because replacements tended to be more trouble than they were worth. British trawlermen and union officials continually complained about "deadbeats" who had been recruited from "pubs and clubs" to work on trawlers. Sometimes unskilled men bribed their way onto vessels after building relationships with a ship's runner or husband (terms for men who recruit crewmembers). Sometimes, "merely because he had at some previous time had a drink with the runner," a man was given a job. S. W. Mills, a TGWU district organizer, argued that such tactics ensured that any "Tom, Dick or Harry" could take the "living from a regular fisherman." In addition to creating "understandable annoyance" among "genuine fisherman, the situation put the skilled workers into a position of having to cover for the new arrivals"[35] At sea the crew invariably discovered these passengers, as they were called, were "not capable of doing the work necessary and very often . . . [the experienced hands] find that they are saddled with men whose work they have to do."[36]

The "passengers problem" was the result of high turnover in the industry. By the 1960s it was becoming increasingly difficult to recruit new labor on both sides of the Atlantic. As a result, according to the *Financial Times,* fishing was "attract[ing] the wrong type of men." Evidence indicates that the turnover was concentrated among younger men. It was unusual for deck-hands to remain with a ship for more than four trips, and an astounding 85 percent of deckie learners left the industry after their first trip.[37] As a result, the transatlantic workforces were steadily getting older.

Hard labor in appalling conditions gave the men of the North Atlantic fisheries a unique identity. For both British and New England trawlermen, the precariousness of working and living on a constantly shifting platform made their existence frightening and insecure. To cope, they turned to heavy drinking and refused to sail. There were differences in the ways in which fishermen handled, or were forced to handle, their situations. For instance, the New England trawlermen were at liberty not to sail, but their British counterparts were legally obliged to turn up at the allotted time. If they refused to sail they could, and were, penalized with fines.

Nonetheless, the dangers of their job unified the men from both fleets. Although fishermen were generally seen as hardy and hard living, the government and the public mostly ignored their terrible working conditions until disasters struck. In the meantime, the men continued to labor, their industries continued to decline, and the fisheries on both sides of the Atlantic wrestled with how to rectify these problems. As the next chapter will show, trade union activism became key to improving their lot.

CHAPTER 3

TRADE UNION DEVELOPMENT

Both New England and British fishermen were generally reluctant to join unions or participate in regular union activities. Part of the reason was structural; they spent the bulk of their time at sea and were uninterested in using up their shore hours on union business. Of the two fleets, the New Englanders were prone to see the value of unionizing. For them the 1960s were years of engagement and progress, thanks to a concerted drive by the unions to improve their members' pay and working conditions and to counter foreign threats to the fishery. In Great Britain, however, the established fishermen's unions struggled to maintain their worth and identity.

On both sides of the Atlantic, the activity of fishermen's unions was both ongoing and erratic, a pattern with parallels in other laborers' trade unions. By the early twentieth century fishermen's unions had established a foothold with the workers, but an employer backlash after World War I swept away those limited gains. Not until the Depression of the 1930s, did fishermen's unions reestablish themselves in fishing ports, and even then the organizations functioned under considerable constraints. In the United States a given union represented all fishermen, eventually including captains and engineers. In Britain the union structure was based on an older craft tradition, so skippers, engineers, and deckworkers each had separate unions. Another difference was the power of the skipper. A British skipper held a position of unchallenged command, while an American skipper, despite his authority, was limited by his membership in the same union as his deckhands.

Fishermen's trade union activity in the United States began in 1915, when the Fisherman's Union of the Atlantic (FUA) was formed in Boston. Union outreach spread quickly to the Massachusetts's ports of Gloucester, New Bedford, and Provincetown, as well as to Atlantic City, New Jersey, and New York City. By the end of World War I the FUA had established a permanent presence in Boston, Gloucester, and New York City. Its hold on those three ports was so strong that it was able to insist upon a closed shop, which meant that all fishermen sailing out of them were required to be members of the union.[1] The FUA's organizing activity matched the surge in overall trade union membership during the period. The advent of war in 1914 eventually had a stimulating effect on the U.S. industry, and by 1916 the economy had expanded exponentially. Sensing an opportunity, the American Federation of Labor began organizing aggressively, targeting industries that had long excluded unionization, such as coal, steel, railroads, and meatpacking.[2] But such conditions did not last. After the war there was a backlash against organized labor, and anxieties about the Red Scare swept away most of the unions' wartime gains. For the FUA, by the 1920s, negotiations with boat owners over wage payments and fish prices were stymied. In addition, with an abundance of available labor, employers no longer had to take the union seriously. But during the economic collapse of the 1930s, the FUA adopted a more aggressive stance and began to enroll new members, actions that mirrored the resurgence of the American Federation of Labor and the founding of the Congress of Industrial Organizations. Once again conditions were ripe, and the fishermen used them to improve their lot.[3]

By 1940 a new union, the Atlantic Fishermen's Union (AFU), backed by the larger Seafarers International Union, had formed to replace the FUA. Almost immediately it signed a contract with Boston and New York City boat owners. The agreement, which covered all crew members, except skippers, stipulated that union officials would have access to boats and wharves. This enabled shop stewards to check crewmembers' trade union status and ensure that most boats were sailing with union crews. In an attempt to curtail disruption on the voyage, the agreement stipulated that a boat could not "return [to port] if a dispute breaks out over non-union crew." Nor could the crew be forced to paint the ship or polish brass, chores that most fishermen saw as a form of discipline, and the men were promised fishing schedules of six hours on and six hours off. The agreement also addressed problems involving ice and fish weight, stipulating that the cost of ice must now be deducted from the gross price at docking. Earlier, the cost had been taken from the net price, critically cutting into the wages that fishermen had received from the fish weight. Most Atlantic fishermen's wages were aligned with the weight of fish brought to market, so the higher the weight, the larger the share (or "the lay" as it was called in Massachusetts's ports).[4]

Throughout World War II, the AFU battled to keep its members from being recruited into the armed services. Yet even as it struggled with that issue, it was also dealing with the fact that many of the larger Boston trawlers were being converted for military service. Despite these setbacks, the AFU's standing as a trade union was solidified during the war era, and the union began attempting to use the new National War Labor Board to further its power. For instance, it appealed to the board for help in reducing crewmembers' costs. For decades, owners had deducted the price of fuel and lubricating oil, sounding machines, wharfage fees, and ice from the gross catch and the crew's share. Additionally, the crew had also been liable for the costs of lumpers (workers who unloaded the catch from the hold) and "watchers" (who oversaw security). The AFU argued that the board had already recognized that coal miners, for instance, were no longer required to pay for "cost of dynamite and other supplies in mining." Nonetheless, the board rejected the union's request, insisting that the fishermen were "co-adventurers with the owners" and therefore should be liable for some of the operating costs. The board further ruled that accepting the union position would, in effect, increase wages, thus compromising the government's attempts to reduce the wartime cost of living. Not everyone on the board was in agreement with this ruling. In a dissenting opinion, board member, John J. Murphy, argued that the board had ignored its principal duty: "the removal of 'gross inequities' so as to aid the prosecution of the War."[5]

The AFU and many of its members were incensed by the NWLB. While some of the board's actions and decisions had resulted in higher pay and greater representation, many trade union members were complaining about the inordinate time the board was taking to make decisions, while others argued that it privileged white male workers over women and people of color. But most of these workers' complaints mirrored the AFU's—that wage increases were being held steady in hopes of staving off wartime inflation—so the AFU was not alone in being disgruntled because of the lack of pay increases.[6] Thus, at the end of the war the Boston office of the AFU pressed hard to increase its members' share of the lay. Union officials insisted that after deductions for fuel and other fees, the remaining gross stock should be divided as a 60–40 lay, 60 percent to the crew and 40 percent to the owners. The owners flatly refused and insisted on retaining the established 50–50 lay. In response, the AFU, led by Patrick J. McHugh, called a strike in Boston, New Bedford, and New York City. Beginning on December 26, 1945, the strike lasted for more than fifteen weeks and tested the mettle of both strikers and owners. McHugh saw it as more of a lockout than a strike and claimed that the owners had declared that "This is the time to break the union."[7]

By April the strike was beginning to have an effect. One sign was that Thomas Rice, the executive secretary of Federated Fishing Boats of New England and New York threatened to move trawlers to Rockland, Maine, whose port was still open. Declaring that the strike was "the result of unwarranted tactics by McHugh," he did dispatch one trawler, the *Flow,* to Rockland and declared that "without question, [it] would be followed by others in the near future." McHugh responded: "All this talk from Rice shows that the owners are desperate," and he followed with a threat of his own: if the owners sent trawlers to Rockland, "we'll be right there on the docks waiting for them."[8] McHugh then raised the stakes, threatening to send the Boston strikers to ports such as Gloucester that were not involved in the strike. As the *Boston Post* reported, that response would "be coordinated with similar drives in New Bedford and New York City." The tactic was impressive. Transferring the strikers to "sites" on Gloucester boats would maintain striker unity while splitting the power of the boat owners, who knew that larger crews meant an increased catch because "vessels now limit their catch to so many pounds per man."[9]

The owners were clearly unnerved. Rather than representing a depleted and weakened strike force, the AFU had outsmarted the owners by finding jobs for the strikers. On April 22 the owners offered a 55–45 lay. Detecting weakness, the union responded with a "prompt turndown" of the proposal.[10] Within days the owners agreed to meet

AFU officials to hammer out an agreement, and in those negotiations the union gained everything it had asked for. The crewmembers were rewarded with a 60–40 lay and the promise of no discrimination against anyone who had engaged in strike activity. Importantly, and for the first time, the agreement also specified that captains must become members of the union.[11]

The AFU appeared to hold a commanding position. It had won an important victory and was preparing to challenge the costs that fishermen were expected to cover, such as oil and sounding equipment, but once again the political winds were changing. By 1947 the Cold War was underway, and its impact on the domestic scene was startling. Trade unions, which had enjoyed incredible growth during the New Deal and World War II eras, were now facing a conservative backlash. Passage of the Taft-Hartley Act (Labor Management Relations Act) reined in trade union power by making organizing more difficult. Enshrined in the act was the concept of "right to work," whereby no workers could be compelled to join a union or pay union dues even when union representation was present in their workplace. At the same time Congress had begun to investigate Communist ties to the labor movement. Quickly the American labor movement became the object of Congressional attention. Such attention had a chilling effect on trade union growth and emboldened those who opposed unions' power.[12]

In this climate the AFU came under attack from antiunion forces in Boston. Starting in 1947 the AFU was swept up in a legal challenge to its status as a trade union representing northeastern fishermen. The case began in 1947, after Charles Barnes, the attorney general of Massachusetts, brought a bill of complaint against the union. Earlier that year Boston fishermen had negotiated an agreement setting a minimum price for fish, but in February, the AFU insisted the price was too low, so the men refused to unload nearly 1.5 million pounds of fish from eighteen trawlers. Local newspapers cried foul, among them the *Boston Traveler*, which demanded a "full, impartial and unsparing investigation. . . . There is something about the business much fishier than the fish."[13] Almost immediately, Barnes prepared an injunction against the union, and a *Boston Herald* reporter applauded, "More power to Attorney General Barnes in his attack on the fish trust."[14] In the state superior court, Barnes charged that the actions of the AFU were a conspiracy to set the price of fish and was a restraint of trade. The court agreed and fined the union. The AFU appealed the decision but was rejected. Eventually, the case went to the U.S. Supreme Court, but the toll on the union was severe. According to Henry Wise, the AFU's counsel, it had "detrimentally affected" the union's ability to sign contracts with vessel owners from Gloucester and Boston and Portland, Maine.[15] Throughout the 1950s, the AFU was hamstrung and destabilized by legal questions concerning its ability to represent its membership.

The situation created a split in the union ranks. New Bedford scallopers, dismayed by the AFU's inertia, decided to separate from it and form their own organization. Thus, by the 1960s New England fishermen were represented by two trade unions: the Atlantic Fishermen's Union in Boston and Gloucester and the New Bedford Fishermen's Union (NBFU) in New Bedford. Although they were separate entities, both unions were periodically affiliated with the Seafarers International Union. In 1957, the AFU voted to disaffiliate from the Seafarers because of its required per capita dues. The New Bedford men, however, maintained their membership.[16]

By 1960 the AFU had lost a large slice of its membership and was also dealing with a declining demand for fresh fish, primarily because of foreign imports of frozen fish blocks. In addition, its control over its membership and the boat owners was slipping. The success of the NBFU did much to aggravate the situation. As the AFU struggled, the NBFU was maintaining its ties to the Seafarers and cementing its position on the New Bedford waterfront. In 1960 and 1961, under the leadership of its secretary-treasurer, Howard Nickerson, it had negotiated a welfare agreement and a boost in wages. Additionally, it had inaugurated a series of safety meetings with the New Bedford Seafood Producers Association, the American Universal Insurance Company, and the U.S. Fish and Wildlife Service.[17]

The NBFU expanded its activities beyond traditional trade union activity. As a local union, it had deep roots in the surrounding community and used this solid communal foundation to extend its influence and impact. Reviving the tradition of fish celebrations, it organized an annual scallop festival to reach out to both politicians and the larger community. The third such festival was held August 12–14, 1960, when fishermen's wives and children helped prepare and serve cooked scallops. The festival took on the pageantry of community engagement and over twenty thousand people attended. Aware that local politicians could play a big role in the future of the fishing industry, the NBFU invited U.S. senators Edward Kennedy and Leverett Saltonstall and congressional representative Hastings Keith to the festival. All three attended. The NBFU also engaged in other kinds of local outreach, for instance, founding a blood bank to which members contributed ten pints of blood a week and establishing a college scholarship fund for children whose fathers had perished at sea.[18]

The AFU did not enjoy such a period of growth and community involvement. Separating from the Seafarers had a profound effect on the AFU's fortunes. Without a strong ally to provide financial and organizational support the union's membership and activities plummeted. AFU officials knew that the buoyant and energetic NBFU was a model that they should study and copy, and they believed that re-affiliation with the Seafarers was a prerequisite for growth and expansion. As a result, in October 1960, the AFU held a referendum for its 1,600 members. The leadership made their choice for reaffiliation clear on the ballot: "all fishermen and maritime workers have a common bond and must be united for mutual benefit." In the final tally, with *yes* being a vote for reaffiliation, Boston had 337 in favor and 23 against, Gloucester had 148 in favor and 9 against, and New York City had 65 in favor and 3 against.[19] The total number of votes masked the dramatic decline in organizational fervor and numbers. While there were reportedly 1,600 members in the AFU (800 in Boston, 600 in Gloucester, and 200 in New York City), only 585 members voted in the referendum, less than 36 percent.[20]

The AFU hoped its renewed connection to the Seafarers would attract new members and draw former members back. Thomas O'Brien, the union's roving business agent, pledged to recruit aggressively, claiming that there were "1,600 potential members in Gloucester alone" and targeting the Maine fishing ports of Portland and Rockland as new sites for organization. Mimicking the NBFU, the newly energized AFU embarked on a public relations campaign to convince the general public that it was a community organization that could simultaneously address the needs of their members, ship owners, fish processors, and the local port communities.

The AFU pledged to work with industry leaders and experts to raise the "US per capita consumption of fish" and ensure that the "Atlantic fishing industry can again become a well-paying business for all involved."[21]

In 1961 this early optimism seemed justified. Within weeks the AFU reported that 102 new members had joined the union—the first increase "in a long while."[22] Some of the impetus behind this influx of new members was the union's stated determination to negotiate a new contract with boat owners. The AFU was clearly aware that its earlier membership losses had been linked to its lack of union activity and authority; indeed, its last negotiated agreement had taken place in 1946. Thus, O'Brien was hopeful that a new negotiated welfare plan, modeled on the NBFU agreement, would encourage more lapsed members to return to the fold.[23] By August 1961, the AFU did ratify a new contract, which included a new welfare plan with greater employer contributions as well as rules requiring longer stays onshore between trips.[24]

While the AFU was undergoing this revival, the NBFU was maintaining its aggressive posture. Although it already had a welfare plan, it now wanted the owners to increase their contribution, and it also wanted an increase in "cure and maintenance payments" (health care benefits) from $6 to $7 per day. The proposed contract would continue to label fishermen as *employees* rather than *crewmen* to ensure that union members would be "fully protected with regard to employment security, taxes and recovery from injury sustained at work." Likewise, captains would be listed as union members "who are not boat owners." A new condition, however, was the NBFU's demand for a union hiring hall. To sweeten that demand, it agreed that for the hiring hall to work efficiently, members would need to undergo annual medical examinations to prove that members were fit to work at sea.[25]

In July 1961 NBFU members voted to ratify the three-year contract, and in a clear symbiotic display, the members simultaneously organized the fourth annual New Bedford Sea Scallop Festival. They had much to celebrate, not just the hiring hall and increased payments to the welfare fund, but also a promise of increased time off between fishing trips. According to the new contract, for every eight days spent fishing, a fisherman could take five off; for every six days spent fishing, he could take four days off.[26] More than 20,000 attended the festival, serving as a public reminder that New Bedford was the "scallop capital of the world." For the wives, the event was a herculean effort, involving thousands of scallops, "379 gallons of cooking oil, 150 dozen jars of tartar sauce, 22,000 lemon wedges, and about five tons of potatoes for French fries."[27]

Much of the NBFU's success of the New Bedford men can be attributed to Howard Nickerson, who had himself been born and raised in New Bedford. In the 1930s, after a short stint as an automobile mechanic, he was persuaded by a friend to try scallop fishing, and his experience with machines landed him a job in the engine room. Most of the crew, he recalled, were Norwegian immigrants who had come north from Brooklyn and men who had come south from Maine. Once he became a member of a regular fishing crew in 1933, he joined the AFU. Nickerson said that on a standard scalloper eleven men toiled to bring in the catch, but days off from fishing "depended on the Captains' whim." Just as aggravating for Nickerson, was the AFU's unwillingness to focus on improving the lot of its members: "We were paying $3 to $3.50 dues a month, but we got nothing." Scallopers went for years "without any benefits. A long time without even negotiating a contract." Eventually Nickerson "decided that I had to change that." In 1957, with the support of group of young union members, he ran for secretary-treasurer of the newly formed NBFU and won the election.[28]

With help of Patrick C. Harrington, a labor lawyer from nearby Fall River, Nickerson drew up a new contract, which he presented to John Lenahan of the Seafood Producers Association. The contract was eventually signed, and the union's success in this matter did much to attract new recruits, not only from the Norwegian-dominated scallop fleet but also from the Portuguese American trawlermen who worked on the dragger fleet.[29] As he worked to create this stronger more integrated trade union, Nickerson also focused on making the NBFU a permanent and durable presence within the wider community. He was particularly active in the scallop festival, which gave the union an opportunity to cement its communal ties and convinced thousands of people to eat scallops. The festival's cooking competition drew chefs and food editors from as far away as Boston and New York City, thus connecting New Bedford's townspeople and seafood producers with consumers beyond the region. Yet Nickerson also made sure that the union continued to present itself as a responsible and caring local entity. For instance, in 1958 he decided to sponsor a Memorial Day service celebrating the New Bedford men who had lost their lives while fishing. An organ from the chapel known as the Seamen's Bethel was transported down to the pier so that his wife could play it the open-air ceremony. "The Rev. Gene Landry, pastor of the Seamen's Bethel, delivered a memorial address," and Nickerson himself "read the scriptural lesson." A Coast Guard color guard participated, and there was a formal gun salute. After prayers, a wreath was dropped into the water and then dragged back to shore, to be taken later to the fishing grounds by "whichever boat is going and . . . cast upon the waters, where they are going to start fishing."[30]

As local power resurged, the NBFU and the AFU viewed each other as partners in bettering the lives of their members and improving the welfare of the fishing industry. They activated an informal alliance during contract negotiations, staying aware of which benefits the other was negotiating for and working to get the same for their own members. For instance, in 1963–64 the president of the AFU, James Ackert, aggressively insisted on major changes in the fishermen's contract with the Federated Fishing Boats of New England and New York. One demand involved the money to be paid when members were too sick to work. Another stipulated that in the event of a poor fishing trip (known as a "broker" trip), fishermen should be paid the "equivalent of a lumper's pay," and that deductions "for radar and sounding machines [should be] eliminated from the lay."[31] The NBFU had already negotiated versions of some of these benefits, and the AFU was following suit.

When Federated Fishing Boats balked at the issue of removing the deduction for electronic equipment, Boston AFU members cast ballots to decide whether or not to support strike action if the issue could not be resolved. A total of six hundred members voted to strike. With the talks stalled and fishing directly threatened, the Federal Mediation and Conciliation Service dispatched mediator John J. Sullivan to try to bring the two sides together. By mid-1964, after three days of round-the-clock bargaining, the two sides signed a tentative agreement. Although the Boston AFU did not succeed in eliminating the deduction for electronic equipment, its demand for increased maintenance and cure payments was accepted, as was the payment for broker trips.[32]

For its part, the NBFU was celebrating the addition of a pension plan, the first time retired fishermen had ever been eligible. Qualifications included being older than sixty-four, and no longer fishing but with a history of fishing for at least 175 days annually since 1959. Like the Boston AFU, however, the NBFU wanted increases in maintenance and cure payments, guaranteed minimum wages for crew members and captains, and an end to deductions for electronic equipment. Nickerson had been recently replaced by a new secretary-treasurer, Austin P. Skinner. Unlike Nickerson, Skinner, who had represented fishermen and cannery workers on the West Coast, was not a local man but a vice president of the Seafarers International Union. Joining him on the executive board was Jacob Ospensen, a port agent for New Bedford.[33]

Their talks with the owners broke down quickly when the New Bedford Seafood Producers Association insisted that a local arbitrator be appointed to oversee the negotiations. The NBFU officials were deeply suspicious of this move, believing it was a ruse to put in a proassociation representative. They claimed, "it's difficult to find an experienced, impartial arbitrator locally, one who is willing to undertake such an assignment," and instead demanded an arbitrator from the Federal Mediation and Conciliation Service be appointed. As the sides tussled over the issue, the NBFU decided to copy the AFU's aggressive tactics and ask its members to weigh in. In a 429–140 vote the New Bedford men opted to strike if negotiations broke down. Recognizing that the threatened strike action would seriously affect the profitable scallop industry, the association hammered out an agreement with the NBFU. The union got everything it wanted: no more deductions for electronic equipment, a 50 percent increase in health and welfare benefits, and a promise that in future talks either side could take the dispute to the Federal Mediation and Conciliation Service if they could not agree on a local arbitrator.[34]

The Boston AFU paid close attention to the negotiations and the NBFU's impressive win. Their union cousins in New Bedford had achieved clear victories in terms of days off, welfare and pension plans, payments for broker trips, and the removal of added fees for electronic equipment. The Boston AFU was determined to achieve similar goals. Thus in its 1966 contract talks, union officials insisted on a pension for their members, a 50 percent increase in health and welfare payments, and no more deductions for electronic equipment. Likewise, they demanded that federal arbitrators be present during the meetings. The tactic paid off: Federated Fishing Boat Owners agreed to the demands and signed a three-year contract.

By mid-1966 the contract provisions of the NBFU and the Boston and New York City branches of the AFU were nearly identical.[35] As the *Gloucester Daily Times* asked, is "Gloucester next?"[36] But despite such optimism, the Gloucester AFU had a more difficult time convincing local boat owners to make concessions. Initially, the leadership believed that mimicking the other union's aggressive stance would guarantee success. Yet when officials threatened to ballot their members and bring in federal and state mediators, the Gloucester Boat Owners Association showed that it was in no mood to accept what the union had seen as inevitable. It flatly denied the AFU's request for a pension scheme and called for a halt to equipment deductions. The association's resistance was a calculated attempt to maintain competitive advantage over its Boston and New York rivals. For Ackert and his members, however, the association's position was untenable. As Ackert made clear, the Gloucester men were merely "seeking benefits similar to those already negotiated in other major fishing ports such as Boston, New Bedford and New York." He recognized that backing down would undermine the AFU's authority and prestige, so on September 20, 1966, he "ordered picket lines set up on the city's piers," not just to stop fishermen from going to work but also to notify workers on "a number of fishing boats" who were returning from the sea. As he explained, "The crews aboard these vessels will join the strike as soon as they reach home port."[37]

More than thirty fishing boats were affected by the strike. Picket lines were set up throughout the city and work in the once thriving fishing port ground to a halt. By the second week of the strike, the owners' determination began to crumble. Ackert and the union's port agent, Michael Orlando, succeeded in getting the owners of four boats to sign a memorandum of agreement to give the workers a pension plan, stop reductions for radar equipment, and increase wage payments while in port—if the AFU could reach an agreement with the majority of boat owners.[38]

That hope was not realized, however, and the strike dragged on for forty-two days. AFU officials knew that the picket lines were key to winning or losing, so they recruited the support of retired fishermen, many of whom "showed up to help the strikers." The NBFU assisted its fellow union, dispatching men to join the picket lines, and providing financial aid. The Maritime Trades Department of the American Federation of Labor and Congress of Industrial Organizations also gave vital financial support. Thanks to such solid backing, the Gloucester AFU was finally successful in persuading the owners association to settle. Ackert and Orlando negotiated a contract that raised in-port pay from $1.00 per hour to $2.50 per hour, instituted a pension plan, and removed the payment for sounding equipment.[39]

Thus, by late 1966, all the fishery unions in Massachusetts and New York shared equal workplace privileges. Now the fishermen from the ports of New York, New Bedford, Boston, and Gloucester could enjoy revitalized and successful trade unions.

For British deep-sea fishermen, union development and power were more limited, and their existence was riven with tension and frustration. Although the trawlermen had a long tradition of trade union activity, they were unable to achieve the kinds of contract provisions their U.S. counterparts had won. Part of the issue involved their union structure. Unlike the Americans, British fishermen were divided into a number of different unions. Engineers had the Engineers' and Firemen's Union, and skippers had the Trawler Officers' Guild. Deckworkers were members of the Transport and General Workers' Union (TGWU). Yet while most skippers and engineers were union members, the deckworkers were notoriously difficult to organize, and, retain.

In a 1965 report, the TGWU estimated that a total of 7,150 deep-sea fishermen could or should be union members, but it noted that only 3,400 men were in the union at one time.[40] The ports of Hull, Grimsby, Aberdeen, Lowestoft, and Fleetwood were the centers of TGWU activity, and during the early decade union officials had been optimistic about growth. In Hull and Grimsby there was a solid core of trade union members. Trade union reports in 1960 showed that in Hull alone 1,791 fishermen were TGWU members; in neighboring Grimsby the total was 1,258; and a staggering 90 percent of Aberdeen deckhands were union members.[41] There were weak spots, however. In the conservative East Anglian port of Lowestoft, for instance, deckhands were notorious for avoiding union membership, and owners were accustomed to a compliant workforce. In October 1960 only 20 percent of Lowestoft deckhands were "in the union" and that was "still dropping."[42]

In early 1961 the TGWU tried hard to convince owners that registering fishermen as union members would stabilize work relations and lead to a fairer and more efficient method of overseeing the work force. Additionally, problematic or roving fishermen could be culled from the industry. According to Steve W. Mills, a Grimsby union official, "the object of the [registration] scheme is to deal with [the] poorer type of men and to form a disciplinary committee whereby such men could be dealt with." The owners, however, were not swayed by such arguments. H. W. Crampin of the Grimsby Fishing Vessels Owners Association declared that his members had "no enthusiasm whatsoever" for the plan. With local port officials barring the way and the National Joint Industrial Council deadlocked on the idea, an industrial tribunal was formed to decide the issue. It released its decision in the 1961 Fleck Report.[43]

This wide-ranging inquiry into the British fishing industry identified two ports with registration schemes, Aberdeen and Milford Haven, and noted that the union and owner representatives were discussing a similar scheme in Grimsby. Yet authors of the report were not ready to support a national scheme of registration, arguing that as individual ports inaugurated registration plans other ports would naturally follow suit. Moreover, "there is a tendency for a fisherman to stay in the employment of a particular owner, or even fish with a particular skipper; and a good skipper, who consistently brings back a good catch, can to a large extent take his pick of the crew."[44]

Without a national registration plan, fishermen had no guarantee of permanent employment, and they saw little reason to pay dues to the union that was clearly powerless to solve the problem. With the failure to garner a registration scheme the situation quickly deteriorated. In Aberdeen, union officials were faced with a widespread revolt. As one official announced, "a large number of fishermen, especially in the deck section will not pay union dues unless forced to do so." In August 1961 TGWU officials reported "losing members," and by April 1962 they noted a "further decline in the deck section." In contrast, 87 percent of the engineers remained organized.[45]

Recruitment and retention problems had long been common in the industry and the reasons were partly structural. After spending days or weeks at sea, fishermen were in port for only two or three days and were not especially interested in spending that time on union affairs. At a 1964 national meeting of the TGWU's fishing section, officials noted that "traditional methods of recruitment were of little avail. Fishermen, having been away for 7–24 or more days, were not well disposed to listen to an organizer on the corner expounding good ethical reasons why they should be members." Local union members had been seen dashing onto the boats to avoid union officials. In Grimsby, for example, it was reported that it was "difficult to make contact with the fishermen who hurried on board without showing any inclination or desire to discuss their industrial problems."[46]

In response, the TGWU formed a two-pronged plan: it would try to aggressively recruit and retain members, and it would ask owners to dock union dues from the fishermen's wages. In early 1961 a Lowestoft union official, Larry Chapman, inaugurated an organizing drive with two union members acting as collectors at 10:00 a.m. and again at 2:00 p.m. Following a specific daily time schedule, they handed out recruitment leaflets to local fishermen. For his part, Chapman held three union meetings per week, hoping to attract the existing members and recruit new ones. Organizers used a similar tactic in Hull, instituting daily meetings and "vigorous campaigning by circulars." Nonetheless, in October 1962 Chapman admitted that the "results" of the Lowestoft organizing effort were "very disappointing." In his view the union's inability to recruit new members resulted in a strategic weakness. He was "amazed at the [men's] lack of militancy" and was shocked that they would not attend meetings and support his efforts to negotiate better wages for them. Chapman disappointedly remarked that he "had hoped for support from the men, but found himself very much a lone figure." He tried to weather the situation, though he admitted that it required "a lot of hard work and patience." In the meantime, Lowestoft boat owners were quick to take advantage of the situation. By mid-1962 they had left the National Joint Industrial Council and were instead bargaining directly with the weakened Lowestoft men.[47]

Without a solid membership, TGWU leaders could do little to encourage owners to negotiate in good faith. Yet at an April 9, 1965, meeting, they did not primarily blame recruitment for their problems: "It was well known the great difficulty lay, not in recruiting members, but in maintaining continuity of payment of contributions once they were recruited." Owners refused to help out. For instance, when Aberdeen union officials had asked local owners to agree to dock union dues from fishermen's wages, their request was "turned down." According to the union, "until this could be achieved, there will always be a problem of lapsed members." In 1965 sixty new members had been added to the union rolls, but that growth was "offset by the number of lapsed members."[48]

The TGWU's unstable membership colored negotiations with employers. For example, it gave owners an opening to drag out negotiations over long-held grievances about working conditions. Moreover, the union's compromised bargaining position poisoned its relations with the unions that represented the skippers and engineers. In effect, the TGWU's weakness had a negative impact on trade union strength throughout the fishing industry.

Employers had little incentive to recognize trade union power. With no registration scheme, the fishermen were still considered casual workers, and after the end of a fishing trip they had no guarantee of future employment. This "hire and fire" system cooled militancy and encouraged fatalism among the fishermen. With little protection from their trade union membership, fishermen either ignored union pleas for action, or half-heartedly went along with them. Fluctuating membership numbers stretched union resources and patience, and the employers, in turn, resisted most calls for change.

The issue of protective clothing is a case in point. Traditionally, the fishermen were required to provide their own bedding and protective clothing (oilskins, hats, boots, and gloves.) In 1958 TGWU national officer, Peter Henderson, asked employers to provide such clothing, and they refused, arguing at a meeting of the National Joint Industrial Council that fishermen "had always found [their] own protective clothing . . . in consequence [they were] unable to consider the proposal."[49] After being turned down by the council, union port officials tried to get local employers to at least consider the issue. At Grimsby in September 1961, a local TGWU official, P. Grant, declared that "more industries [were now] providing protective clothing" and said that the fishing industry should do the same. The owners instead sent the issue back to the council for further consideration. At the council meeting, owners repeated their earlier contention that "provision of sea gear by the men themselves was an integral part of the wage structure and had been the acknowledged custom and practice over the years." Even though the TGWU raised the issue again in 1962, the owners refused to budge.[50]

Then, in spring 1963, Ken Adams, a Grimsby union leader, tried again with local owners, reiterating that "in other industries, including food processing factories and cold stores, this [clothing] was provided." Adams argued that fishermen should simply enjoy what other workers already had. This time, owner representative J. R. Copley "accepted the principle of the provision of protective clothing at concessionary prices." By May, "concessionary buying had been brought into operation."[51] Now other ports scrambled to get the same benefits. While Hull was successful, Aberdeen was not. By the end of the year, only Grimsby and Hull owners had agreed to provide clothing at a reduced cost, leaving the other ports waiting for a decision that never came.[52]

As I have mentioned, fishermen had no permanency in employment, which made union recruiting and retention difficult. In addition, unlike workers in shore-based industries, fishermen did not have close ties or access to their shop stewards. In other industries the stewards worked alongside their members, but in the fishing industry they were not allowed onto the fishing vessels. To counter this problem, the TGWU proposed that shop stewards should also sail, a request that owners met with hostility and that also alienated allies such as the Trawler Officers' Guild.

By 1967 it was clear to the TGWU's local and national officers that the membership had stabilized but had not grown above 50 percent of the entire workforce. They also knew that the lack of trade union representation onboard ship was seen as equally freighted. For the men, the lack of representation was perceived as a critical problem. At sea, problems with skippers could fester, and once a skipper had decided to take action against a fisherman there was no intermediary available to him. It was common for skippers to hand out legally sanctioned fines during a fishing trip, and deckhands had no recourse until the boat had docked in their home port. For shore-based workers, the presence of a shop steward ensured at least a semblance of protection from such arbitrary power.

Skippers and engineers regarded the lack of trade union commitment by deckhands as a strategic weakness.

In Henderson's view, low union membership, combined with the men's lack of fighting spirit, was causing friction with the other fishery unions. While most industries were experiencing an "expansion of membership, . . . [people] in fishing could report no such progress and naturally this was causing concern all round." Henderson believed that "engineers, firemen, fish lumpers, etc., with a long history of [trade union] membership were becoming increasingly restive at non-unionism among deck crews, bosuns, cooks, etc." They were becoming so "restive that they might be prepared to [take] action, if necessary without official sanction, to enforce membership."[53]

Henderson also thought that bringing shop stewards onto the ships was the only effective way to cement a union presence in the fishing industry. In 1966, correspondence with another national TGWU leader Jack Jones, Henderson agreed that the "sovereignty of the Master [skipper] ought not be challenged" but insisted that there were circumstances in which "shipboard representation" was required. Such examples were overtures made to the skipper to stop fishing in hazardous conditions. As Henderson pointed out, "Is it not right that deckhands, for example, should be able to register protest at being ordered to fish in force 8–10 gales, or in 'black ice' conditions?" But deckhands had little recourse in such situations because maritime law prohibited any challenge to a skipper's authority. Not only could the skipper log the offence, but he could also hand out fines for insubordination. Henderson suggested the solutions of removing the "disciplinary powers" and subjecting fishermen to the "same disciplinary code as shore based workers. Certainly nothing more severe should obtain." According to him, the 1894 Merchant Shipping Act was "archaic in the extreme and we will do our utmost to persuade the Government of the day to bring this into line with twentieth century thinking."[54]

During discussions to reform the Merchant Shipping Act, the TGWU argued forcefully that skipper fines should be abolished, which the union saw as "harsh in the extreme." Officials declared that a skipper should not be the "judge and jury in disciplining of fishermen." Instead, he should merely log the behavior as a "deterrent to further misconduct."

The union recognized that penalties should be imposed for "disobeying a lawful command relative to the safety of the vessel and those on board." But it believed that in most cases fines were handed down for a "simple act of cussedness or bloody mindedness."[55] The solution, according to the TGWU, was onboard representation, a "good deal of petty friction—and even more serious trouble—could be avoided if accredited representatives of the crew had the right to approach the Skipper to present grievances for attention." The TGWU pointed out that the merchant navy had shipboard representation and that no serious problems had been reported. It also reported that crews concerned about fishing in "Force 8–10 gales" should have their protests "entered in the log."[56] The Labor government supported the TGWU's arguments. In a memorandum to J. K. L. Taylor of the Ministry of Labor, A. W. Wood of the Board of Trade wrote, "We are of course eliminating the powers of the skipper to impose fines." Taylor agreed, insisting that skippers should simply log the offence and then allow a tribunal of union and employer representatives to make a judgment on the issue.[57]

But the TGWU also had to contend with the Trawler Officers' Guild. Throughout 1967 union officials pressed the National Joint Industrial Council to address the issue of shop stewards onboard ship. Guild members were furious. Skippers were used to holding unquestioned authority onboard the trawlers, and their union refused to accept the TGWU's proposal. It perceived anything that threatened the skippers' command as unwarranted and insurrectionary.

A schism was developing at the local level between TGWU and guild representatives. According to Ken Wardle of the Grimsby TGWU, the point was to improve relations onboard. As the situation now stood, "if a few of the lads go to the bridge and tell the skipper they think the weather is too bad, they get prosecuted for combining to disobey a lawful command." If a union representative were able to make a complaint, however, it could be put into "the log." The guild's secretary, John Jacobs, quickly dismissed that reasoning, "The skipper is master of the ship. We could not have any interference with control of the ship. Of course we will vote against the idea [at the National Joint Industrial Council meeting]."[58]

During a May 31, 1967, meeting, the council decided to establish a subcommittee to examine the issue of shipboard representation. The

Trawler Officers' Guild was not pleased. Its representative on the council's trade union side questioned the "wisdom" of such a move, pointing out that shop stewards onboard ship would undermine the skipper's command and declaring the fishing "industry was not ready for such an innovation." Tension in the meeting increased after the guild officer made "derogatory" remarks about the "men's attitudes to wages and conditions generally."[59]

Amid this fraught atmosphere, the TGWU "agreed to press" for shop stewards. The guild was clearly unhappy about this move, and on February 14, 1968, the council's trade union side met to discuss the issue further. The guild representative "made [it] clear that under no circumstances would [the skippers] tolerate any suggestion of 'shop stewards' representation on their commands." Jack Jones, the meeting chair, recognized that the issue might have "serious repercussions [for] the future harmony of the Trade Union side." Yet he believed the issue had to be taken seriously, and he was prepared to charge ahead.[60]

Jones's gamble did not pay off. In April 1968, Laurie Oliver, the secretary of the Hull branch of the Trawler Officers' Guild, declared that his organization was leaving the trade union side of the National Joint Industrial Council. According to Oliver, the guild had once "felt that we could count on the support of the T.&G.W.U. in any negotiations which we may have with the Owners but the situation has changed of late and we feel we would now prefer to fight our own battles with the employers." The issue of onboard union representation was the final straw: "As you are aware, we cannot accept your proposal of ship-board representation on trawlers." He was apologetic about leaving the council, and emphasized his "personal high regard for [Jones's] ability and efficiency but I am sure you will understand."[61] Jones's response is unknown.

Relations between the TGWU and the guild had been problematic for years. As I discuss in chapter 5, friction had developed between the two organizations during the 1958–59 Icelandic cod war. This subsequent disagreement over shipboard representation was merely one aspect of a rift that that had long been coming. The British unions' bifurcated organizational structure ensured that tensions at sea would overflow into the respective union hierarchies that represented deckhands, skippers, and engineers. Skippers had long held a privileged position both at sea and on land. Moreover, rather than living close to the docks, they had begun moving to the surrounding suburbs, and thus their residential separation mirrored that of their work and union environments. In contrast, the New England skippers, engineers, and deckhands all sat in the same union halls. Their unified stance created a powerful alliance during contract negotiations, and conflicts over working conditions.

By the late 1960s American fishermen appeared to be content with the actions of the AFU and NBFU. With the unions' aid, they had achieved important gains during the decade, including better pay, welfare and pension agreements, and an increased number of days ashore. The unified workforce in the union halls gave them a powerful identity and cemented commitment to union membership and action. British fishermen, on the other hand, seemed to be paralyzed by the casual structure of their employment, which led to longer periods spent fishing and to shorter rest periods on shore. Their fatalistic attitude toward work meant that they were not inclined to become active participants in their trade unions. Trade union officials were far more militant in their outlook and political posturing than their members were, and they were constantly frustrated by the fishermen's apathy. Without significant political power, the TGWU was unable to accomplish much until the winter of 1968 when the British distant trawler fleet suffered a series of disasters. As I show in the next chapter, these tragedies brought the hazards of the job into the public spotlight and triggered an alliance between TGWU leaders and the once silent and overlooked wives of the men who went out to sea.

CHAPTER 4

THE WIVES' CAMPAIGN

Mothers, wives, daughters, and sweethearts shared the anxiety of waiting for the men to return safely from their voyages over an unforgiving ocean. Rescue services could do little to save trawlers that were foundering in the far reaches of the Atlantic, and the fears of the British women were heightened by the fact that the men might be fishing thousands of miles away from port. As I show in this chapter, a series of disasters in the British far distant fleet confirmed their worst fears. In an extraordinary series of events, three Hull trawlers were lost in the space of few weeks, leaving in their wake a devastated but galvanized group of women.

Both fishermen and their loved ones recognized the hazards of the job, including injury and death caused by accidents and fatigue. Family members had to cope not only with the actuality of such terrors but also with the fear of them. British families dreaded the arrival of clergymen representing the Royal National Mission to Deep Sea Fishermen. Their knock on the door could only mean death and accompanying despair.[1] Generally such moments were tempered by the support of relatives and neighbors, but when a trawler went down with all hands, the whole fishing community was affected.

In the early winter months of 1968 the port of Hull suffered an astounding loss. Known as the Triple Trawler Tragedy, it began in January as the *St. Romanus,* a six-hundred-ton trawler sailed along the Norwegian coast. The ship's last radio message was on January 10, but this silence was not initially worrisome as boats often kept radio silence to avoid giving away their position to other trawlers. Because a radio operator was not sailing on the *St. Romanus,* the skipper, James Wheeldon, was supposed to be operating the radio. So even though he was not responding to radio calls, the boat owners assumed he was busy fishing.

The *St. Romanus* was sighted off the Norwegian coast on January 13, but the radio silence continued and no further sightings were reported. After ten days without a word, the crew's worried relatives asked the owners for information about the "silent trawler." The owners insisted there was "no cause for anxiety," but just to be sure they asked other vessels to keep a lookout for the *St. Romanus.* By January 25, without any news, the owners were forced to request an official search of the North Sea along the Norwegian coast.[2]

By this point Hull's Hessle Road fishing community was in shock not only because of the silent trawler but also because of the owners' reluctance to seek information about the vanished *St. Romanus.* Jack Ashwell, the TGWU's local fisheries officer, echoed the concerns of family members about the owners taking nearly two weeks to admit there might be problem linked to the radio silence. Additionally, Ashwell charged that it was irresponsible to sail without a licensed radio operator: "When the ship is fighting bad weather the skipper has to be on the bridge. How can he send out a distress signal?" He declared, "This is a matter we shall not drop."[3]

On January 29, as the search continued for the *St. Romanus,* Hull was rocked by reports of another missing trawler. The 650-ton *Kingston Peridot* had been fishing off the north coast of Iceland. The boat had been in regular contact with its owners, but when it failed to report in at its regular twelve-hour interval, they immediately reported her missing. Within a day a rubber dinghy and life rafts had washed up near Kópasker, on Iceland's northern shore. Wreckage, including signal lights and rocket containers, was sighted off the coast, as was a "long oil slick." Now two air and sea searches were underway in the northern seas.

The Hessle Road fishing community was in deep distress. The sheer scale of two trawlers lost brought to the surface deep-seated fear tinged with anger. A reporter with the *Hull Daily Mail* wrote, "The 40 missing men are on everybody's minds. Forty husbands, sons, brothers, sweethearts. Forty cousins, nephews and mates." A resident said, "The waiting is awful. Everybody's just waiting." The loss was also forcing the community to revisit past tragedies. Speaking of a woman who had lost family members in previous disasters, a friend explained: "It brought everything back to her. It must have brought it back to a lot of people."[4]

On February 2, the *St. Romanus* was officially declared lost. But while this ended the families' hopes of finding survivors, it began a new era in community activism. One prime mover was Lillian Bilocca. She had been born in Hull and was the daughter, wife, and mother of fishermen. She herself was employed in a fish-processing plant near the docks.[5] When the *St. Romanus* and the *Kingston Peridot* were reported lost, her son was out to sea on another boat, so she understood the terrors that families were facing. Another major activist was Yvonne Blenkinsop, a locally well-known cabaret singer whose father had died four years earlier.

The loss of the trawlers enraged both women. As Blenkinsop remarked to her family, "It can't go on like this. There must be a way to improve on things. We have lovely planes and outer space things happening now, so why haven't we put more technology into our [fishing] business?" She always had a sense of community responsibility. She was not one to stand by while an injustice was committed. She credited her mother with giving her such a heightened sense of justice and dignity, which was instilled in her at a young age: "If anybody was at school, if anybody was in trouble, I would always stand up for them. Always. It's the only way to be. And my mother taught me that." Blenkinsop's fearlessness put her in dangerous positions at times. In one instance, a crowd of men were beating a man in a local restaurant. She broke up the fight single-handedly by shouting at the attackers, "yelling they were cowards and [how] would they like it if someone did that to them?" Another incident saw her protecting a street Bilocca and bus driver from attack. A young man with a "belt . . . wrapping around his hand" had cornered the bus driver in his "little cubbyhole" and began "hitting him." Blenkinsop confronted the attacker: "I thought of every rude word I could think of and shouted as loud as I could. And he ran away at the finish." As she explained later, "How could you sit there and let somebody bash somebody like that? With a belt buckle and do nothing?"[6]

As the drama of the lost ships unfolded, Blenkinsop was unable to "sleep at all; I couldn't clear my mind." She met on the street Bilocca and other interested and traumatized women. It was just "four or five of us talking and someone says, 'Why don't we get the keys to Victoria Hall?'" Galvanized to action, she and Bilocca booked the community hall and called a meeting of fishermen's family members. On February 2 Blenkinsop set up the "amplification equipment" she had used in her cabaret shows, and the two waited, not knowing who might appear. In fact, hundreds of people showed up. Blenkinsop was amazed at the large turnout at Victoria Hall: "you wouldn't believe the people who turned up. I don't know where they came from. It was as if they [fishermen's wives] had all headed there, it was full."[7] During the chaotic event, various future activists emerged from the audience to speak. Although Blenkinsop had not intended to be a central figure, she found her voice that day, declaring, "Our men are fools, with hearts of gold to do it." She pointed out in her speech that trawlers should have better signaling equipment as well as "luminous paint for easy recognition in the dark or half-light of the Arctic winter."[8]

Mary Denness also stepped out of the shadows to take a leadership position. Denness was a Hull native, a wife of a trawler skipper, and a daughter of a fisherman. After leaving school at the age of fifteen, she went to work in a factory that made fish boxes. Bored by the job, she took the extraordinary step at the age of seventeen of trying to get a job as a stewardess on merchant ships that also carried passengers. She was initially waved away and told to reapply when she had turned twenty-one. She persisted, and at the age of nineteen, she was hired and sent off to London to catch her first ship. Thus she had "started a short but very enjoyable sea going career." The job, she said, "opened my eyes to the world, and I had been halfway around the world. I came back, maybe not educated to a higher degree academically, but certainly more worldly than I had left."[9]

Denness credited her four brothers with pushing her to take risks. As the lone daughter in a household full of boys, she had no encouragement from her "mother [who] kept me as a drudge." But her brothers encouraged her to be "more ambitious." She said, "I learned to be strong, assertive, and that stood me in good stead later in life." As her brothers headed off to sea, she merely wanted to follow them: "I wanted to be doing what my brothers were doing—to go to sea in ships." "So, yeah, my brothers were my mentors. Without a doubt."[10]

After returning to Hull, Denness met and married a fishermen's mate, Barry Denness. Soon her husband was promoted to skipper, and their lives began to change. They moved to a small suburb outside of Hull. Being married to a skipper ensured that their standard of living would rise: "It was, for me, a real step up the ladder. . . . This was the first house I had lived in that had its own bathroom. Wow, that was luxury, believe you me." The couple had three children in quick succession, and Denness's life fell into a predictable pattern of a fisherman's wife. Like most of them, she had to run the household alone. As she explained, "The fishing community was very much a matriarchal system. The women brought up the children, saw to everything onshore, paid the bills. Anything that had to be seen to was done by the women." A husband's return was invariably awkward: "My routine was put on the back boiler. Chaos ensued cause it was all eats, sweets, days out, and before we had drawn breath . . . he was a way again."[11]

Denness's childhood and work experience as a ship stewardess, had given her an independent spirit, but they had also made her acutely aware of the injustices that fishermen faced in their working lives. While merchant seamen enjoyed strong unions and good benefits, fishermen did not. Denness had witnessed firsthand the better working conditions onboard merchant vessels. She also understood, as most fishing families did, how the trawler owners "mistreated their employees." As I have discussed, the casual nature of the job ensured acquiescence and a fatalistic attitude. Unlike coal miners, for instance, who finished their shifts at the same time and "could mass together in a hall," fishermen came into port a "few ships at a time." On shore the men were not interested in union meetings "but [in] going out and enjoying themselves. So getting a strong union was very difficult and that's where the trawler owners ruled."[12] Blenkinsop, too, blamed the owners for refusing to improve the lot of fishermen: "If any of the men folk spoke up of things that they knew were wrong on the ships—the first thing that was done—they didn't have a ship!" Although the owners "didn't keep them out indefinitely," the lesson was clear: "It was enough so that you were scrimping and scraping and you've got kids to look after. And this happened all the time."[13]

After the first trawler losses, many community members were irate about what they saw as the owners' coldheartedness. According to Blenkinsop, the owner's ten-day delay in sharing *St. Romanus* news with the families "infuriated the entire fishing fraternity." Denness says it was seen as "outrageous. So that started that anger building up." So word came in of terrible weather in the North Atlantic, especially around Iceland, and fear became endemic throughout the community. Reports that the *Kingston Peridot* had gone down began circulating around town, yet other trawlers continued to fish in the vicinity. As Denness recalled, "we were now fearful that if two trawlers had gone down in the space of a couple of weeks, it wasn't going to stop." When the loss of the second ship, the *Kingston Peridot* was confirmed, "panic, fear, plus the anger all melted into one pot and like a volcano, erupted."[14]

Denness was deeply affected by the sheer scale of the tragedy. She had never lost a family member at sea, though she had "lots of friends" who had. But in most cases, fatalities had occurred in single incidents, perhaps because a man had been ill at sea or been washed overboard. Now, with the loss of two trawlers, she knew, "dozens of names" among the forty men who had gone down with the ships. Incredulous and angry, she joined hundreds of women at the first Victoria meeting, but as the wife of a skipper, she was wary about fomenting problems with crewmembers' families. Out at sea, her husband "was God Almighty because he was the only law that governed that little space on board that ship." She knew that others resented that power, and her apprehension was realized soon enough. When Bilocca asked for volunteers to join a deputation to meet the owners, Denness shouted, "Well, I'd volunteer if no one else wants [to]." Another audience member responded, "We don't want a load of skippers' wives representing us!" But Bilocca was not going to allow any disunity in the wives' ranks. She asked, "Did the skippers come home? Did the skippers go down with their ships or did they come home?" After her words, there was "a deathly silence" in the room. Then Bilocca continued, "They went down with their ships. So they have a right to be represented." Attendees voted to allow Denness to join the deputation.[15]

Following the meeting, Bilocca led a delegation to the docks and demanded a meeting with the owners. The women carried with them a hastily put-together petition and a six-point safety charter. The owners refused to meet them. Furious about such indifference, Bilocca declared,

"There's only one way to make these people meet us and hear our case and that's by taking direct action. We are determined to fight this to the end, whatever the cost." She was as good as her word. The next morning she led a group of wives to the docks to monitor trawlers that were leaving for the fishing grounds. As the trawler *St. Keverne* was sailing through the lock gates crew members yelled to the assembled women that no radio operator was on board. At that point, Bilocca—along with Mary Pye, who had lost her second husband on the *St. Romanus*—attempted to jump the fence and climb onto the *St. Keverne*. Police moved in to hold the women back, and there was a melee of "shouting, fighting and screaming." Pye told reporters, "I have five sons and all are trawlermen. I have come here to protest about the safety conditions on the trawlers. A lot more could be done. For the next three weeks [while her sons were fishing] I shall be living in fear and anxiety." Although the Hull *Daily Mail* noted the protesters' low turnout numbers, Bilocca insisted, "Nevertheless, I shall carry on this fight to the bitter end."[16]

The small turnout can be explained by the women's long-standing reluctance, tinged with superstition, to visit the male-dominated fish dock. In Hull, St. Andrew's fish dock was traditionally a male-only space. According to Elizabeth Musgraves, a fisherman's wife, the tunnel onto the dock led into "a strictly man's world. It has been that way for generations and won't change any more than the cruel elements of the sea can ever change."[17] Even Blenkinsop avoided the dock protest: "I would not go down the dock when the men were going out because I think it's bad luck." She admitted to being "very superstitious" and was unwilling to take any action that might threaten the men's lives.[18]

Nonetheless, the direct action, small as it was, had its intended effect. Reporters witnessed the tussle at the lock gates and covered the incident in the newspapers and on television news. Local TGWU officials and Labour Party politician Kevin McNamara, who represented Hull in Parliament, were actively calling for better safety conditions after the two disasters, and they saw the women as useful allies. McNamara helped the women arrange a meeting with trawler owners and then arranged a visit to Parliament so they could meet with Fred Peart, the minister of agriculture and fisheries, and Joseph Mallalieu, the minister of the Board of Trade. Jack Jones, the assistant executive secretary of the TGWU, was also involved in setting up that meeting. Initially, he had asked the prime minister, Harold Wilson, to speak to the delegation, calling it a "matter of extreme urgency" and a way to "prevent repetition of these tragic events." Wilson, however, declined, saying that the ministers "will of course inform me of your discussions with them."[19]

On Monday, February 5, Denness, Bilocca, and Blenkinsop were at the hairdresser getting ready for a meeting with boat owner Mark Elliot of Elliot Brothers trawling fleet, when they suddenly heard the devastating news that another Hull trawler had gone down. The *Ross Cleveland,* and several other fishing vessels had been trying to shelter from hurricane-force winds and snow in a fjord on Iceland's northwestern coast, but the wind was blowing off a nearby glazier, creating icing conditions. The crews on the assembled boats recognized that the situation was dire. Sure enough, as the ice began to build up on the *Ross Cleveland,* the trawler became top heavy and slowly began to capsize. At midnight, the other ships heard the following radio message from Skipper Phil Gay of the *Ross Cleveland*: "I am going over. We are laying over, help me." There was a slight pause and then the words: "I am going over. Give my love and the crew's love to the wives and families."[20]

Christine Smallbone, the fourth member of the women's delegation, had not yet heard the news when she turned up for her hairdressing appointment. When the other women told her what had happened, she was appalled: her brother was Philip Gay, the skipper of the *Ross Cleveland.* Later that day, she somehow managed to turn up for the meeting with the boat owner, but Denness was apprehensive about her mental state. She remembered that Smallbone "was red-eyed and hardly able to stand up. And I thought, 'Oh my God, how is she going to get through this day?'" Elliot chose to meet the women in the boardroom, sitting "in a big fancy chair" while they were invited to sit on "ordinary dining chairs." The seating arrangement convinced Denness that he did not take their delegation seriously. What she saw was a "man on his throne lording [it] over these females." As she felt herself "getting angrier and angrier," she kept an eye on the increasingly upset Smallbone, who sat across from her. Though Denness "could see right through" Elliot, she refrained from interrupting the proceedings. She explains that she, "had to think of the other ladies and Christine was keeping me subdued because of her despair." Eventually, Smallbone could endure the meeting no longer and was escorted out of the room by the port chaplain.[21]

The three remaining women began their presentation to Elliot. They told him they knew that the owners must be aware of the dangers faced by their crews and insisted that something be done to improve safety. The women gave him a list of demands, including a mother ship to provide weather information and medical support, a ban on fishing in rough weather, and improved communication equipment. Denness, however, remained convinced that Elliot was not taking them seriously: he merely "saw us as women of Hessel Road; not terribly educated, straw in our hair, don't know what we're talking about really." With hordes of journalists waiting outside, he did not want to "be seen as the big bad wolf so I'll just humor you for a little while [longer]." She claimed, "He didn't [think] . . . that we were going to do anything because we hadn't the skills. However, he was to learn a hard lesson."[22]

After the meeting, Lillian Bilocca vented her frustration and anger. Turning to a nearby group of fishermen, she shouted, "Another ship has gone down . . . more lads have died. Don't go lads. No one gives a damn about you." For the Hessle Road community this third loss came as a terrible shock. As one journalist wrote, "the news hit them like the blow that fells an already groggy boxer." Older fishermen "talked of black ice and towering seas: 'These ships are built to take those sort of seas, it is the ice that gets them.'"[23]

Now the women were even more determined to speak with the government ministers in London. To prepare, Bilocca, Denness, and Blenkinsop met on February 5 with Jack Ashwell and Kevin McNamara at TGWU's district headquarters in Bedenhouse. According to Denness, both men were "very, very helpful." They coached the women on how to approach the ministers, saying, "you ought to ask this and you ought to ask that." Denness found "their advice was invaluable."[24]

On the following day, February 6, the three boarded a train to London's King's Cross Railway Station. Christine Smallbone was still too distraught over her brother's death to take part, but McNamara and a posse of journalists accompanied the delegation. According to Denness, so many "pressmen . . . were onboard the train" that "we could hardly find seats." Throughout the rail journey, the three women were "continuously interviewed," yet they were unprepared for the size of the crowds that awaited them at King's Cross Station. To control the onlookers, police had been forced to set up barriers along the railroad platform. When the women stepped off the train, however, the crowd fell eerily quiet. A female reporter from the BBC's Woman's Hour grabbed Denness by the arm and steered her into a nearby bathroom for an impromptu interview. Then the women and McNamara piled into a taxicab and drove quickly to the House of Commons. Denness recalled the pace as "manic." Jack Jones, TGWU's assistant executive secretary, met the delegation outside the House. Once inside, the visitors were given lunch and then ushered into their meeting with Fred Peart and Joseph Mallalieu.

Well before this meeting, the ministers had felt pressured to provide solutions to the crisis in Hull. They knew that Denness had already declared, "We don't want promises. We want action." She had threatened to "stay in London until we get something definite done," and Bilocca had suggested that they should sit on the steps at 10 Downing Street until their demands were met.[25] Days before the women arrived in London, Peart's parliamentary secretary was prepping him on how to greet the delegation. On February 5, the day before the meeting, Peart and Mallalieu had met with the prime minister, Harold Wilson, at 10 Downing Street to discuss the issue. The ministers agreed that the fishing industry in general was in deep trouble. Hundreds of fishing boats were unfit for service, and the owners' "19th century capitalist attitude" could not continue. Though an independent inquiry was crucial, Wilson was adamant that it should not "stand in the way of taking any immediate action that was considered necessary for the safety of vessels currently at sea."[26]

At the February 6 meeting at the House of Commons, the women were joined by twenty-one other people, an amalgam of trade union leaders and ministry officials from the Board of Trade, the Ministry of Agriculture and Fisheries, and the Ministry of Labor. Peart opened the meeting by expressing his sympathy for the terrible losses endured by the people of Hull and asking the delegation to "speak frankly on any ideas which they had." Jones, the TGWU official, responded by demanding that the government focus not just on the loss of the three trawlers "but on all problems of the trawler fishing industry and the safety of its men." He insisted that shop stewards needed to be on board ships to "raise . . . questions of safety" with the skippers. Additionally, he believed that the government should declare the waters north of the Arctic Circle off limits during winter and said that safety and training should be the mainstay of employment relations.[27]

Yvonne Blenkinsop spoke next, declaring that boats should be equipped with ice-clearing technology, mother ships should be standing by to provide medical and weather support, owners should be supplying fishermen with protective clothing (a situation that "had not been changed since her grandfather's time"), and deckie learners should not be allowed to sail in winter. Then Lillian Bilocca stated that the women had asked for this meeting in order to convince the government "to overcome the indifference of the owners." Above all, she believed ships should always sail with "a radio operator (not the skipper) on board." A. D. Shenton, the secretary of TGWU's Humber district, reiterated Bilocca's emphasis on the owners' "indifference." He "felt compelled to say that the lives of the trawler men were a secondary consideration with the owners," and he argued that the men's long working hours "were outrageous" and "naturally led to mistakes through fatigue." Michael Neve, TGWU's Hull-based fishing officer, explained that fishermen needed a union registration plan if they were to counter the enormous power of the owners and avoid being penalized when raising safety issues. At the end of the meeting, Peart and Mallalieu thanked the assembled stakeholders and declared they would call for an official inquiry of the fishing industry as a whole, and with a specific focus on safety at sea. In a parting shot, Mary Denness warned them that the "mood in Hull is now emotional, but tomorrow it would be militant" if the families' concerns were not adequately addressed and if "some effective action" were not forthcoming.[28]

The women returned to Hull after the meeting, feeling grateful that the government ministers and assembled trade union officials had taken their concerns seriously. At the same time, they were somewhat disturbed by the behavior of Mallalieu, who Denness recalled had "turned up late and very drunk." Peart ran the meeting, and for the most part Mallalieu stayed quiet. But when he did speak, "he was [only] slightly coherent . . . [And] oh dear, the alcohol fumes!"[29] They were heartened, however, by Peart's promise that the government would immediately insist on regular twelve-hour radio contact, require ice-clearing machinery to be installed on ships, close fishing grounds during extreme weather, and mandate that a mother ship be standing by to provide weather updates and medical attention. Bilocca was impressed by the meeting, exclaiming: "The wheels are moving. . . . We have got further today than others have in years and years and years." Denness was also happy about the outcome: "Every detail was discussed. They were really wonderful." Their spirits rose even more when they learned that one crewman from the *Ross Cleveland* had managed to survive the disaster. When the boat capsized, the mate Harry Edom, had scrambled into a rubber dinghy with two other crewmen. Both perished within matter of hours because of hypothermia, but Edom had managed to stay alive and get himself to land. There he found an empty summer home and waited under a shelter. The following day a shepherd boy heard his cries for help and escorted him to a farmhouse, where he was given warm clothing and food.[30]

As Hull celebrated Edom's miraculous survival, the three women called a meeting of the fishermen's wives to detail their trip to London. In "blunt workmanlike speech" (as one journalist reported), Bilocca explained the government's promise to institute immediate safety improvements and establish an official inquiry that would look at safety across the industry. After each item, "the audience applauded and cheered," and when she had finished speaking they gave her "three cheers." The *Hull Daily Mail* reported that the audience "roared with cheers." Denness later testified that there "was thunderous support" for what the three women had achieved.[31]

Using their newly found skills for public speaking and organization, they not only brought Hull's local tragedy into national prominence but also convinced the government to institute substantial safety improvements in an industry that was solely in need of change. Despite their success, however, internal divisions soon began to rock their fledgling organization. In particular, many locals became dissatisfied with Bilocca's leadership. Although she had been the lightning rod for the spontaneous movement, people became increasingly uncomfortable with her aggressive manner. In interviews with reporters she was invariably blunt and outspoken, and her working-class South Riding accent embarrassed some listeners. The backlash against Bilocca began in earnest after the government and the trawler owners forbade fishing above the Arctic Circle. In letters to the *Hull Daily Mail*, some locals accused her of taking work away from fishermen. For instance, H. Harling asked in a letter to the paper, if Bilocca was pleased that foreign trawlers ("German, Russian and Icelandic") would now take the fish left by the departing British. "Surely," Harling wrote, "it rests with the fishermen themselves where and when they" go fishing. Nonetheless, other locals continued to support Bilocca. One fisherman's wife wrote, "I think Mrs. Bilocca is fabulous. She has great courage in supporting our fishermen heroes."[32]

More trouble soon followed. During an interview with the television personality Eamonn Andrews, Bilocca remarked that the wives had begun the campaign because the men were away at sea most of the time, and on their return, they looked forward to a few "bevies" (beers) and did not have "time to sort out their affairs." Some wives took offense at the suggestion that the men were interested only in drinking a few "bevies." One wife wrote to the *Hull Daily Mail*, "I am sure hundreds of wives, along with myself, will feel ashamed to mention outside our city that they are fisherman's wives." She emphasized that she and many other local women were not "putting on airs and graces" like Bilocca was.[33]

Bilocca and her colleagues believed they could weather such remarks. but just before delivering a speech to students at the University of Strathclyde in Scotland, Bilocca learned she had been fired from her job as a fish processor. Her husband, Charlie, had told her not to worry because "she had the whole world with her." She agreed, recalling that the sacking "made me even more determined to battle on." She stood up before an audience in Strathclyde and suggested that perhaps the fishermen should strike to teach the owners a lesson. She also mused (or was misrepresented as doing so) that perhaps the wives should withhold sexual favors until their men stood up for themselves.[34] The backlash was immediate and damning. Leading members of the wives' campaign, including Denness, were vocal in their annoyance. Denness said that the idea of a strike was "ludicrous," and claimed that Bilocca was "making this whole thing into a one-woman crusade." Denness was frustrated: "As we take one step forward this happens and we go back again. We are losing support through this kind of talk." Blenkinsop agreed, describing the idea of a strike as "downright stupid," and declaring, "I still support most strongly the basic ideas of this campaign, but no one wants to be talking of striking."[35]

In later years, Denness was more sympathetic to Bilocca, whom she believed had been manipulated to spout out a militant posture. As Denness put it, "Words were being put into her mouth by the questions they [reporters] were asking. A more educated, a more astute [person] would have said whoa. No, she didn't see it so I think she was unfairly judged." But at the same time, Denness thought that Bilocca had crossed the line. Bilocca's comments had "divided the men from the women." For her part, Blenkinsop could not forgive Bilocca for suggesting a sex strike by the wives: "Do you think we're going to cut off our own noses to spite our faces?" She continued, "I won't say that I won't have sex with my husband for three weeks or six weeks or nine weeks, however long it went on. I certainly won't have my husband talked to like that."[36]

For Jack Ashwell, the local trade unionist, Bilocca's comments at Strathclyde came at a bad time. The government was finally ready to confront the long-standing safety concerns, but her talk of strikes had slowed momentum. He told reporters that he would try to discover what Bilocca had been saying in Scotland, and then he called a meeting of the wives to discuss the issue. Bilocca, meanwhile, tried to distance herself from her strike statements. She pointed out to reporters that she was not "trying to do the union's job." Indeed, she explained, men ruled the roost in Hull: "If people are beginning to think that trawlermen are tied to apron strings they should come to Hull and see for themselves." Her husband, tried to portray himself as fully supportive of his wife: "I think Lil is doing the right thing to fight for better safety conditions on trawlers." But he could not conceal the family's strain, admitting their household was receiving a deluge of letters, and "some of them are nasty."[37]

Bilocca knew that Ashwell had called the meeting to discuss her future as leader of the wives' campaign, so beforehand she tried to approach the other leaders. She telephoned Denness to explain her version of the unfolding drama, and Denness pledged to withhold final judgment until the meeting, but matters were soon out of their hands. After TGWU officials visited Bilocca to find out what had happened in Strathclyde, they announced they "had cleared up the matter with her." Nonetheless, they had determined that the wives' campaign needed to end. A union spokesman, Michael Neve, explained, "The wives association is not going to be for industrial purposes. The trawlermen and the union are capable of looking after this side of our affairs." Instead, the TGWU had decided that wives should take on a supportive role such as comforting grieving widows who had lost their husbands at sea, or arranging social events for fishermen's families. During a February 23 closed-door meeting with the wives, TGWU officials made it clear that they were eager to regain control of the situation and to harness the wives' power.[38] They also wanted to rein in excess publicity. According to Ashwell, the closed meeting prevented people from "making speeches for the Press rather than for the good of the new association." Mary Denness and Christine Smallbone were voted in as joint chairs, and Lillian Bilocca was ousted from her leadership role, but she joined seven other women on the executive committee instead. Bilocca claimed she was happy with the result: "Everything went off lovely. We are all united again." Her enthusiastic portrayal was tempered by Smallbone's comments, "[There was no] unpleasantness between Big Lil and the rest of us. But we cannot say she has been accepted back completely."[39]

Among the wives, Smallbone was a major force behind the change in tack from fighting for fishermen's safety to becoming a welfare organization for fishing families. She explained that the women remained keenly interested in the "safety of our men folk [but] we have decided to leave that to the union representatives."[40] Not all of her colleagues agreed, however. Blenkinsop left the meeting after forty-five minutes, declaring to reporters who had assembled outside the venue, "We came here to talk about safety and not about social work." She felt betrayed by the new direction: "I certainly don't want to go into a bloody mother's meeting."[41] Another woman, Dianne Horsfield, agreed: "They have gone right off the point. We want to know about the safety angle and we don't want anything to do with welfare."[42]

In the end, this change in direction and the loss of women like Blenkinsop doomed the organization. The original leaders had waged a successful campaign to pressure the government and the boat owners to make substantive improvements, but when the group became welfare-oriented, many wives lost interest. In the meantime, the original activists were paying a personal price. Bilocca was inundated with hate mail. Others faced troubles in their marriages. Denness recalled that Smallbone "got a lot of blitzing from her husband. . . . And she moved on, and he was left back." Denness herself felt a strain in her marriage. After the organization refocused on welfare activities, her husband told her, "C'mon, you've done your bit, now come out of it." But Denness had discovered "a strength that was not being used and should be used for the good [of all]." "But," as she explained, "I had a husband who didn't want a strong wife, and so, I'm afraid, divorce finished up on the cards. Not there and then, but a few years later."[43]

Most of the leaders felt they had been shunted aside by the fishermen and union officials. Blenkinsop believed "the men were doing their best to shove us back out of the way and not have any say." In her view they were implying, "We can do it now. That's fine." Denness agreed, adding that some men felt emasculated by the actions of the women. Although they were grateful, "We thank you very much for your help," they nonetheless felt that other men "were laughing at them because they had left the women to do the fighting." This "affront to their masculinity" became a powerful tool for pushing the women to the sidelines.[44]

The women leaders came together for a final time on March 8, 1968, at the memorial service for the fishermen who had been lost in the three trawler disaster. At the service, the bishop of Hull asked those who would conduct the official inquiry to follow it with "meaningful" reforms. If effective action could be taken, "then indeed they will not have died in vain." But, he went on to say, "Like all seafarers they had their own philosophy which comes from living close to the rigors and realities of the natural world, more perhaps than we who live in man-made cities."[45]

Thanks to the wives' campaign, people all over Great Britain learned about the hazards of working on trawlers and the cruelty of the sea. For a brief period in the winter of 1968, people began to understand what trawlermen endured to provide fish for the nation's dinner plates. On an individual level, the women's spontaneous actions were also hugely influential. Mary Denness "saw the whole world in a different light after that campaign." The effort had galvanized the women to look beyond their immediate domestic concerns, to challenge an industry that did little to protect its own. Briefly, these women assumed the mantle of protector; they became the guardians of their husbands' working lives. Because of that experience, they began to recognize their own power. As Denness said, "at the end of the campaign, the only thing I regret is that I didn't start sooner, shout louder, and make it last longer."[46] While tragedies of sunken boats with all hands periodically staggered local fishing communities and the general public, a more ominous threat was becoming evident. Nations around the world were examining ways to protect fish resources close to their shores. Iceland, in particular, would challenge the British trawlermen's livelihood with a series of devastating cod wars.

CHAPTER 5

THE COD WARS

For British fishermen, access to foreign fishing grounds was tantamount for their survival. Thus their territorial disputes with Iceland, which became known as the cod wars of 1958–59 and 1972–73, challenged their very existence as fishermen. As the cod wars made clear, the nation's long-distance fishing fleet was economically vulnerable, and when Iceland decided to impose coastal fishing limits, British fishing interests went on the defensive immediately. Even before hostilities broke out, both the fishermen's unions and the fishing crews were demanding naval protection from marauding Icelandic gunboats. Nonetheless, during skirmishes on the high seas, the British trawlermen found themselves on the front lines, and frustrated with their government's inaction, they began threatening to withdraw from the fishing grounds, a political and economic red flag that the government was forced to take seriously.

Tensions between Iceland and foreign fishing fleets were grounded in Iceland's argument that fish stocks around its coast were seriously declining and in danger of devastation. The fish industry comprised 80 to 90 percent of the nation's exports. Only 1 percent of its land was cultivated, and only 23 percent was used for animal grazing. More than 76 percent was made up of "uninhabitable wastes of mountains, glaziers, lava fields, lakes and sands."[1] Thus, Icelanders saw any threat to their fishery as a distinct threat to their entire economy and maritime way of life.

As Icelanders mulled over the need to defend their coastal fishery, they were influenced by evolving international laws. For centuries, a nation's territorial waters had been generally established at three miles, which was the maximum distance traveled by a shell or cannonball fired from a warship. But following World War II, Harry Truman, the president the United States, had issued a series of proclamations extending maritime jurisdiction. Known as the Truman Proclamations, the basic point was that the United States wanted to protect mineral resources beyond the continental shelf and beyond the three-mile limit. The proclamations also declared that conservation zones should be created to protect fish stocks. The American stance opened the way for other coastal nations to expand their territorial limits, and Chile, Ecuador, and Peru rushed to extend their maritime sovereignty to two hundred miles. In 1951 Norway used these territorial movements as precedent when it declared that its limit should be extended to four miles. The International Court of Justice ruled in Norway's favor.[2]

As this movement to increase fishery limits was gaining legal and political momentum, Iceland announced it was enlarging its territorial limit to twelve miles. In response, the British government argued that international law did not recognize such unilateral declarations, and it appealed to the newly established United Nations Conference on the Law of the Sea for redress. This conference had been tasked to overseeing and making judgments on issues of international maritime law such as freedom of passage, freedom of the seas, and territorial limits. Its creation was part of an overall movement toward international collaboration and control following World War II. During the nineteenth and early twentieth centuries, there had been several attempts to legislate territorial fishing boundaries and fishing limits, but after 1945, as advances in science and technology led to larger fishing catches and better ways to gauge them, the need for international control became paramount. At the same time, decolonization movements in the developing world added to global concerns about the increase in catches and the corresponding declines in fish stocks. The conference was founded to address these issues.[3]

The First Conference on the Law of the Sea took place in Geneva on February 24, 1958. Eighty-seven nations were represented. At the gathering, the Icelanders and the British presented their respective cases. Iceland's delegates argued that its fishery was being depleted by other European fishing fleets, especially Great Britain's, and that a twelve-mile limit was needed to protect fish stocks. The British delegation made the point that international law still recognized the three-mile limit as the standard for a nation's territorial limits. They also argued that their nation's trawlermen had fished off Iceland's coast for decades and thus had historical precedent for continuing to do so. After much discussion, representatives at the conference could not come to an agreement about the case and referred it for further consideration to the Second Law of Sea Conference, scheduled to be held in 1960.[4]

With the failure of the talks, Iceland was determined to extend its territorial limits to protect its coastal fishery. In May 1958 it declared that starting on September 1 it would impose a twelve-mile territorial limit. In response, the British Conservative government announced that it was staunchly opposed to any such action without international approval. It therefore pledged to provide naval support for British fishermen who fished within that zone. To some observers, Great Britain, despite its stature as a declining world power, seemed to behave like a bully. Yet in the ensuing daily confrontations with Icelandic gunboats, the British were on the defensive.

After Iceland's government declared that its twelve-mile limit would begin September 1, some members of Trawler Officers' Guild threatened to stop fishing in those waters without guaranteed support. Leading the charge was Dennis Welch, the secretary of the Grimsby branch of the guild. In a closed-door meeting on April 22, 1958, he and his guild members passed a resolution stating that skippers out of Grimsby, Hull, and Fleetwood would refuse to sail to Iceland unless the British government banned Icelandic trawlers from unloading fish in British ports. Welch also predicted that Iceland's territorial actions would divert more British trawlers to the North Sea, "which is already over-fished and will soon be barren." Foreign Office officials reacted angrily to Welch's statements and the guild's resolutions. In a memorandum forwarded to Paul Gilchrist, Britain's ambassador to Iceland, they exclaimed that the guild meeting had included the votes of only the Grimsby skippers, not the total membership in other ports, and they dismissed Welch as "not a practical fisherman." The Foreign Office also insisted that the trade union officials should not be acting as power brokers, saying the employer group "The British Trawlers' Federation is anyhow the important body on policy matters." Clearly the Conservative government, historically inclined to favor owners over unions, did not consider the guild officials worthy of serious consideration.[5]

While the Grimsby guild was passing resolutions, the British government, working closely with the British Trawlers' Federation, was establishing its own strategy to protect trawlers that chose to fish within Iceland's newly established twelve-mile limit. The plan was to keep Royal Navy ships standing by to counter any interference from Icelandic gunboats, and to make that task easier the government encouraged trawlers to work in designated protected areas.[6] In a memorandum forwarded to all trawler skippers, the British government outlined its strategy. It insisted that skippers who fished outside safe zones would "do so at their own risk" and noted that the position of all Icelandic gunboats should be reported immediately to the nearest protection vessel. If gunboat crews attempted to board a trawler, "the skipper should protest vigorously and seek to prevent his vessel from being boarded." The memorandum warned that firearms or explosives should not be used to defend the trawler but did suggest possible ways to "delay Icelandic [boarding] operations" through passive resistance. For example, skippers should "immobilize engines by removing and hiding an easily replaceable part." Additionally, skippers were instructed to ignore any signals from Icelandic fishery aircraft.[7]

The Icelanders were also preparing for the coming confrontation. Their tactics became clear to the British on September 2 when the gunboat *Thor* approached the trawler, *Northern Foam,* which was fishing inside the twelve-mile limit. Once alongside the British trawler, the crew of the *Thor* linked the two vessels with grapples and a party of ten men jumped onboard the *Northern Foam,* but the trawler had already sent a radio alert to HMS *Eastbourne* for assistance. The *Eastbourne* arrived shortly thereafter, and it too sent a boarding party onto the *Northern Foam.* Outgunned, the captain of the *Thor* was forced to admit defeat, but he refused to allow his own boarding party back onto the gunboat. The embarrassed naval officers had to transfer the Icelandic boarding party to the *Eastbourne* and hold them until the two nations could reach a diplomatic solution.[8]

The British Foreign Office ordered Ambassador Gilchrist to lodge a protest with the Icelandic government about the refusal of the *Thor*'s captain to take his crew back. Gilchrist was eager to comply, declaring, "I am doing my best to make the Icelanders ashamed of themselves." At the same time, he cautioned British officials against making too much of the incident: "On the whole the less fuss we make about this the better." Although he agreed that the Icelandic ambassador in London should be given "a dressing down," he also believed that "amused contempt seems the best line." Gilchrist's acidic attitude reflected the sense of isolation he felt in Reykjavík. Since September 2 the British embassy in Reykjavík had been under siege, with an unruly crowd of Icelanders massing outside the building and bombarding it with stones and other missiles. In a memorandum to the Foreign Office, Gilchrist commented on the embassy's broken windows, remarking sarcastically that "local glazier delighted with five of his men on full time duty at the expense of the Icelandic government." Although he reported no injuries, the ambassador was expecting a "big all-party demonstration" outside the embassy, where he predicted "we shall have some fun."[9]

The *Northern Foam* incident set the scene for further confrontations throughout September. Icelandic gunboats made numerous attempts to set grapples onto the British trawlers, with the goal of holding the "ships together to assist boarding" and then seizing the trawlers and taking them back to Iceland. Skippers responded by turning hoses onto the invading crews as deckhands cut the grapple ropes with axes. In some cases, the gunboats tried to grapple the warps of nets. While not useful for boarding purposes, such actions were seen as an added "nuisance." In one incident, deckhands threw fish at Icelandic crews to keep them from boarding, and the Icelanders retaliated, throwing the fish back at the British. But as British naval officials reported, the "trawlermen's morale is very high. They are cheerful, defiant and determined to repel boarders." One skipper even told a defending navy frigate that "he was out to capture a boarding party and take it to Hull as a trophy."[10]

Even when the Icelanders were able to board a trawler successfully, they had to contend with an irate crew. For instance, on September 26 the *Paynter,* a British trawler that had just arrived on the fishing grounds, "was taken by surprise mainly due to the fact that being outside [the] 12 mile limit she was taking no special precautions." The gunboat *Odin* had led the assault with one unarmed officer and six crewmembers scrambling onto the *Paynter.* As the boarding party surged around the trawler, the *Paynter*'s skipper and crew "immobilized[d] engines and anchor." Still, when the Icelanders entered the wheelhouse, the trawler skipper ordered his crew to remain calm. The situation escalated quickly, however, after another gunboat, the *Maria Julia,* had trained its guns on the trawler. Now a second boarding party—this one also composed of an officer and six crewmen, "carrying rubber truncheons"—jumped aboard the *Paynter.*[11]

After a brief on-deck scuffle over the immobilized anchor, two members of the *Maria Julia*'s boarding party went below to restart the engines. As mentioned earlier, engineers perceived their engine rooms as sacrosanct. At this point, tempers flared and one of the engineers was "badly bruised" with a rubber truncheon. The *Paynter*'s fireman and third mate joined the fray, and the Icelanders beat a hasty retreat to the deck where they confronted an "unfortunate galley boy who happened to be passing with dinner." Both the third mate and the galley boy suffered "minor bruises." As the uproar continued, the two boarding parties suddenly began retreating to their respective gunboats: they had spotted a protective vessel, the HMS *Diana,* advancing to the rescue. Now some of the *Paynter*'s crewmembers decided that the more antagonistic Icelanders should not be allowed to escape. They grabbed the "most aggressive Icelander on board but a rifle was pointed from *Maria Julia* whose Captain threatened that it would be fired if the man was not released. He then was."[12]

As this incident shows, the Icelanders could be aggressive when British naval ships were not on the scene and threatening to toss them into the brig. In the *Paynter*'s case, their delay in getting the trawler engines started gave the *Diana* time to arrive so that the gunboats would back off. Nonetheless, the incident highlighted both sides' determination to maintain their respective positions. The same was true on the policy level. After learning about the events on the *Paynter,* Gilchrist immediately lodged a protest against the actions of the *Maria Julia* and the *Odin.*

He reiterated the British view that such actions had taken place on the high seas and were therefore unlawful. He made it clear that the British government would not tolerate the "molesting of British fishing vessels on the high seas around Iceland" and would "reserve all [its] rights" in protecting British trawlers.[13]

For their part, the Icelanders reacted to British statements about freedom of the high seas with incredulity and suspicion. In response to the *Paynter* incident, Iceland's journalists began asking why more was not being done to curtail the activities of the British fishing fleet. One newspaper, the *Morgunblaðið*, published an interview with the *Thor*'s captain. When the reporter asked why he had been so "cautious" in arresting British trawler crews, he explained that his orders were to "seize trawlers not under protection of warships." Still, during the "nerve war," as he called it, seventy-nine trawlers had been warned for fishing illegally. According to the captain, British crews were generally behaving themselves during their interactions with gunboats, and "scarcely any abuse was now heard from them." When pressed about the decision-making process involved in capturing trawlers, the captain emphasized that the gunboats had little hope of capturing any that were under naval protection. Indeed, as the *Paynter* incident showed, "it was no good boarding a trawler if the only result was to have part of his crew captured." Nonetheless, he remained optimistic. He noted that confining British trawlers to small areas kept their catches correspondingly small and made the "owners . . . extremely apprehensive about the course of events."[14]

Despite the captain's declared optimism, Icelandic frustration over Great Britain's lack of respect for the twelve-mile limit grew throughout the autumn, and it led to another notable incident involving the gunboat *Thor*. On November 12, the trawler the *Hackness* was sailing along the Icelandic coast trying to avoid heavy seas during a gale. According to its skipper, Ernest Holt, the boat "took two very heavy seas on the starboard side which laid my ship right over." He recalled that the "list was so severe [that] the water was lapping the bridge veranda" and fishing gear washed off the deck when lashings failed. Holt slowed the engines to allow the ship to right itself and then ordered his crew to lash down whatever remaining gear was left on deck. He sent a radio update to Robert Hutcheson, the skipper of the nearby *St. Just*, who informed him that the *Hackness* was roughly six miles off the Icelandic coast.[15]

As the *Hackness* regained stability and Holt began to steer the ship toward a group of British trawlers, he saw another vessel rounding the coast close to Stalberg. At first he thought it was a trawler, but after it fired a warning shot, he realized it was the *Thor*. When the *Hackness* approached the assembled trawlers, *Thor* fired three more shots, one with live ammunition. The trawlers began circling around the *Hackness*, trying to protect it. At this point the HMS *Russell* arrived on the scene. In a heated exchange, the *Thor*'s captain accused the *Hackness* of fishing inside the old three-mile limit, and insisted that it should be towed to an Icelandic port. The *Russell*'s captain refused to allow this. In taped conversations, the *Thor*'s captain declared that international law was on his side and that he would "shoot on him if he is going away." The *Russell*'s captain retorted, "If you open fire on the trawler we will sink you." With this threat hanging in the air, the *Thor*'s captain turned conciliatory: "We are still ready to talk with you and we would much prefer to talk than shoot." After a short discussion in which the *Russell*'s captain assured the Icelanders that the *Hackness* would return to England, tempers cooled. Still, when the *Hackness* set a bearing for England and sailed away, it was shadowed by both the *Russell* and the *Thor*.[16]

Following the incident, both sides presented their own versions of events as well as their differing readings of international law. The *Thor*'s captain insisted that the *Hackness* had been fishing illegally inside Iceland's three-mile limit and that the *Russell* had steamed "full speed towards the *Thor* with her guns manned." Ambassador Gilchrist, on the other hand, argued that the chase was unlawful "from the outset" because the *Hackness* had not been fishing but was attempting to avoid sinking after taking on heavy waves. The *Russell* was therefore lawfully protecting a British vessel on the high seas.

The British Foreign Office believed that the incident might serve as a test case in the United Nations' International Court, but Gilchrist disagreed: "It is all very well to score debating points at the United Nations, [but] we must devote our best and promptest efforts to hitting real targets which is Icelandic opinion."[17] Yet the confrontations continued, and Gilchrist's hopes were dashed when all of Iceland's political parties cemented their opposition to the "invaders" in a united rally to protest the British actions. In a stirring speech, Magnús Kjartansson, a member of the People's Alliance Party, declared, "We don't deal with the Brits, we beat them."[18] This was more than bluster. The Icelanders were a small nation battling the bullying British Empire, and thus they believed they held the higher moral ground. They were not cowed by the British navy, even when it was thwarting their attempts to board and impound British trawlers. The establishment of safe havens could work only on a short-term basis, and the Icelanders felt they could afford to wait and see what would happen. British trawlers had already lost their flexibility; they were not able to follow shoals of fish because they feared arrest. Hundreds of miles from their home ports, they could no longer enter Iceland's ports to drop off sick fishermen or for repairs of their boats. And while Icelandic gunboats could retire to port during severe weather, British trawlers and naval ships did not have the same option. Indeed, admiralty officials quickly realized that maintaining their protective squadron was a hopeless task. Refueling at sea was dangerous at the best of times, but it was exceedingly difficult during rough weather. The same could be said for operating on sick or injured fishermen. Just as problematic were the battering seas around Iceland, which were damaging the hulls of naval frigates. As a member of the Icelandic coast guard gleefully declared, "Hitler and Napoleon made it to the gates of Moscow, but they did not survive a northern winter."[19]

To add to the government's frustrations, many nations in the international community did not support Britian's actions. While the United States and a few others sympathized with their position, as the conflict dragged on, Iceland's position gained strength. Americans were rattled by statements from Icelandic socialists and communists who questioned the worth of continuing as NATO members. They also worried about threats to the U.S. air force base in the Icelandic town of Keflavík. The British clearly recognized they would not win the propaganda war. Despite Gilchrist's eagerness to keep up the fight, the Foreign Office could not counter the impression that this was a war pitting a tiny nation against an overbearing world power.[20]

Meanwhile the confrontations continued with the Icelandic gunboats constantly harassing the trawlers and naval ships alike. By March 3, 1959, their gunboats had made twenty-nine attempts to board British trawlers. Although only two had succeeded, the cost of naval protection was becoming prohibitive.[21]

The British government thought that the Second Law of the Sea Conference, scheduled for March of 1960, might clarify the situation, but it merely clouded the waters. A proposal to set the territorial limit at six miles, failed by one vote, and the cod war continued. The failure to accept a standard convinced the British government that little could be achieved by continuing the cod war. By mid-1960, the government was ready to accept the twelve-mile limit, but first it had to convince trawler owners and unions that the war could not continue.[22]

The Trawler Officers' Guild and the TGWU were fully aware of the impact that the conflict was having on their livelihoods. Nonetheless, while the TGWU leadership was willing to go along with government efforts to find a peaceful solution, the guild officers were not so compliant. This disconnect reflected long-standing tensions between the two unions. The guild had complained for years about the TGWU's political stasis and its fluctuating membership. Thus, as the government quietly began negotiations with Iceland, the unions watched the unfolding discussions with both apprehension and distrust.

Trouble brewed from the beginning. In early 1960 Peter Henderson, the national secretary of the TGWU's fishery section, agreed to join a fishery union delegation to speak with Iceland's ambassador in London. After the meeting with the ambassador, he met with a journalist from the *Daily Express*. Unfortunately, however, Henderson neglected to mention the role played by the guild's Grimsby representative, Dennis Welch, in setting up the meeting. Welch, who was inclined to be prickly, fired off an angry letter to Henderson condemning him, writing that there "were bitter feeling[s] at the Icelandic landings," and that Henderson "[had] not even mentioned" that Welch had "been at the meeting," though Welch claimed that he himself had allowed Henderson to handle the press. Welch declared, "Incidents such as this will undermine the confidence all members of the Committee will have in each other's integrity."

In response, Henderson telephoned Welch and explained that he was also "disappointed" by the newspaper's failure to mention all the names of the committee members. Henderson blamed the journalist and the paper's subeditors, claiming they were trying to "create further dissension."[23] But in a candid letter to Robert Head, the regional secretary of the Grimsby branch of the TGWU, Henderson made it clear that he disliked Welch. He told Head that he was "aware of Welch's tendencies to give the impression abroad that he is the only person working in or for the fishing industry" and complained that he had lived with this situation for more than two-and-a-half years: "Indeed, I can say frankly I have tolerated things from Welch that I would not have thought possible purely in the interests of maintaining peace in the industry." Henderson saw the incident as a question of trust. Although the National Joint Industrial Council meetings were supposed to be confidential, he believed it was "useless to expect this character [Welch] to maintain a confidence." Moreover, he saw Welch's inflammatory threat to call all fishermen to strike as rank interference with the TGWU's independence.[24]

Henderson had more to worry about than Welch's hurt feelings or his interference into TGWU affairs. The fishery unions were "bitterly disappointed" by the failure of the second conference to establish international territorial limits. When negotiations recommenced between the British and Icelandic governments, Iceland continued to insist that it would phase in its new twelve-mile limit within three years. Despite his antipathy for Iceland's position, Henderson understood that the TGWU must not do anything to prejudice the talks. In a September 29, 1960, circular to all fishery port officers, he spelled out his concerns. While recognizing that guild officers in Grimsby and Hull wanted to engage in industrial action to influence the negotiations, he insisted: "We must not and cannot yield to these pressures. It would be criminal folly to prejudice the talks." Henderson made it clear that he understood how frustrated the guild officers felt as they watched Icelandic fishing boats offload their catches in British ports, but he urged them to remain "cool and let the Government get on with the job of negotiating a settlement."[25]

A month later Henderson was not so sanguine, as it became clear that the government was going to cave in to Iceland's demands. In October 1960, he lamented the government's weakness, declaring that the "outlook was grim" and "that the price being asked by the Icelanders was far too high."[26] After joining a delegation from the fishery unions in a visit to the Ministry of Agriculture and Fisheries, he came away deeply concerned about the government's intentions. He told TGWU's national secretary, Edward Birkett, "I am convinced that the Government is prepared to sell the Distant Water Fishing fleet down the river for the sake of NATO and so-called Western unity. In other words, we appear to [be] becoming another military and economic satellite of the [US] State Department." Henderson could find no remedy for this situation, yet "I do not think we can stand by and allow this to happen if, in fact, we can do anything to prevent it."[27]

What could be done? Eventually, Henderson took the dramatic step of visiting Iceland himself and talking with its trade union officials. After contacting Jón Sigurðsson, the president of the Icelandic Seamen and Fishermen's Union, Henderson flew to Iceland in late October. He met with Sigurðsson, as well as with the minister of fisheries, and E. Jónsson, the chairman of Iceland's Trawlers Owners' Association, and various journalists. Henderson reported that his hosts gave him "a cordial and courteous welcome." He was also "impressed by the obvious anxiety of the Icelanders to reach an agreed settlement."[28]

Meanwhile, at a gathering in London on October 10, officials from the Ministry of Agriculture and Fisheries and the Foreign Office met with trawler owners and trade union officials to update them on the negotiations. The fisheries minister, Sir Christopher Soames, explained that the Icelanders were continuing to insist on the twelve-mile limit but would allow British vessels to fish in "certain boxes" within that limit, although only for a five-year grace period. In addition, they wanted a reduction in the British tariff on frozen fillets. The foreign secretary, Sir Alec Douglas Home, followed up by stating the Icelanders "were generally anxious to reach an agreement," and said they had agreed to "restrain their trawler owners from landing fish at British ports for the time being." But he also warned that the Soviet premier, Nikita Khrushchev, was monitoring the situation and was eager to become involved in the dispute. Therefore, Home wanted to resume public negotiations with Iceland, and he expected the British trawlers to stop fishing inside the twelve-mile limit.

Major-General Sir Farndale Phillips, representing the trawler owners, expressed his frustration with Iceland's position but pledged "to assist the Government in its difficult task."[29] Likewise, Henderson stated that he wanted the negotiations to continue and did not wish the TGWU "to be held responsible for talks being broken off." In contrast, Welch (from the officers' guild) and G. H. Harker (from the Grimsby Engineers and Oilers Union), refused to pledge support before they had spoken with their membership. In a follow-up meeting on October 25, the trade union delegates met with the fisheries minister again, and Welch now declared that their combined memberships had found the proposals "completely unacceptable." He argued that the twelve-mile limit was an arbitrary line and said that the tariff issue should be dismissed out of hand.[30] He also continued to insist that Icelandic boats should not be allowed to offload their catches in British ports. Welch's saber rattling made the TGWU very nervous. Henderson was clearly concerned that his members might be pulled into some form of industry-wide action to support the officers' guild. As he explained to Bob Sontley, the secretary of the International Transport Workers' Federation, "tremendous pressure is being put on our port labor in Hull and Grimsby to black [boycott] Icelandic fish." He was resisting such action because he didn't want "to be blamed for causing the talks to break down."[31] But Welch's influence among the deckhands in Grimsby—and, to a lesser extent, Hull—was unsettling local TGWU officials. From Hull, Robert Head (regional secretary of the Grimsby branch of TGWU) wrote to Henderson expressing his frustration with Welch's attempts to embroil the TGWU in the controversy: "I personally am getting very tired of this individual's statements on behalf of other people."[32]

Although the British government recognized the concerns of trawler owners and the unions, it continued to work to reach a negotiated settlement with Iceland. In a series of high-level meetings, the two nations hammered out an agreement, which they signed in February 1961. Conceding to most of Iceland demands, Britain accepted the twelve-mile limit and a reduction of British fishing off the Icelandic coast. British officials required Iceland to agree that any future controversy between the two nations would be adjudicated by International Court of Justice in The Hague. For them, keeping the NATO alliance intact and countering any Soviet threat were "more important than the interests of the Humber trawler owners and fishermen."[33] For its part, Iceland's government promised that it would impose no further unilateral extensions of fishing limits.[34]

British government ministers met separately with the owners and the unions to discuss the agreement. While the owners reluctantly accepted the government's agreement, the unions were less easy to persuade. At first, Welch and Laurie Oliver, who represented Hull's trawler officers, refused to accept it at all. Sir Christopher Soames agreed to meet the two men, along with Harker on February 24. He had hoped that Henderson would also be present, but the TGWU official was in hospital for a back injury. Therefore, before his meeting with the guild representatives, Soames dispatched his assistant, Sir Basil Engholm, to visit Henderson in hospital. After listening to Engholm's explanation, Henderson told him that the TGWU would fully support the government's position, and said that he hoped the officers' guild would do the same.[35]

Prepping for the meeting with the three union officials, Soames understood the dynamic between the three union leaders. Soames was convinced that Harker was "very much a satellite of Captain Welch" and predicted he would "say little at the meeting." That turned out to be correct. While Harker remained silent, Welch and Oliver complained angrily about the government's inability to protect their members. Nonetheless, they were powerless to stop the momentum toward an agreement. The officers' guild had to admit defeat and accept it.[36]

Henderson, however, still had a problem: he had to convince his membership to support, or at least tolerate, the government's settlement with Iceland. In a circular distributed to TGWU members, he admitted he was "bitterly disappointed" with the agreement, but was forced to accept its terms as a "fait accompli." He wrote that he "had no brief whatsoever for this [Conservative] government" but pointed out that the dispute was "a diplomatic and not an industrial matter." Thus, the controversy could not "be resolved by industrial action." Henderson reassured the members that Iceland had agreed to abide by international law and would not unilaterally extend its limits. If it attempted to do so, the TGWU "would certainly not hesitate to apply such sanctions as we could." Henderson never spelled out what those "sanctions" would be, but presumably they would have involved blocking Icelandic trawlers from unloading fish in British ports.

He was certainly aware that Welch was prepared to take such action. In a March 22, 1961, letter to Jón Sigurðsson, Henderson wrote that he was pleased that the dispute had been resolved, but he remained concerned about actions that Welch and others might take. He knew Welch had threatened strikes if Icelandic trawlers attempted to land fish in Grimsby, but he promised Sigurðsson that the TGWU would "not be a party to this and will do our utmost to combat any such attempt."[37]

Henderson's fears were realized in May 1961, when Welch made good on his threat. After an Icelandic trawler unloaded fish in Grimsby, Welch and Harker called for a strike among the officers and engineers. As a result, by the end of May more than 2,500 fishermen were "thrown on the beach," unable to work without the skippers or engineers to manage the boats. The TGWU's passivity enraged its membership, and the situation got worse when Grimsby deckhands decided to join a breakaway union, the United Fishermen's Union (UFU). In response, the TGWU pledged to isolate the UFU and "to convince the fishermen of Grimsby" that the TGWU was "best suited to represent their interests."[38] For several months, the UFU drew members away from the TGWU, managing to spread from Grimsby to Lowestoft. But by September 1962, TGWU officials reported that the UFU had "completely disintegrated in Lowestoft" and "it had lost a great deal of its dynamic" in Grimsby.[39] Its insurgent leader in Grimsby was S. W. Mills, a former TGWU port official, who was not popular with his former employers. In a national meeting on June 16, 1963, a TGWU spokesperson declared that "if this person [is] as effective with his new employers as he had been with us, then we ha[ve] little cause for concern." Although the UFU did not go away quietly, it did eventually lose momentum, and in 1966 it folded into the TGWU. As a nod to the militants, one local UFU leader, Edward Hall, was retained by the union for "special organizing duties."[40]

Although the TGWU survived the UFU insurgency, the whole episode gave it a black eye. Clearly members were frustrated with its accommodationist stance. What role Welch and the officers' guilds played in this controversy is difficult to gauge. The cod war had certainly damaged collegiality among the various unions. It had also highlighted their inability to influence government action concretely. Most importantly, it had shown the Icelanders that they could protect their own fishery, even when they were out-gunned and out-muscled.

In 1972 the Icelandic government announced its intention to further extend its territorial limit to fifty miles by September 1, and Great Britain's Conservative Government declared its determination to oppose such action. Officials at the Ministry of Agriculture and Fisheries detailed the dire consequences for the distant fleet if the fifty-mile limit were to go into effect. According to a ministry report, the fleet's average landings of groundfish between 1960 and 1970 equaled "about 154,000 tons valued at over £12 million making up 45% by weight and 49% by value of all UK distant water landings." By the early 1970s, more than two hundred British trawlers were fishing around Iceland's shores. Thirty-six of them were freezer trawlers that were equipped to fish longer and farther out to sea than the rest of the vessels were. These boats could divert to more distant fishing grounds, such as Greenland's, but the remainder would have to retreat to closer destinations in the North Sea or the North Atlantic.

The British recognized that such moves would risk triggering other countries to extend their fishery limits. For example, if the distant trawlers diverted to fisheries around Denmark or Norway, "it would almost certainly lead to over fishing which could well prompt [these nations] to announce 50 mile limits purely as a defensive measure and further increase chaos in the industry that the Icelandic extension must cause."[41]

Even if the distant water trawlers stayed in the North Sea, they would find themselves in direct competition with the near and middle distant trawler fleets, and "the increased competition on these grounds would depress catch rates further." With nowhere to go, the distant fleet would be in a vulnerable position. Older vessels would most likely be scrapped and not replaced, "a loss of a considerable national capital asset." At the same time, the British public's heavy consumption of groundfish would ensure that imports would increase, especially from Icelandic fishing vessels. Such imports and a corresponding increase in prices, would adversely affect the country's "balance of payments."[42]

Iceland's territorial limit change would have had a disastrous effect on fishermen and workers in related industries. In 1972 Britain had a total of 17,600 full-time fishermen. Although the exact number of distant fishermen is difficult to determine, at least four thousand were engaged in that sector. According to the ministry's report, these men did not have "marketable" or transferable skills; thus, erasing their jobs would have a devastating impact. In addition to affecting thousands of trawlermen, it would cripple "the ancillary industries of ship-building and repairing, packing, transport and marketing." In Hull alone, up to seven thousand ancillary workers "derive[d] their livelihood directly from the fishing industry." In the nation as a whole, "some 40 to 50 thousand" ancillary workers would be affected. For the distant fishing ports of Hull, Grimsby, and Fleetwood, the closing of the Icelandic fishing grounds would be calamitous. Hull and Grimsby were already suffering from "a severe shortage of jobs," and the end of fishing would decimate the local economies. The speed of the changes would be just as damaging. The report estimated that the fishermen would be dispersed after twelve months, and the shore-based industries would be so "disrupted" that "an early return to the *status quo ante* [would be] impossible." The report concluded, "it would be idle to suppose that any industry could recover, if it recovered at all, from a disaster of [this] magnitude."[43]

The government had to act. Its ministers met immediately with officials from both the British Trawlers' Federation and the Scottish Trawlers Federation to come up with a strategy. It also appealed to the International Court for redress. In the meantime, it informed the federations that it would protect fishing vessels, but its frigates would remain outside the fifty-mile limit while processing the appeal. The government did promise to employ seagoing tugs to provide protection within the fifty-mile limit.

In August 21, 1972, a circular was sent to skippers and crews, urging them to avoid any action that could inflame the situation while the government was appealing the Icelandic decision. The federations also issued guidelines on how to behave while fishing inside the fifty-mile limit. It stressed that the unions and owners had agreed that "*the UK should not appear in an aggressive role*" (italics in original) so naval ships would stay out of the disputed territory. However, if gunboats attempted to commandeer British vessels, the government had authorized the "use of naval vessels for the protection of our trawlers up to the 12 mile limit."[44]

The federations also decided to institute a fleet system of fishing, where vessels "should always fish in company with at least one but preferably two other British trawlers." The support ship *Miranda*, "in her capacity as a Holland-Martin safety ship," would be on call outside the fifty-mile limit to provide medical services as well as radio operators who could repair trawlers' communication systems. In addition, the *Miranda* would carry a diver in case a trawler needed underwater inspection. The skippers were told to avoid Icelandic ports to avoid arrest. Only when a crewmember was "seriously injured" or the vessel was "unseaworthy" should a skipper make for an Icelandic port.[45]

Skippers were ordered to take "every reasonable precaution to avoid [their] vessel being boarded." Tactics such as laying out "bobbins, floats and nets" from the side of trawlers were acceptable, but the use of "firearms, explosives, [and] lethal or dangerous weapons" was prohibited. When ordered by gunboats to stop fishing, skippers were to reply, "The International Court of Justice has ruled that 'Iceland should refrain from taking any measures to enforce the [Icelandic] regulations of July 14, 1972, against vessels registered in the UK and engaged in fishing activity in the waters around Iceland outside the 12 mile limit.'" When in communication with the *Miranda,* or British naval vessels, skippers should use special codes, and if boarded by Icelandic personnel, they should "destroy or effectively dispose of all codes and written instructions."

The federations instructed skippers to inform the crew of plans to repel boarders and to let them know that such confrontations would involve an issue of "fundamental importance to the livelihoods of everyone in the British fishing industry, both ashore and afloat."[46] Crewmembers who had been active in the previous cod war would know what to expect from Icelandic patrol vessels. In earlier confrontations, the gunboats had carried cutters that protruded from the front or bow of the boat. Circling to the back of a fishing vessel, a gunboat would use those cutters to slash the warps that held the net in place while fishing. Such a maneuver on the high seas was potentially dangerous, but it was an effective way of stopping a vessel from fishing, and it ensured that the fishermen lost both their gear and their catch.

As British crews headed to Iceland in the latter days of August 1972, they must have felt considerable trepidation. The Icelandic government had made it clear that, starting on September 1, they would proceed with their plan to rid their waters of foreign fishing boats. Indeed, the first confrontation took place on that day when the Icelandic gunboat *Aegir* attempted to cut the warps of the *Newby Wyke.* On September 5, the *Aegir* cut the warps of the *Peter Scott,* and another gunboat, the *Odin,* tried to cut the warps of the *Boston Explorer.*[47]

A more serious confrontation took place on September 8, when the *Aegir* approached the *Wyre Conqueror,* which was fishing inside the fifty-mile limit, and ordered her to stop. British skipper Alfred Watson gave the standard scripted reply, but the *Aegir* captain insisted "that the International Court of Justice meant nothing to him." Watson replied that he was "a British subject," and said he "would . . . accept no order from other than the British Government whilst on the High Seas." The *Aegir* shadowed the *Wyre Conqueror* until the trawler began to haul its net up to the surface. Then the gunboat began to maneuver alongside, and Watson noticed that it was lowering a "manned inflatable boat," suggesting that his trawler was going to be boarded. At the same time, the *Aegir*'s captain had trained a searchlight onto the trawler's bridge and was "blinking it very rapidly in order to blind me which he succeeded in doing."

Watson's bosun reported that the *Aegir* had "dropped boarding fenders on [the] starboard and the port side." He ordered his radio operator to send a distress message to the *Miranda,* but the *Aegir* jammed his signals. He then told his crew to pull in the net as fast as they could and "stand by to repel boarders." Once the catch was secured, Watson ordered "Full Ahead and Hard-A-Starboard," a motion that took him no more than a "few feet" from the *Aegir*'s stern. Then his tactic was to steer toward the *Miranda* and a nearby fleet of Fleetwood trawlers. Watson also ordered the engineer "to padlock the engine room from the inside," while he himself locked the bridge doors. Although the *Aegir* continued to shadow Watson for a two more hours, it eventually gave up and returned to port.[48]

But a few days later it reappeared while the *Wyre Conqueror* was fishing. This time it was successful in cutting the boat's warps, "with the result that we lost the complete gear." During the process, some of Watson's crewmembers "did throw missiles aboard *Aegir* with the intention of scaring him off." After the gunboat departed, the fishing crew "rigged [the *Wyre Conquerer*'s] spare gear and carried on fishing," but the *Aegir* returned yet again, this time shinning a "powerful searchlight on us which blinded the crew." Watson demanded that the gunboat turn off the searchlight as his crew managed to haul their gear back into the boat.

To prevent boarding, Watson stationed half of his crew "on the boat deck with battens and chains." Faced with such a display and knowing that the net was safe inside in the ship, the *Aegir* sailed away. But on the following morning, the gunboat returned once more and forced Watson and the other Fleetwood skippers to haul in their gear and stop fishing.[49]

The volatile process continued again, but this time it resulted in the British trawlers attempting to ram the Icelandic gunboats. On the evening of September 21, eight Fleetwood trawlers were fishing seventeen miles off the point of Kópanes when the gunboat *Odin* arrived and threatened to cut warps if the trawlers did not stop fishing. The trawlers countered by surrounding the vessels that were currently fishing to protect them from harassment. The *Odin* left but returned the next day and targeted one of the trawlers, the *Wyre Gleaner*. When the captain of the *Odin* shouted, "Haul your gear and leave the area, I hope you won't cause any trouble," the trawler skipper refused. *Odin*'s captain retorted, "Well I think I will cut off your gear then." His crew was unable to do so, however, and he turned his attention to another trawler, the *Kennedy*. The *Kennedy*'s skipper told the *Odin*'s captain that he was simply following British government instructions to continue fishing. The *Odin*'s captain replied, "You got your orders, I got mine," and the gunboat "nipped in smartly and cut [the] Kennedy's gear."[50]

Then the *Odin* targeted yet another trawler, the *Wyre Captain*, and cut its gear as well. This action infuriated the assembled Fleetwood trawlers. The skipper of the *Wyre Corsair* declared to the *Odin*, "You are now responsible for any action we take in defending ourselves. So look out." Skipper A. Bushini of the *Robert Hewett* recalled, "Everybody's tempers were up [because] of the unseamanlike behavior of *Odin* [which] must result in a serious accident before long." The *Kennedy*, the *Wyre Victory*, and the *Wyre Corsair* "in fury tried to box [in] *Odin* and ram her." But the *Odin* easily outpaced the chasing trawlers, and the *Odin* captain boasted, "You will have to move faster to catch us."[51]

The tactics of the Icelandic gunboats were having an adverse effect on crew morale. Two Fleetwood skippers, A. Bushini and A. H. Vickers, testified to officials from the fisheries ministry that the trawlermen were tiring of the constant confrontations. The skippers charged that British naval ships were doing little to protect their vessels. They "were not pleased" that the Royal Navy was stationing its ships outside the fifty-mile limit and thus had not been able "to *defend us* against attack by *Odin*." Likewise, they were angry with trawler skippers from other British ports, charging that, "Hull and Grimsby trawlers are not doing their part in fighting for the cause by staying 30 miles off the land."[52]

Vessels from Hull and Grimsby went to sea primarily in search of cod and haddock, fishing on shoals that were relatively far from the Icelandic coast. Fleetwood's trawlers were in pursuit of plaice, which tended to congregate closer to shore. Thus, they were far more likely to be targeted by gunboats, and this vulnerability, according to Bushini and Vickers, meant that "morale amongst the crews is falling rapidly." They told the ministry officials, "Crews will not be willing to sail to Iceland if they are continually losing money and being exposed to the extra danger arising out of these incidents." In the skippers' view, the British government should compensate the crews "for earnings lost."[53]

Throughout the next several weeks, Icelandic patrol boats continued to appear when British trawlers were fishing and attempted to cut their warps. Eventually, on October 11, a significant confrontation took place. The Grimsby trawler *Aldershot* was fishing off the Kjölsen Bank (thirty-four miles from shore) in the company of "30–40 [other] Hull and Grimsby trawlers." The *Aegir* approached the *Aldershot* and ordered it to stop fishing. Its skipper, Edward I. Collins, ignored the gunboat, and with the support of another trawler, the *Ross Revenge*, continued fishing. Eventually, however, Collins cut his engines and tried to pull in his net. The *Aegir* used this opportunity to pass between the "two vessels at approx. 20 knots and succeeded in cutting the *Aldershot*'s gear." The sea was rough and winds were high, and as Collins explained, "Due to the action of the sea our stern lifted and set down heavily on [the gunboat's] starboard quarter." The *Aegir* was able to sail away, but the *Aldershot* was damaged and was taking in water. The crew quickly "effected temporary repairs by means of mattresses and deck board which partially stemmed the intake of water." Then, under the escort of another trawler, the *Aldershot* made its way to the Faroe Islands for repairs. After the repairs were complete, the *Aldershot* returned to Iceland to fish.[54]

In the meantime, the Icelandic ambassador in London was publicly blaming the trawler for ramming the *Aegir*, claiming that it had "put on a full speed astern and rammed the patrol boat slightly abaft of center and glided sternwards." Icelandic officials insisted that had it not been for the gunboat's "skillful maneuvering," it would have been "crushed between the two trawlers."[55] As in most of these cases, it is difficult to tell which side was interpreting the event more accurately, but it is clear that such incidents fuelled everyone's resentment.

Between January 1 and February 23, 1973, the British recorded more than twenty-five incidents of warp cutting and general harassment by Icelandic gunboats.[56] Although no serious incidents occurred in this period, fishing crews continued to express safety concerns, particularly about the dangers of warp cutting. On March 2, 1973, for instance, the trawler *Brucella* was acting as a guardian for another trawler, the *Vanessa*, when the *Aegir* appeared and ordered them to stop fishing. Both trawlers responded by changing course and heading toward the gunboat. The *Brucella*'s skipper, M. Patterson, claimed that changing course was "just a gesture to warn him off." The *Aegir* directed both vessels to steer away, and then fired two blank shots for effect. Four days later the gunboat again confronted the *Brucella* and this time succeeded in cutting the trawler's warps as the "crew were on the deck in hauling stations." The cut warps "whipped back sharply," recalled the skipper, "and it was fortunate no-one was hurt." The British government filed a letter of protest, making it clear that cutting warps was "dangerous to life and limb" and emphasizing "it is only through good fortune that British fishermen have not been injured." The letter repeated the British policy of continuing to fish outside the twelve-mile limit while the case remained under review in the International Court of Justice, and it asked Iceland to stop cutting warps and engaging in the "dangerous maneuvering of coastguard vessels and other forms of harassment of British vessels on the high seas."[57]

Despite the letter of protest, conflicts continued to intensify. On the night of March 12, the *Aegir* again confronted the *Aldershot*. This time two ships came to the rescue: one was a support tug, the *Englishman*, the other a fellow Grimsby trawler, the *Arsenal*. As the would-be rescuers sailed in to help, the *Aegir* shone a searchlight into Skipper Collins's wheelhouse. In response, Collins turned off his engines. Until this point, the *Aegir* had been in radio communication with the British vessels, but when the *Englishman* arrived at the scene, the *Aegir* broke off contact.

Unfortunately the *Arsenal* was now approaching the area "at a fair speed." Although the *Aldershot* and the *Arsenal* attempted to avoid each other, a collision occurred. As the *Arsenal*'s skipper, J. Loades, explained, "We were on top of him before I could see a thing because of the searchlight." Both vessels were damaged and went to the Faroes for repairs.[58]

Previously, the gunboats had not tried to cut the British warps at night, but a March 12 incident marked the beginning of a more aggressive, and more dangerous, approach to disabling the trawlers. Trying to cut warps at night had raised the stakes. In April, J. Blackburn, the skipper of the *Irvana,* testified that he was "extremely angry about the deliberate departure from good seamanship by the Icelandic gunboats." While accepting the Icelanders' right to cut warps, he was incensed that they were using undue speed when the "harassment takes place." In his view, "this could involve loss of life," and "it was only a matter of time before a serious collision takes place due to the lack of judgment or breakdown of gear."[59]

Although Blackburn accepted the Icelander's right to cut warps, other skippers did not. David Platten, the skipper of the *St. Leger,* was fishing on the night of March 26 alongside an Icelandic trawler when the *Aegir* appeared without warning and cut his warps. Platten was convinced that an Icelandic trawler had called in his position to the gunboat. Moreover, he accused the Icelandic trawler of "playing provocative music over the radio." After "suffering the loss of his gear," Platten "los[t] his temper and steamed towards the Icelandic stern trawler." He lowered "his anchor and 3 lengths of cable," clearly with the intention of "retaliate[ing] on the stern trawler's gear." The *Aegir* ordered Platten to stop interfering with the Icelandic ship, but the *St. Leger* still held its course and the gunboat fired at least "6 rounds, believed to be blanks."[60]

British and Icelandic officials exchanged letters of protest over the incident. The clash had come at an awkward time because diplomats from both countries were about to begin talks at the "ministerial level." A British Foreign Office spokesman predicted that "it will cause extra difficulty in the matter of talks," but to industry spokesmen, Platten's actions were understandable. Charles Hudson, the president of the British Trawlers' Federation, described the gunfire as "extraordinary." The owners of the *St. Leger* also voiced incredulity over the clash. Jonathan Watson Hall, a company manager, stated, "Even if he [Platten] had tried to cut an Icelandic vessel's gear then I have every sympathy with him. After all, he was on the high seas when he was attacked."[61]

Beginning in July 1973, British protection and naval vessels became involved in confrontations with Icelandic gunboats. On July 1, the *Aegir* attempted to cut the warps of the German trawler, the *Dusseldorf*. The British frigate, the *Leopard*, witnessed the action. Following two unsuccessful attempts to cut the *Dusseldorf*'s warps, the gunboat opened fire on the trawler. The commander of the *Leopard* warned the *Aegir* that the shots were "within ten degrees of *Leopard*'s bearing." Receiving no reply, the British commander ordered action stations and "warned [the] *Aegir* on Channel 10 VHF that if he continued to fire in my direction, fire would be returned at him." The commander asked if the *Aegir* had "understood my warning. No reply was received." The two vessels proceeded to circle one another, both with guns manned. Eventually, the *Aegir* covered its gun and cleared away toward the south. The British commander "immediately de-escalated" by cancelling "action stations."[62]

The navy continued to offer protection to British trawlers during the summer of 1973. In some cases, however, they also had to prevent trawlers from fishing in unprotected areas. In one case, a fleet of fifteen trawlers decided to move out of designated fishing areas to ones nearer the shore. The skipper of the navy control ship, the *Lloydsman*, pleaded with the "rebel" skippers to return to the designated zone. The trawler skippers refused and continued to fish. William E. Brown, the defense commander of the *Lloydsman*, expressed his frustration: "We now find ourselves in much the same position as an employer, or for that matter a government, faced with a determined but unofficial strike." Brown conceded that "no one had lost their temper" but said that the rebel group was undermining the majority of skippers "who are abiding by the rules," and consequently were "over-stretching our line of defence."[63]

The Icelandic gunboats were also creating problems for the British commanders. For instance, on September 7, the HMS *Lynx* drove off the gunboat *Thor*, which had been harassing three trawlers. In retaliation, the *Thor* sailed to within "one foot" of the frigate and attempted to "bump [the] *Lynx* gently beam to beam but was kept off by [a] big wave or Guardian Angel." As the vessels came side to side, the *Thor*'s crew "hurled abuse and potatoes. The latter were returned." A few days later, on the night of September 10, 1973, the HMS *Jaguar* was protecting the trawler *Volesun* when the gunboat *Thor* appeared on the scene. As the *Thor* was targeting the trawler, it cut in front of the bow of the *Jaguar*. Such a maneuver was extremely hazardous in the dark. As the British commander reported, "I do not fathom a mentality that will turn across a frigate's bows from 30 feet at 18 knots at night."[64]

British naval captains and trawler skippers were unified in their condemnation of these kinds of near misses on the high seas. Such actions were very dangerous and could be potentially fatal, as could mutilated fishing gear. Cut warps, wildly swinging back toward the deck, might easily injure or kill a fisherman. Damaged trawl doors were also a hazard. During one incident in September, the gunboat *Albert* had its cutter stuck in the trawl door of the *St. Alguin*. As the *Albert* tried to wrest itself free, the "heavy trawl door [began] swinging across *St. Alguin*'s deck most dangerously."[65] Despite these perilous situations, however, no one on the British ships were killed or even seriously injured.

Ironically, the only person who died during this period was an Icelandic engineer. The circumstances surrounding the fatality, which took place on the *Aegir* on August 30, 1973, are still in dispute. The Icelanders claimed that the HMS *Apollo* had ordered the tugboat *Statesman* to intersect the *Aegir*'s path. In response, the gunboat decided to veer back inside the twelve-mile limit. Unfortunately, its second engineer, Halldór Hallfreðsson, had been mending a leak with an electric welder. As the *Aegir* began to move away, a large wave struck the gunboat while "he was still holding the electric welder. He got an electric shock and lost consciousness immediately." Attempts to resuscitate him were ultimately unsuccessful. The British refused to take any responsibility for Hallfreðsson's death, merely stating that the *Statesman* shadowed the *Aegir* to the twelve-mile limit but had always remained at least a mile away.[66]

But the Icelandic government and the general public were incensed by the tragedy. A Icelandic government spokesman declared, "This event is a deplorable result of the violent measure which the Royal Navy and support ships have used against Icelandic patrol vessels." The engineer's death even spurred opposition figures in Iceland to call for extending the territorial limit to two hundred miles.[67] At the same time, Icelandic authorities increased tensions by insisting that British trawlers found sheltering from storms in surrounding fjords could be arrested. Additionally, by insisting that trawlers themselves bring sick trawlermen into Icelandic ports and not support vessels, the government was creating another opportunity for arresting the boat crews.[68]

By the end of September, the Icelandic government declared it had had enough: it was ending diplomatic relations with Great Britain. This gesture was a calculated gamble, an attempt to isolate Great Britain from its NATO allies. Pressure grew on the British government and the prime minister, Edward Heath, to respond. Weary of the conflict, Heath declared on October 1 that he had instructed naval ships to withdraw from the fifty-mile limit, insisting that the move would allow talks to recommence. In a letter to Iceland's prime minister, Ólafur Jóhannesson, Heath wrote, "I believe the sooner we meet the better."[69] But trade union leaders were frustrated by his action, calling it an unnecessary retreat. Jack Evans, the president of the Grimsby branch of the Trawler Officers' Guild, described it as "capitulation," and said that he was a "very worried man." The *Hull Daily Mail* published a telegram from a skipper on the fishing grounds, who asked, "Is there not one proud Englishman left in the British Government?"[70]

Despite the frustration of fishing crews, the cod war had effectively ended. In the negotiations that followed, the British accepted Iceland's demand for a fifty-mile limit and eventually signed an agreement that would stay in effect until 1975. Like the previous cod war, this one had been a disheartening experience for British trawlermen and their unions. In both, they had battled boarding crews and warp-cutting gunboats. While the navy had provided a semblance of protection, it could not sustain such aid, and the costs had been prohibitive. Time had been on Iceland's side.

The 1971–72 cod war revealed deep divisions in the fishermen's unions. The skippers' and engineers' unions wanted to battle out the dispute, either in confrontations on the high seas or by boycotting Icelandic fishing vessels that were trying to unload fish in British ports. The TGWU, on the other hand, was more willing to follow the government's lead in negotiating with Iceland for a peaceful solution. That stance not only alienated the skippers and the engineers but led also to turmoil within the TGWU itself. Everyone's feelings were bruised. The British government had been forced to back down from the Icelandic onslaught, while the trade unions were bystanders to the larger drama. Although the trawlermen served alongside the naval crews as combatants, they were not able to concretely influence military or diplomatic policy. In the meantime, as I will discuss in the next chapter, foreign fishing fleets were creating concerns on the western side of the Atlantic Ocean. Echoing the Iceland authorities and fishers, New England fishers demanded that their fisheries be protected from these marauding foreign fishing fleets.

CHAPTER 6

NEW ENGLAND FISHERMEN AND FOREIGN COMPETITION

New Englanders had dominated the fishing areas along their extensive coastline for centuries. Well into the nineteenth century, however, fishing remained a small-scale affair. Boats generally sailed close to the coast or only a few miles offshore in search of groundfish. Some vessels used the dory method in which a relatively large boat would sail to a promising spot and then release several small dories onto the ocean. The two-man crew would set lines to catch fish on the dory. The work required incredible physical endurance. Not only did the men have to handle the lines but they also had to load the catch onto the deck of the dory and then row back to the larger sailboat and transfer the catch to that deck.[1]

Since the colonial period, New Englanders had been trying to regulate the industry, whether it involved the building of rock weirs or managing estuary fishing. Fishermen had always understood that heavy fishing could have a dramatic impact on fish stocks. Now with the advent of steam-powered boats, fishing intensified, as did the size of the catches. Otter and beam trawlers could travel to more distant reaches, such as Georges Bank, and they were also better able to withstand the wild weather and high seas of the North Atlantic. During the latter part of the nineteenth century, there were heated debates throughout New England about the overuse of trawl nets, which critics argued caught too many fish and damaged the seabed. Supporters of trawling, on the other hand, countered that fishing in dories was too dangerous. Adrift on the high seas, these dories and the men onboard were sometimes lost.[2]

Fishery scientists and North Atlantic coastal nations had long been aware that fish stocks did not have a national identity, that is, they spawned, grew, and swam across international boundaries. The scientists and their political allies knew they had to learn more about the hydrographic and biological development of North Atlantic fish, so in 1902 they founded the International Council for the Exploration of the Sea (ICES) to oversee issues of marine science and territorial limits.[3] However, the council did not have regulatory control over fishing efforts, especially after 1945 when diesel-powered trawlers became available. Thus, in 1949, the International Commission of Northwest Atlantic Fisheries (ICNAF) was established under the auspices of the newly formed International Convention for the Northwest Atlantic Fisheries. The convention had been signed that year by Canada, Denmark, France, Iceland, Italy, Norway, Spain, the United Kingdom, Newfoundland, and the United States. Other nations, including Poland, the Federal Republic of Germany, and the Soviet Union joined later. All of these nations fished in the northwest Atlantic and were thus eligible to join the new organization. The ICNAF was tasked with conservation measures in the region, including denoting open and closed seasons, establishing size limits and mesh sizes, prohibiting certain kinds of fishing gear, and establishing quotas.[4]

The scientists involved with ICES were, to a certain degree, responsible for the creation of the ICNAF. They had long complained that an enforcement arm was needed to supplement marine science findings of their council. There had been a few regulatory attempts before World War II, for instance, when the United States had sponsored international meetings intended to set standards for mesh size of trawl nets. The momentum was interrupted by the war, but as the fishing effort mushroomed after the war, it became increasingly obvious that fishing efforts needed to be monitored and controlled. With support from the United States, ICES pushed hard for a new regulatory organization.[5]

The ICNAF's central task was to gather data and make recommendations at its annual meetings, the first of which was held in 1951. It was composed as a two-tier structure of commissioners and advisors, the commissioners were generally fishery officials from government agencies of its member countries, while the advisors were fishery scientists, trade union leaders, and local fishery officials. Notably, a number of the scientists from ICES served on the commission. Although the ICNAF's mission and methods were broad, by 1963 it had accomplished only one aspect of its mandate, which was to recommend and enforce minimum mesh sizes.[6]

Nonetheless, this was a major regulatory step. Throughout the 1950s the ICNAF concentrated on gathering data and acting as an international forum for fishery scientists, officials, and related political entities. Each member nation shared scientific information and analysis, and this unprecedented collaboration, with its emphasis on scientific enquiry, is clearly evident in the ICNAF's reports and periodic reviews. The scope and detail of the data was impressive, for each of the signatory nations had multiple research facilities and tools for examining biological and oceanographic conditions. Interpreting these data, alongside the scientists were fishery officials, trade unionists, local politicians, and business leaders. This broad spectrum of stakeholders nourished interesting intersections.

Yet as foreign fishing increased exponentially on Georges and Browns Banks and in the Gulf of Maine during the 1960s, the ICNAF came under attack from within and from without, and the combined onslaught broke the commission's ability to regulate the fishery. Before 1960, New England's principal fishing ports—Boston, Gloucester, and New Bedford—had enjoyed mostly unfettered access to their coastal fisheries. Only Canadian fishing vessels and a few Norwegian and British trawlers ever appeared in the areas. This changed quickly when large foreign fleets of modern trawlers and factory ships moved in the fishing grounds and began to compete directly with the New Englanders.

In 1961 about one hundred Soviet fishing vessels were sighted on Georges Bank. In 1962 a fleet of 219 Soviet vessels was spotted fishing for herring in the same area.[7] By 1964 the Soviet ships had been joined by vessels from Norway, East and West Germany, Poland, Spain, and Japan. As these foreign fleets switched from herring to haddock and cod in the mid-1960s, the New England fishermen found themselves hopelessly outmatched and outclassed. Their otter trawlers could not compete with the larger foreign factory ships and stern trawlers, and as a result their landings of haddock, cod, and herring correspondingly plummeted.[8]

The Soviet Union led the charge in establishing integrated fishing fleets, beginning in the late 1950s. In an integrated fishing fleet, modern trawlers unloaded their fish onto five-hundred-foot-long factory ships (also known as fish transports) where hundreds of Soviet workers, both male and female, processed the catch. As each factory ship returned to port with its loads of fish, another factory ship immediately replaced it at sea. Oil and water tankers supported the trawlers and factory ships, which meant that fishing could be continuous.[9] The factory ships also offered onboard medical support services, including "doctors, well-equipped medical and dental facilities, two 12-bed hospital wards, and an outpatient clinic." When mechanical or medical emergencies occurred, ocean-going tugs acted as support ships. Fishing and processing crews usually worked at sea for thirty-eight days at a stretch until passenger ships arrived with replacement crews. A base chief organized the complex routine of finding fish, dispatching large trawlers to capture them, and organizing the catch's transfer to the factory ships.[10]

Soviet fishing was having an enormous global impact on the king crab, halibut, herring, ocean perch, sole, cod, and shrimp fisheries. In 1963 as more than two hundred Soviet vessels were fishing off the New England and Middle Atlantic coasts, the U.S. Bureau of Fisheries was reporting that more than four hundred were fishing off the coasts of Alaska, Washington, Oregon, and California. Using Cuba as a base, the Soviet fleets also maintained a heavy presence in the Caribbean and off the coasts of the Carolinas and Florida. The impact extended beyond North American waters; the Soviets were also exploring fish stocks off the coast of western Africa and in the Indian Ocean. With its expanded and integrated fishing fleets, the Soviet Union was now able to fish for "prolonged periods at greater distances from home ports and had become the world's dominant fishing nation."[11]

While their fleet system gave the Soviets an edge, their modern fishing vessels gave them the greatest advantage over their competitors. With heightened stability, their large factory stern trawlers had significantly more hauling power than side trawlers did, and because it was more efficient and less dangerous to haul from the stern (the rear of the boat), the catch was proportionally larger often fifteen tons per trawl set. Onboard the ships, a hundred or more crewmembers processed the catch into fillets, and fish meal. Nothing was wasted; fish livers were processed for their oil, and two hundred cans of fish-liver paste could be packed daily.[12]

The Soviet's North Atlantic fleet generally sailed from the port of Murmansk, nicknamed the "Barrel City," which was home to more than three hundred thousand people and served as both a military base and the fishing industry's transfer hub. By 1968 fleets were unloading more than a million metric tons of fish in the port. Further processing took place on land where workers smoked and cured redfish, cod, catfish, and herring. Murmansk also housed a small army of marine scientists and their staff. In large facilities, they studied fish behavior, fishing technology, and the migratory patterns of groundfish. This concentrated scientific effort strategically supplemented the Soviet technological superiority, as is evidenced by their rapidly expanding catch (see table 6.1).[13]

Table 6.1. Soviet Union's Catch in the Northwest Atlantic (Metric Tons)

SPECIES	1956	1962	1963
Cod	3,000	100,791	81,658
Herring		160,404	100,036
Whiting		50,725	230,380
Ocean Perch	12,500	32,269	37,535
Haddock		5,135	6,504
Other	1,500	20,290	35,333
Total Catch	17,000	369,614	491,446

Note: Figures reflect data collected from areas of the North Atlantic included in the ICNAF convention.
Source: Commercial Fisheries Review 21 (January 1966): 40–43.

Concerned about this dramatic increase in catch, the U.S. Bureau of Fisheries and the U.S. Coast Guard began "extensive aerial and sea patrols" of the foreign fishing fleets that were working off the American coastlines. During these sorties, they not only counted the fishing vessels but occasionally boarded them to verify their fishing gear adhered to established ICNAF regulations, for instance, to make sure they were using the correct size of mesh in their herring nets, although the inspectors were not able to enforce regulations in any widespread way.[14] The agencies also took note of what kinds of fish the foreign fleets were pursuing. In the Soviet case, they discovered that the fleets had initially concentrated on herring, but by 1963 had switched their attention to cod and especially haddock, which had hatched in abundance in the late 1950s. Indeed, it was clear to all of the ICNAF nations that the haddock stocks were outstanding, and the Bureau of Fisheries reported that "local [U.S.] fishermen can make adequate preparation for harvesting this important fish."[15]

But the outdated New England fishing fleet was unprepared for the foreign onslaught on their fishing grounds. By 1964 the total haddock catch had increased by 40 percent to 140 million pounds.[16] Within a year, the ICNAF was "concerned over the increased fishing on Northwest Atlantic fishery resources," which "appeared to be at or beyond the point of maximum sustainable yield." ICNAF members agreed that catch quotas should be imposed or mesh sizes changed, but as these regulatory discussions began to take shape, the intense fishing continued[17] The Soviet haddock catch alone increased from 6,031 tons in 1964 to 90,070 tons in 1965. The U.S. Bureau of Commercial Fisheries reported, "This catch was more than the combined catch of haddock by both Canada and the United States." Canadian and American ICNAF members desperately tried to steer the commission's discussion toward regulating the haddock catch but discussion was tabled for future meetings.[18]

The New England fishermen's unions, the Atlantic Fishermen's Union (AFU) and the New Bedford Fishermen's Union, treated the arrival of foreign fleets on their traditional fishing grounds as a serious threat. Indeed, they were so worried that the AFU reaffiliated with the Seafarers International Union of North America, reasoning that in order to counter the foreign threat, it needed powerful allies "to make any headway in preserving their industry and their jobs."[19]

The fishermen's unions were right to be concerned. Joining the Soviet fleet off the Atlantic coast were fishing vessels from Spain, Poland, Norway, East and West Germany, Romania, and Greece. At times these foreign fleets were extremely large. For example, in 1966 thirty Spanish and fourteen Polish trawlers were spotted on Georges Bank.[20] Some of these boats had crew and officers from different countries: a Polish captain, fishing officer, processing machinery engineer, and two fishermen led the workers on two Romanian trawlers. Not all the foreign fleets were huge (in 1964, only three British factory stern trawlers were seen fishing off Georges Bank), but the combined onslaught of hundreds of modern fishing boats quickly depleted the haddock. The ICNAF reported in 1966 that the Soviet haddock catch had increased from 5,483 tons in 1964 to 81,882 tons in 1965.[21]

By 1967 foreign fleets were fishing up and down the North Atlantic coast. In April 140 were spotted in coastal waters. In May 171 were recorded. As the fish stocks fluctuated throughout the year, so did the number of fishing boats. In October a reduced fleet of sixty Soviet ships was seen fishing on Georges Bank and off Long Island, along with stern trawlers from East and West Germany, Poland, and Romania.[22] Throughout late 1967 and into 1968, these fleets continued to fish in these areas as well as further south along the coasts of New Jersey, Maryland, and Virginia. The fleets constantly shifted their positions to follow the fish, using sophisticated equipment to identify where and what types of fish were swimming. They would fish for haddock or cod in one area, and they would pursue ocean perch, herring, or menhaden in another.

In monthly reports, the U.S. Bureau of Commercial Fisheries kept track of these foreign vessels, recording both their numbers and positions. By June 1968, observers noted that Soviet fishing fleets had been seen off California and Alaska, and before the end of the month, three huge Soviet fleets were fishing simultaneously off the Pacific and Atlantic coastlines and taking in enormous amounts of fish. Correspondingly, fish landings by American fishing boats had begun to fall. Hopelessly outmatched by the foreign fleets, American fishermen could not compete.[23]

In the northwest Atlantic, haddock stocks declined precipitously. By March 1968, the bureau reported that the 1967 class had been the "weakest ever measured." The June *Commercial Fisheries Review* reported that landings of haddock had dropped by 34 percent, noting "4 successive small year classes on Georges Bank [of] below-average abundance" warning that "[poor] landings are expected to continue, at least through 1971."[24] Records of haddock landings in the three principal New England ports highlight the deteriorating situation (see table 6.2).

Table 6.2. Haddock Landings in Major New England Ports (in Millions of Pounds)

YEAR	BOSTON	GLOUCESTER	NEW BEDFORD
1960	76.7	12.1	9.2
1961	84.1	15.0	12.0
1962	83.1	16.0	12.3
1936	75.1	17.2	10.2
1964	76.3	22.9	12.1
1965	75.7	24.4	11.8
1966	65.5	27.1	15.7
1967	51.0	19.3	10.9
1968	35.6	15.1	7.4

Source: U.S. Bureau of Commercial Fisheries, *Food and Fish Situation and Outlook* (May 1969).

Much of this decline was blamed on foreign competition, which was affecting both domestic landings and imports. In 1958 the United States had imported 38 percent of its fish, but by 1968 those imports had rocketed to 76 percent. Soviet dominance of the fishing grounds had forced New England fishermen to concede defeat. Indeed, Coast Guard commander Adrian L. Lonsdale declared, "The Soviet Union has won the battle of the fishing grounds." Using "task force operations and the latest fishing techniques, they are exploiting to the limit traditional American fisheries."[25] When it came to haddock, that limit had obviously been breached.

The huge Soviet fleet devastated the groundfish off the New England coast. In June 1969, eight years after the first Soviet vessels had arrived on the scene, 140 vessels were seen at one time on the fishing grounds, included were twenty-eight factory stern trawlers, ninety-six medium-sized side trawlers, six factory-base ships, nine refrigerated fish transports, and one tanker. The number dropped to 75 in August, and then rose to 102 in September. A total of 256 foreign fishing vessels were reported in the northwestern Atlantic in December; 107 were Soviet.[26]

New England fishermen and others cried foul. As the international fleets switched from haddock to redfish, herring, and flounder, those stocks also began to decline. The ICNAF's Research and Statistics Committee tried to deal with these new circumstances, warning in its report at the 1965 annual meeting that the commission would need to adjust its rules about mesh sizes, catch quotas, and closed seasons to protect the fisheries. The research committee identified two primary challenges: collecting scientific data to support conservation measures and convincing member countries to restrict their fishing. As its report explained, "there is rarely any such a thing as painless conservation. National delegations must be prepared to over-ride short-term sectional interests to ensure a productive and profitable fishery."[27]

Three years later, however, very little had changed. At the ICNAF's 1968 annual meeting, held in London, it was clear that deteriorating fish stocks had become the major problem. This time the ICNAF moved more decisively, closing the season on haddock and introducing quotas for redfish and yellowtail flounder. By the 1970 annual meeting, held in Halifax, Canada, participants recognized that even these restrictive measures were not enough. Canada's minister of fisheries and forestry, Jack

Davis, directly addressed the critical situation. Although he applauded the delegates for supporting conservation, he also warned that continued overfishing would devastate his country's maritime economy. Davis closed his remarks with an ironic farewell, "To all of you I say bonne chance."[28]

For New England fishermen the problem of overfishing was critical but so was their inability to compete effectively with the larger foreign vessels. As James Ackert, the president of the AFU, had testified to Congress earlier in 1963, they were literally being forced off the fishing grounds: "There have been several incidents of harassment of our boats by the Russian fishing fleet. . . . [Using] a new checkerboard system, . . . they take areas and block them off, which shows a military standout, in my mind. In other words, this has been planned by military men and they keep criss-crossing areas . . . until [they are] completely swept clean of fish." The New England boats were also in danger of being rammed by larger vessels. Ackert testified that in one incident, a Soviet patrol ship steamed toward the New Englanders "and completely forced our fleet off the bank. We had to haul back and get the devil out of there. It was impossible for us to fish, they harassed us so bad." Boston otter trawlers were no match for huge Soviet factory and military vessels. As Ackert explained, "You take a [Soviet] vessel that is 200 feet in length and you are in a vessel 90 feet in length, [and] you know might is right!" It was more than size that gave the Soviets the edge. The increased horsepower of their engines were better able to negotiate the swirling ocean currents of Georges Bank. As Ackert explained, "That is the trouble. They have so much more power. They are more maneuverable." He blamed the decrepitude of the New England vessels: "Our vessels, due to overage, the engines are run down, when the tide catches you, a heavy tide going on the bank it is impossible unless you have a lot of power. . . . The power is not there. We have to scratch as best we can."[29]

James Callis, a trawler captain from Virginia, echoed Ackert's contention that the Soviet vessels were bullying the American boats. Callis had been fishing in his small trawler, the *Dragnet,* when a Russian boat "veered towards it and nearly rammed it." Although Callis complained about the incident to the State Department, "nothing came of it." In his view, the larger Soviet vessel had simply brushed him aside: "A lot of those Russian boats just want to hog the bottom—and since they're bigger than we are, there isn't much we can do about it."[30] These episodes of Soviet intimidation epitomized the task faced by American fishermen. While the ocean was seen as a common site for fishing, the large foreign fleets could easily push away the smaller American boats. When the holds of the American fishing vessels were full of fish they returned to port. But the integrated foreign fleets were able to keep on fishing, further highlighting their strategic advantage.

This infuriated trade union representatives and fishery officials, who also accused the foreign vessels of using illegal fishing nets. The unions charged that the mesh size of these nets was too small, and thus the trawls were capturing small spawning fish, another step in devastating the New England fishery. Ackert testified that the Soviet "smaller mesh twine . . . will deplete our fishing grounds." He offered as evidence a Soviet net found by the trawler *Massachusetts* on August 17, 1963. Although it was marked as a herring net, it was found in an area where no herring gathered. Manuel Lewis of the Gloucester Fisheries Commission stated that "only a cigar could get through" such a net. Hastings Keith, a Democratic Representative from Massachusetts, declared that "the most telling comment on their [Soviet] thoroughness is that you never find seagulls following their ships. There's nothing left even for the birds."[31]

The AFU and the NBFU were unified in their political response, which focused on targeting key congressional committees and demanding that they respond to the crisis. Modernizing the American fleet was crucial, but the unions were hampered by the 1792 law that forbade American fishermen from landing fish in the United States from a foreign-built ship. Thus in 1963 Ackert, and Howard Nickerson of the NBFU and the Seafarers, told Congress that if owners could buy boats on the free market, the current poor state of the fishing fleet would be remedied. Nickerson testified that "it is strange, but only in America are fishing vessels as aged as ours allowed to go to sea." In other foreign countries, "They would be condemned."[32] Nickerson was not averse to using scare tactics and Red-baiting rhetoric to bolster his argument. He alluded to Cold War fears of nuclear Armageddon when he argued that "in the event of an atomic attack on the United States, the only food available for consumption would be products from the sea." Ignoring the toxic impact of radioactivity on the oceans, he hammered away at this claim that "the people of the future are going to have to look to the sea for food to survive in case there ever should be an atomic attack."[33]

Various state and federal officials supported union efforts to modernize the fleet, but on the whole, the federal government was slow to acknowledge the complex, multifaceted problems facing the New England fishermen. In October 1967, during a speech to fish processors, David S. Black, the undersecretary of the interior, declared that the U.S. fishing industry urgently needed to catch up to other countries. He insisted that the potential to catch more fish was "unlimited." Black thought the problem was merely the lack of modern fishing boats. Because the New England fleet had been left unscathed by World War II, he explained, the boats had not been modernized. In contrast, the fleets of other nations were devastated by the war, with the ironic consequence that those countries "had to start from scratch and rebuild, and as a result, their floating stock is newer and far superior to ours today." H. E. Crowther, the director of the Bureau of Fisheries, agreed that the U.S. fleets were far behind other nations, but he was optimistic that they could catch up. In his annual report for the bureau, he repeated his assertion that "postwar inertia" had created outdated fishing fleets. American fishermen, he claimed, were unable to "challenge foreign fleets off our coasts," but with increasing governmental attention they would prevail.[34]

A year later, in 1968, Commander Lonsdale of the Coast Guard spoke far more pessimistically. Declaring that the Soviet Union had already "won the battle of the fishing grounds," he called the U.S. fishing fleets hopelessly outdated and blasted the government's inadequate investment in fishery research. Lonsdale detailed the Soviet dominance of the high seas and called for a massive "resuscitation" of the fishing industry, insisting that the federal government should revitalize marine research and begin an extensive shipbuilding program. "Something akin to our urge to get to the moon first is required."[35]

At the 1972 ICNAF annual meeting in Washington, D.C., gloom and doom were the order of the day. The sticking points were national quotas and enforcement, and the meeting promised to be stormy, primarily because the United States had decided to withdraw from the commission. In opening remarks, James Lynn, an undersecretary at the

Department of Commerce, called for "revolutionary change within the Commission equaling the revolutionary change in fishing." According to him, American fishermen were "not overwhelmed with the success of ICNAF." The loss of the haddock fishery had forced them to turn to other coastal catches "only [to] find them already the objective of massive fishing effort." Lynn made it clear that the U.S. government was pushing to extend territorial limits to protect the 'American' fishery."[36]

The 1974 ICNAF annual meeting in Halifax roiled from one crisis to another. K. C. Lucas, Canada's senior deputy minister of fisheries, argued that while his government saw a continuing need for the ICNAF ("even if its terms of reference may change"): "Canada is on the side of those nations favoring extension of coastal state jurisdiction for fisheries purposes." Like the United States, Canada had decided that extending its territorial limits was a better way to protect its fisheries.[37]

The crisis point had been reached. New England fishermen, their trade unions, and their local political representatives were pushing hard to extend territorial limits. In a series of House and Senate hearings, they vigorously made their case that this was the only way to protect the fishery around Georges Bank. Gerri Lovasco, the vice president of the Gloucester Fishermen's Wives Association, testified that foreign competition and obsolete fishing vessels were dragging the industry into a downward spiral. In fact, as I show in chapter 7, this loss of control was what had forced the fishermen's wives to act. As Lovasco made clear in 1970, the wives of Gloucester and New Bedford fishermen stepped into the fray because, "our men are at sea most of the year and are unable to act on their own behalf." The solution was simple, according to the New Bedford women: "Let's wake up to the fact that we can no longer give our natural resource to the rest of the world. Let us establish the 200 mile Fisheries Limit now to save whatever is there."[38] Their shared anger would fuel their fight and garner support from other stakeholders.

CHAPTER 7

FISHERMEN'S WIVES AND TERRITORIAL EXPANSION

Wives hold a special place in fishermen lore. While the men are at sea hunting fish, women have traditionally been left alone to manage their homes, finances, and families. As I show in chapter 4, in my discussion of Hull fishermen's wives, many also worked outside of the home in order to earn a steady income as a hedge against poor fish catches. A number of anthropologists and sociologists have studied these women's roles as child rearers and financial controllers.[1] Yet while such support roles have been well documented, researchers have generally ignored the women's work as active political agents. In this chapter, I shine a light on the political movements that New England fishermen's wives established and ran, and I consider how such activity influenced the debates over territorial fishing limits.

One such organization, the Gloucester Fishermen's Wives Association of New England, was particularly engaged in those debates. In some respects, its members' actions fit a so-called "feminine" model: that is, rather than directly challenging their established gendered roles, they "use[d] these gendered roles as a justification for their activism."[2] At the same time, however, they asked other groups, with different activist agendas, to support their work. This multiorganizational, or "meso" approach demonstrates how skillfully they were able to recruit allies to their cause.[3] Along the way, leaders emerged from the women whose drive and energy marked them as "political entrepreneurs."[4]

In contrast to the Hull wives, the Gloucester women were not propelled into action because of catastrophic accidents at sea, but the threat to their coastal fisheries pushed them forward. Nonetheless, the two movements were related most obviously by the women's shared urge to protect their men. Most of the Gloucester activists were the wives of skippers or boat owners. Long accustomed to taking part in the family's fishing enterprise, they already possessed the necessary skills they needed when seeking help from other women's organizations or environmental groups. In other words, they found it relatively easy to move out of domestic spheres and into public debates about protecting the fishery and ultimately their husbands' livelihoods.

As the Gloucester wives began to organize, trade union leaders were also embarking on a campaign to protect the fishery. Sometimes the two entities collaborated; at other times they went their own way. Nonetheless, when working as a combined force, the wives' organizations and the trade unions brought the concerns of New England fishermen into the spotlight, and their unique insight gave them credence as they spoke about those issues to political leaders. They intimately understood the vagaries and hazards of fishing, and how foreign fleets were disrupting, if not destroying, the New England fisheries.

In 1962 a fleet of Soviet fishing vessels appeared off Georges Bank, and within two years, they were joined by fishing boats from East and West Germany, Norway, Spain, Greece, Romania, and Japan. For nearly two hundred years New England fishermen had combed the bank for cod and haddock, but now foreign fleets were threatening the New Englanders' dominance and the fishery's survival.

In February 1969 fishermen's wives in New Bedford formed the United Fishermen's Wives Organization (UFWO) with backing from the NBFU. The UFWO's lead organizer was Janet Connors, the wife of a dragger owner. After acquiring a list of union members from the NBFU, she began phoning their wives to ask for support in starting a "group that would help the fishing industry." Acting on the advice of the NBFU official Austin Skinner, the group began meeting in the union hall. Skinner suggested using a West Coast group, the National Fishermen and Wives, Inc., as a template for the new entity. The women agreed, and they voted on March 21 to establish a permanent organization. Ann

Mackay, a fisherman's wife, read aloud the UFWO's bylaws and officers were elected. The organization established platforms that included "curtailment of foreign fleets off our shores" and "strict enforcement of the 12 mile fishery limit." To ensure that such protection should be applied, the UFWO insisted that Congress should enact "legislation that is beneficial to all fishermen."[5]

Following the UFWO's lead, fishermen's wives in Gloucester formed the Gloucester Fishermen's Wives Association (GFWA) in the same year. According to Grace Parsons, one of its early leaders, "We were inspired by the New Bedford and Seattle organizations." They also studied a group in Brookings, Oregon, that had organized specifically in response to foreign fishing off the Pacific Coast. In the GFWU's first newsletter, they quoted Sandra Sappington, the secretary Brookings group, who said there was a "likely possibility [that] foreign fleets may deplete our [fish] stocks."[6]

The GFWA's founding leaders were all linked to Gloucester's Italian and Sicilian community. Gerri Lovasco was born in Garfield, New Jersey, but had moved to Gloucester and married a fishermen. She became the first vice-president of GFWA and remained an officer throughout the 1970s and 1980s. Grace Moceri Parsons, who had graduated from Salem State Community College, became the corresponding secretary for the GFWA. Lovasco described Parsons as a "very liberated young woman."[7] Grace's sister, Ann Moceri, was the organization's treasurer. Lena Novello, another leader, was a Gloucester native.[8] Lovasco, Parsons, and Novello were all married to skippers who owned their own boats and independently fished out of Gloucester.[9]

Parsons and her husband, Peter, were the driving force behind the group's formation. Both were already members of Action Inc., a local environmental and community group, and they were also engaging in more personal forms of community activism, primarily through their monthly newsletter, *Pisces*. The first issue, which appeared in October 1969, immediately set the tone by attacking fish dealers who unfairly weighed the catch at the fish piers. Another article accused fish processors of mislabeling foreign-caught cod as haddock and then selling it to "mid westerners who don't realize the difference." The issue commented on ocean dumping, exploitation of fish resources, and the inability of governments to regulate the fishing effort. It also published recipes for

New England clam chowder.[10] Subsequent issues hammered home the theme that Gloucester's fishermen were enduring hard times. In an effort to boost fish sales, *Pieces* called for Gloucester schools to put fish on the lunch menus. And as the GFWA came into being, the newsletter called on all fishermen's wives to join the new organization: "To unite the industry, we need the wives of all fishermen (not just the owners)" [to join].[11]

Although the Parsons were the drivers of *Pisces*, other GFWA stakeholders also began to get involved. Novello wrote the recipe column, while another active member, Margaret Sibley, commented on the state of fishing in various New England ports. The newsletter's primary focus, however, was on extending the territorial fishing limit to two hundred miles. In May 1970, as Representative Don H. Clausen was introducing legislation into Congress to extend the limit, *Pieces* was urging its readers to support the legislation. According to the newsletter's editorial, this was the "most important of our goals." The editorial continued, "These foreign vessels, gigantic, and equipped for months of continued fishing, have depleted our historic fishing grounds of the bounty that rightfully belongs to American fishermen. We must receive the same help as our farming brothers. . . . What the United States of America must remember. . . . is that any nation that is able to feed itself will always be rich."[12]

Soon after the legislation was introduced, the New Bedford and Gloucester wives' organizations were invited to present their cases at congressional hearings in Massachusetts and Washington, D.C. Senator Edward Kennedy of Massachusetts, who was intimately connected to the state's fishing industry, was propelling these hearings. An avid sailor, he had long enjoyed a connection to the sea and was pushing legislation to support the ailing New England fishing industry. As the foreign fleets began devastating the haddock fishery, he became even more determined to protect what remained of it.

The first hearing took place in New Bedford on February 11, 1970. The assembled fishery officials, politicians, and fishermen voiced concerns about the ways in which foreign fishing fleets were undermining them, and many of the speakers called for two-hundred-mile territorial limit. State senator William Q. MacLean Jr. opened the proceedings by urging Kennedy to support the idea: "I think nowhere in the world is a greater fishing area than off of our coast." But unlike "some of the South American countries" that have imposed two-hundred-mile limits, he said, the New Englanders were hamstrung by congressional indifference. Kennedy agreed: "If we have oil that goes out 200 miles, that is considered part of the United States natural advantage. But we provide one set of reasoning for oil resources and an entirely different set of conditions for fish."[13]

Austin Skinner, of the NBFU, echoed MacLean's comments. While acknowledging that the problems involved an array of issues including lack of investment, older fishing boats, and declining fish stocks, he believed that extending the territorial limit would "probably eliminate a good many of the problems of the local fishing fleet and any American fishing fleet as far as that goes." Lucille Swain, the president of the UFWO, spoke after Skinner, lamenting the fact that the foreign fleets were now turning their attention to hake and herring after devastating haddock stocks. She explained that if they continued fishing unchecked, "I am afraid that New Bedford will not only be remembered for her whaling port but [for her] fishing port too." Swain blamed the International Commission of Northwest Atlantic Fisheries (ICNAF) for failing to enforce its regulations and agreed it would be prudent to extend the limit. Kennedy met with representatives from Gloucester later that day and heard essentially the same story.[14]

Then Kennedy organized more formal hearings in Washington, and on March 12 and 13, 1970, Parsons and Lovasco of the GFWA were scheduled to speak before the Senate Subcommittee on Energy, Natural Resources, and the Environment. Initially, Lovasco was asked to testify alone, and she nervously tried to persuade Parsons to go in her place: "You are the college graduate. You get up and go." But Parsons responded, "No, G, you've got to do it." They settled on going together. To bolster her courage and commitment, Lovasco called on her "guardian angel" and asked, "Help me out on this."[15]

In their testimony before the subcommittee, Parsons and Lovasco made clear that the New England fishing industry was in dire need of government support. Parsons spoke first. Her presentation concentrated on fish imports, both frozen and fish. She explained, that, because of foreign fishing activity, fishing jobs were being lost. Frozen fish blocks were flooding the market, she noted wryly, but at least they were being "processed into sticks and portions thereby providing employment for

American labor." Parsons also made the point of justifying the political activism of the Gloucester women: "We who are their wives, widows, and daughters know the problems facing our fishermen." She continued, "We are proud of our traditions and hopeful for the future, but we need the Government's support now."[16]

Lovasco, for her part, slammed the poor state of the New England fishing industry and the lack of government support. She explained that the women of Gloucester had organized "to work for the benefit of our husbands and fathers," and said the men were "overwhelmed with the problems facing them today." To add weight to her testimony, she focused on "a real life situation:" her husband's financial "problems." With costs increasing for the upkeep of his fishing boat, he was "not only in debt, but has mortgaged his home." Lovasco implored the senators to help: "I hope and pray help will come before it is too late." Recalling her testimony later, she admitted she was proud of what she had done: "I'm just amazed myself that I could do something like that, you know. But it came from my heart.[17]

Now congressional politicians had to put a human face on the huge problems facing the New England fishing industry. With this success behind them, Parsons and Lovasco began creating organizational links with the New Bedford women. In March 1971 the two groups joined a protest at the annual ICNAF meeting, held that year in Boston. According to Parsons, they were determined to show the public that the ICNAF was "merely a mouthpiece of the U.S. State Department." She charged that the commission only "reacts to situations such as haddock depletion. It never acts to prevent such disasters." She also emphasized that she and the other Gloucester women were "grateful to the UFWO of New Bedford for their hard work in protecting the rights of the unrepresented American Fishermen." In the meantime, the two groups maintained their contacts with the Brookings women on the West Coast. That organization had forwarded a newsletter including a statement about the two-hundred-mile limit: "Resolved: that we will continue our campaign to extend the fishing jurisdiction of the United States to the 200 mile limit." Parsons commended the resolution by remarking, "Right on."[18]

By the middle of 1971, *Pisces* was no longer being published. Nonetheless, the fishermen's wives continued their agitational posture, not least because of their unique position as business partners. Their husbands may have been business owners, but the small scale of their fishing ventures (with no more than seven men on board) meant that the wives were fully involved with bookkeeping and other support tasks that gave them a detailed knowledge of the industry. Moreover, the women understood that "the men are unable to fight for themselves. They are at sea much of the time and when ashore, they are plagued with all sorts of preparations for the next voyage."[19] As one wife explained, "If they have got a problem, it becomes our problem. There's no way we can avoid getting involved."[20]

The women shouldered more than bookkeeping for their husbands. Part of their organizational prowess grew from the fact that they had to manage almost everything. One fisherman admitted, "I spent 99% of my holidays on the boat. . . . I never saw them [children] grow up." Lovasco recalled that her husband "missed so many of the good times with the children. . . . At first (when Peter came home from fishing trips) the children would . . . shy away from him."[21] Fishing was exhausting work, and as one observer put it, "When the men come back, they're tired. They want to rest and be with their families. They don't want to be bothered with politics, with a fight."[22] The ramifications of being largely absent at sea or tired made for a disorganized political defense of the fishing grounds. Thus, because the fishermen were largely ineffectual as a political force, the women flowed into the vacuum.

But good bookkeeping and letter-writing skills did not always transcend easily into political action, and some women were clearly better at the task of organizing. For Lena Novello there was urgency to her commitment. She had been diagnosed with cancer in 1969, and doctors told her that she had little time to live. She used her condition to spur her on: "I made up my mind I had three years to live. I started getting involved in things, and the busier I got, the better I felt. . . . I believe, if you do good, good will come of it." Nurturing her was a deep Catholic faith in the righteousness of her cause: "When Almighty God created the world he made one Georges Bank, and he blessed us with it. It's up to us to protect it."[23]

According to most members, Novello became the lightning rod for the organization partly because she was well known in Gloucester. Grace Favazza, one of the early members, recalled, "Lena, I knew from the day I was born because she lived by the fort [in Gloucester]. . . . She was a neighbor. My mom knew her. I knew her all my life." Novello did much of the GFWA's recruiting: "She was in the Fishermen's Wives, and she told us to join, and we did. . . . It got us out of the house, and we loved it."[24] Margaret Favazza echoed her sister's recollections: "Oh Lena Novello, she was a sweetheart. . . . She knew everything. She came from a well-known fishing family. . . . She was a peach." Another early member, Rosalie Laiachino, noted that most meetings began in Novello's house: "We always went to her dining room. We sat around and we made plans how to help the fishermen."[25]

During the early 1970s, the Gloucester women outlined a strategy to educate the surrounding community and their elected officials about the value of their husbands' work and the critical role that fish played in people's health. To that end, they decided to hold fish expositions at local supermarkets and other venues. Margaret Favazza would ask her husband to get some haddock from a local fish plant, and "he would cut it in pieces that we wanted." At other times, it would be donated by fishermen or fish processors.[26] At supermarkets or festivals, the women would demonstrate how to cook the fish. Grace Favazza recalled that Novello was particularly good at marketing their product. If a reluctant shopper refused to eat some of the cooked fish, she would insist, "Try it. Do it for me. Try it." Thanks to these demonstrations, most of the fish would be sold. Indeed, supermarket managers were so impressed they would ask, "When are you girls coming back? While you girls were here we sold the most fish we ever have."[27]

The Cape Ann League of Women Voters was an important supporter of these cooking expositions, offering tactical advice and providing some start-up funds for a cookbook that soon sold thousands of copies. Now, with $20,000 earned from the cookbook and raised at expositions, the GFWA could afford to become more active. The organization bought stationery and sponsored trips to Washington, D.C., so that its activists could lobby members of Congress. Meanwhile, Novello kept fearlessly advocating for the fishermen. Another fishermen's wife, Angela Sanfilippo, said, "She doesn't care that she's a woman or not; she goes to the fishermen, to the groups and to the individuals."[28]

Yet at first, some politicians and men in the industry refused to take Novello seriously. In 1978, Carolyn O'Connor of the Cape Ann League of Women Voters called her "the most underutilized resource in the city [of Gloucester]. Until recently, snobbery kept her out—the men in the fishing industry refused to acknowledge her."[29] Maybe some of that distrust arose from her unorthodox methods. During a stormy meeting with the mayor of Gloucester, Leo Alper, Novello remarked on the shoddy condition of the drapes in his office: "If I'd known. Leo, I would have brought my needle and thread." In a follow-up meeting, Alper recalled she actually "took out some thread. Before I knew it she was mending my drapes." While such behavior could be unsettling, in the long run her tactics did much to ease the tension.[30]

Margaret Sibley supported Novello in important ways. Unlike most of the women in the GFWA, Sibley was not of Italian or Sicilian extraction. She had been born in England into a middle-class household. She had planned to attend Oxford University, but at the start of World War II, she chose to serve in the Women's Royal Navy (WRENS), where she met her future husband, Bill Sibley, "a homesick Gloucester boy." She eventually transferred from the WRENS to the First Aid Nursing Yeomanry because "the navy was very well fed" and the change made her feel like "I was doing my part." Shipped to Ceylon (Sri Lanka), Sibley engaged in "exciting work" with British special forces. For her, the conflict was a "good war, a very lucky war."

After the war ended, Sibley joined Bill in Gloucester, where they married and raised five children. She opened the English Bookshop, which specialized in children's books, and during the early 1970s, she became involved in the GFWA. Like other fishermen's wives, Sibley became an activist because "our men don't have time to fight these battles. They're off at sea, so it's important that we be their spokesmen."[31] But she also cited her war experience as critical to her political development. According to Sibley, she had served with a group of British women who were "absolutely free, utterly committed." In her view "they were an excellent cadre of women who were prepared to do anything."[32]

Sibley was well respected by other GFWA officials and members. As Laiachino said, "She was great. . . . She was a strong woman." Laiachino saw Sibley, Novello, and Lovasco, as "the voice. We were just the followers. You know what I mean? They told us to cook. We cooked. They told us to go over here, we went. But they were the voice. They were the speakers."[33] The three women became political fixtures not only in Gloucester but throughout New England, and they pressed the GFWA to support or attack causes that hit close to home, whether it be development of the waterfront, boat safety, the dumping of tires into the ocean, Canadian fishing intrusion, or oil development. The GFWA became a sophisticated defender of Georges Bank partly because its members learned where the real power lay. For instance, if quotas were the issue, then they targeted the New England Regional Council. Once the women discovered "who directed things," they could continue the fight.[34]

Although some government officials grumbled about the women of the GFWA, most came to recognize their validity and drive. John Rittgers, an executive officer for the National Marine Fisheries Service, said, "It makes good sense to me for the wives to be involved. Who could be more articulate in expressing the concerns of their husbands and their families?"[35] The Conservation Law Foundation saw the GFWA as a strategic ally in its environmental work. Douglas Foy, the executive director, recognized they had a remarkable moral authority when presenting their case before Congress: "They speak with an emotional energy, and they are well-informed, kind and appealing people. When they testify in Congress, the average politician has to listen to them because they are directly involved with the fishing industry. Their lives and their livelihoods depend on it."[36] Spurring on the leadership was a personal commitment. These women moved beyond the world of managing a domestic economy, and the family fishing enterprise, to taking on vested interests that threatened their family world.

They were certainly aware of their growing political acumen. They had very good relations with New England politicians, especially Senator Kennedy. As Lovasco triumphantly recalled, "Oh Kennedy, he was one of us. Yes. And he felt the pain that the fishermen were going through, and he did everything he could possibly do for us."[37] The 1969 hearings in ports around the state had convinced Kennedy that solving the fishermen's problems meant protecting the fisheries. Along with senators Warren G. Magnuson of Washington State and John O. Pastore of Rhode Island, he convinced Congress to pay attention to the foreign fleets threatening the Atlantic and Pacific fishing industries. He was particularly hostile to the ICNAF, which he implicated in the incredible destruction of New England's haddock fishery. Kennedy was not alone: fishermen's unions, the wives' organizations, local fishery officials, and state and federal allies were all frustrated with the commission's inertia. It was clear that the ICNAF's luck was running out.

Anger at the ICNAF flared up in 1971, when enormous Soviet vessels began trawling through Atlantic lobster beds—destroying traps and pushing lobster boats out of their way. The captain of one of those lobster boats, the *Wily Fox*, reported that on April 1, April 30, May 8, and May 12, 1971, the Soviets "had trawled through fixed lobster gear." During one of those incidents crew members on the *Wily Fox* had tried to tell the Soviet ships they were destroying lobster gear, but the Soviets had ignored the alert.[38] In a hastily convened meeting of the House Subcommittee on Fisheries and Wildlife Conservation, members of Congress asked State Department officials what they planned to do about the matter. In response, Donald L. McKernan, a special assistant to the secretary of state, testified that he had met with a Soviet commander who had pledged that such incidents would cease. But the owners of the lobster boats were skeptical. Joseph S. Gaziano, an industry leader and owner of the *Wily Fox*, complained: "When they come through the area, we cannot ward them off. They will not give way." In the short term, he wanted to be compensated for his losses, but he agreed with other fishermen that expanding the territorial limit was the ultimate solution: "We need to extend the fishing rights off our coast to 200 miles. If the fishing fleets of the foreign nation are going to behave like hoodlums, we should kick them out. We need help. I hope Congress will hear us."[39]

Many members of Congress did hear the fishermen. In October 1972, the House Subcommittee on the Coast Guard, held a hearing in the port of Stonington, Connecticut. The subcommittee's chair, Frank M. Clark of Pennsylvania, made his support for extending the limit clear. In his opening statement he said that the hearing had been arranged "to gather information . . . with respect to the damage to the [New England] lobster and fish industries by Communist bloc fishing vessels in our contiguous water."[40] Numerous witnesses testified about Soviet disruption of New England fishing. Gaziano, who had become far more aggressive about the issue, told the gathering that his corporation had lost "more than $750,000 in gear and income" due to the aggressive tactics of Soviet fishing vessels. While he was thankful for Coast Guard support, he noted that it could only do so much: "As our Captains say, when the big white fellow arrives, everybody is a good boy. However [the Coast Guard] can't be everywhere at once." Gaziano's fury was clear: "I daresay if we had a 3-inch gun on the bow of our fishing vessels, [the Soviets] might be cooperative with us." From the audience, there were shouts of "Hear. Hear."[41]

Russell T. Norris, the regional director of the National Marine Fisheries Service, was questioned about the idea of extending the territorial limit to two hundred miles. He suggested in his response that Congress would be better off waiting until delegates could bring up the issue at the 1973 Law of the Sea Conference, more than a year in the future. He also spoke favorably of the ICNAF, insisting that it was working effectively to oversee fishing limits and quotas. But Representative Robert H. Steele of Connecticut was not impressed with Norris's arguments, and he blasted the idea that the fishing industry should wait for a decision at the Law of the Sea Conference. As Steele pointed out, the exhausted fishing industry had waited long enough for the State Department to act: "This is one of the things that bothers me. Are we to continue to rely on the State Department and its good wishes, its good will, and its eagerness to explore the problem? When are we going to have some concrete action?"[42]

New Bedford's Howard Nickerson also testified at the hearing. He had switched jobs by this time. He was no longer the leader of the NBFU but was now a representative for the port's Seafood Dealers Association. Like most of those at the hearing, he supported the proposed two-hundred-mile limit and blamed high fish prices on foreign overfishing. Jacob Dykstra, the president of Rhode Island's Point Judith Fishermen's Cooperative Association, agreed, calling the ICNAF's attempts to regulate the fishery "Band-Aids on a big problem." For Dykstra, any solution required getting "foreign fishermen off . . . those stocks." Likewise, Hugh O'Rourke, the executive secretary of the Boston Fisheries Association, supported instituting the proposed territorial limit to "protect what we ha[ve] left and possibly work toward rebuilding our areas so we'll have supply."[43]

A crisis point had been reached. Senator Magnuson, the powerful chair of the Senate's Commerce Committee, sponsored a bill to extend the territorial limit to two hundred miles. His cosponsors were Senator John O. Pastore and Senator Ted Stevens of Alaska, and initial hearings on the proposal took place in early December 1973. The senators opened by sharing 1973 statistics highlighting the dramatic decline of fish landings on both coasts. In the north Pacific, they showed that large numbers of Soviet and Japanese vessels were fishing for salmon, king crab, perch, and pollock. In the North Atlantic, foreign fleets were fishing for herring, mackerel, squid, and hakes. Off the Florida panhandle, Cuban fishing boats were fishing for snapper and shrimp.[44]

In April 1974 members of the Senate Subcommittee on Oceans and Atmosphere took to the road. Their first stop was California, where they heard testimony from fishermen and representatives of the cannery workers' unions. During the hearings, Stevens, in an extraordinary comparison, declared that Iceland's strategy in the cod wars should be an example for Americans to follow: "I just wonder how long it takes before we get some backbone. Little Iceland, they had a cod war and won." The parallels for Stevens was obvious, "They won in 1957. Everyone condemned them." Just as impressive, in the more recent 1971–72 cod war: "They extended [the fishing limit] to 50 miles, put up their backbone, and . . . defeated Great Britain."[45] In Stevens's view, Iceland had set a precedent for ignoring international treaties and had ultimately won its case.

In May the subcommittee traveled east to Providence and then Boston. Senator Pastore opened the Providence hearing by announcing that the "time for waiting for international negotiations to succeed is over." He blasted the unfortunate ICNAF as "tragically ineffective." In Boston, Senator Kennedy reiterated his colleagues' urgent demands for extending the territorial limit: "We in New England . . . cannot afford to wait. We need this act. We need this legislation. We need it now."[46]

A procession of industry officials, including Dykstra and O'Rourke supported the senators. Union leaders and fishermen's wives also spoke at the hearings. Austin Skinner, of the NBFU, noted that fishing was an integral part of New England's history and economy and warned that its founders would be horrified by the way in which current practices were wiping out fish stocks: "Thank God they cannot see how these fisheries have been desecrated in the last 15 years." Skinner blamed the Law of the Sea Conference and ICNAF for failing to correct the situation. In the meantime, as he pointed out, "the fishermen had to stand by and watch the depletion of the major stocks of fish on which we [are] dependent for our livelihood." Representatives from the New Bedford wives' UFWO asserted that foreign vessels "dwarf the American fleet with their catches." The solution was obvious: "Let's wake up to the fact that we can no longer give our natural resources to the rest of the world. . . . Let us establish the 200 mile Fisheries Limit now to save whatever is there."[47]

Remarkably, the Gloucester women did not even attend the hearings. Like the Hull women, they had found themselves sidelined by the fishing interests around them. As Gloucester's wholesalers, processors, and local and state politicians shouldered the fight to extend the territorial limit, the GFWA began to shift away from the issue. In a 1978 interview, its new president, Angela Sanfilippo, explained that this did not mean the GFWA was going dormant. Rather, she said, it was focusing more heavily on cooking expositions in order to meet its expenses.[48]

Novello began championing a new cause in early 1974. She was angry that the Department of Labor was categorizing fishermen as unskilled workers and argued this mislabelling was having a negative effect on Gloucester's dragger business. For many years owners had relied on Italian immigrants to work on their boats, most of whom came to the United States by jumping ship or marrying into an American family. They could not enter the country through usual immigration channels because their unskilled status meant that they were not given immigration priority. The result was a growing shortage of fishermen in the dragger fleet.

Novello successfully convinced both the city's political leaders and its state representative, Michael J. Harrington, to press the Department of Labor to change the unskilled designation.[49] In other words, even as the territorial debate raged in Congress, the GFWA continued to advocate for their husbands' fishing businesses. Unlike the Hull women, they did not disappear from the stage. They merely moved to another one, where they continued fighting to protect fishermen and the fisheries.

By 1974 many government officials seemed to be leaning toward adopting the two-hundred-mile limit. Yet the powerful Senate Foreign Relations Committee remained vehemently opposed to it, as did the State Department. In hearings department officials claimed that unilaterally extending the limit would endanger multilateral fishery agreements proposed under the Law of the Sea and would encourage other nations to exclude American fishermen from their shores. For instance, they noted that Pacific tuna fishermen worried that South American countries would subsequently declare their own two-hundred-mile limits, thus pushing

U.S. tuna boats out of prime fishing areas. And in a reference to the cod wars, they argued that the proposed limit would "risk serious confrontations as in the Iceland-United Kingdom fishery dispute."[50]

Forced to revisit the issue, the House Committee on Merchant Marine and Fisheries held a new set of hearings in March 1975. Dykstra, of the Point Judith Fishermen's Cooperative Association, once again argued passionately for the mile limit. Focusing on the uproar over damaged lobster gear, he explained that the captains of foreign vessels were under intense pressure to catch fish. Thus, "when a foreign captain gets out there, although he knows our gear is there, it is my opinion in many cases he simply goes where the fish are, whether the gear is there or not." Even though the ICNAF had established catch quotas for all of its member nations, it was not enforcing them. As Dykstra pointed out, when New England fishermen unloaded their catches in their home ports, and the fish were inspected. But who, he asked, was checking the fish catches of the foreign fleets? While he sympathized with the Pacific tuna fishermen, he emphasized that the Atlantic fisheries were in jeopardy: "While we delay, the resources off our own coasts are going by the boards."[51]

Patrick Harrington, an officer in the NBFU, reinforced Dykstra's main points. He argued that his union as well those of the AFU had an "intimate connection with the catching, marketing, and processing of the product" and were thus "in a better position than employees in any other industry to understand the forces that are shaping their economic future." He said that they knew "the fish just aren't there anymore" and recognized that foreign fishing boats were the principal threat: "[The fishermen] do not have to search out an economist or political scientist to tell them that they have a problem. They see it nearly every working day in the presence of vast foreign fishing fleets on the fishing grounds that traditionally have been the domain of the New England fishermen."[52]

It was left to Howard Nickerson, the former union leader and U.S. Delegate to ICNAF to deliver the body blow. He said that the ICNAF "has failed the American fisherman." Its slow reactions and lack of enforcement power had allowed foreign fleets to devastate the haddock and cod fisheries, and now, as Nickerson explained, flounders and lobsters were being similarly exploited. The final speaker was a lobster fisherman, Greg Mayhey, who played the Cold War trump card: "I spent a year over there supposedly fighting foreign intervention in South Vietnam, and primarily the Communist threat, and within 12 miles of [Martha's] Vineyard, I see the hammer and sickle." Mayhey called on the committee to pass the law establishing the two-hundred-mile limit.[53]

On October 9, 1975, following the recommendation of the Committee on Merchant Marine and Fisheries, the U.S. House of Representatives voted 208–101 to impose a two-hundred-mile territorial fishing limit. On January 28, 1976, the Senate also approved the bill, this time with a vote of 77 to 19. On April 13, 1976, the Magnuson Fisheries Conservation Act was signed into law.[54] After a long and strenuous fight, the fishermen and their supporters could celebrate an important victory. For the first time in years their traditional fishing grounds were once again their sole domain. By successfully convincing political elites to join in the battle, this organizational and familial alliance had helped usher in a new era in which nations accepted the need to protect fish stocks. But there were losers as well—not only the ICNAF but also the foreign fishing fleets who now had few alternative sites to fish.

Yet even during this period of celebration, the GFWA kept working to convince the public to eat fish. They also began pushing companies to portray fish in a more favorable light. In 1975, Novello began an attack campaign against Avon and Lysol, both of which were running advertisements that used the smell of rotten fish as a rationale for buying cleaning products and fragrances.[55] Throughout the late 1970s and into the 1980s, the GFWA pushed for marine sanctuaries, tried to stop the practice of dumping car tires into the ocean, and worked to restrict oil exploration and development close to Georges Bank.

Since 1969 the GWFA and the New England fishermen's unions had been struggling to convince Congress to impose a two-hundred-mile territorial fishing limit. For them, the Magnusson Act was an enormous victory. But for the British fishermen who were nervously looking on, the passage of the act was ominous. Like the foreign fleets who were now barred from New England's fishing grounds, they and their government allies recognized that their industry was now under serious threat. Once again, Britain's far distant fleet would have to grapple with a recalcitrant Iceland, which was determined to follow the U.S. lead and impose its own two-hundred-mile limit.

CHAPTER 8

THE FINAL COD WAR

By 1975 Iceland and Great Britain were gearing up once again for talks regarding the fishing and territorial expansion. The agreement the two nations had signed in 1973 was scheduled to end on November 13, and the British were worried. To analyze what the future might bring, the Labor government established a working group comprised of officials from the Ministry of Agriculture and Fisheries, the Foreign Office, and the Ministry of Defense. As these officials discussed the forthcoming negotiations, boat owners and crews waited anxiously for news.

By the time the deadline rolled around, everyone understood that another cod war was in the offing. Once again, the Icelanders, now emboldened by the moves that other nations had made to institute two-hundred-mile limits, targeted the warps of British trawlers. But in a clear escalation, the gunboats began ramming Royal Navy vessels. The British had to decide whether to defend themselves or back down. Their decision to stand their ground ratcheted up the potential for violence on the high seas, and NATO members saw the situation of two warring members as a worst-case scenario.

The British government clung to its long-held claim that the sea's bounty was there for taking. While open to negotiation, it saw Iceland's protective approach as archaic and unwarranted. Yet given the global shift in attitudes to territorial fishing, the British stance had become a defensive one.[1] By September 1975 the Icelandic government announced its intention to extend its territorial waters to two hundred miles. As

Matthías Bjarnason, the minister of fisheries, explained, "the fishing waters are our only mines." He was confident that the British had learned from their folly during the previous cod wars, which had "resulted in a loss of prestige for that country," and he thought it was "unlikely that Britain will use that force again." In his view, the Icelanders were merely doing what nations such as the United States had already done.[2]

Unfortunately, Bjarnason was too optimistic. As soon as it learned about Iceland's decision to extend the territorial limit, the British Labor government began planning ways to protect their trawlers with Royal Navy vessels. In a confidential memorandum to members of the working group, Robert Lowson of the Ministry of Fisheries wrote that it is "essential to avoid provoking the Icelanders into action against our trawlers." While "there was a major area of uncertainty over how the Icelanders would behave," he believed that Britain must not take the first step in escalation. Lowson was significantly concerned about public perceptions of his government's actions, in large part because Iceland had spent the last cod war portraying itself as the bullied smaller country. As Lowson noted, "the UK had very much the worst of the publicity last time."[3]

The trawler owners were also concerned about the upcoming confrontation. In instructions to its skippers, the British Trawler Federation laid out the ground rules for fishing off the Icelandic coast. Skippers were ordered to follow naval instructions about where and with whom to fish, and they were required to maintain radio contact. They were told to avoid Icelandic boarding parties and, if arrested, to refuse to speak until they had received legal counsel. Finally, they had to keep their crews informed about fishing tactics. The federation emphasized that the forthcoming cod war was of "fundamental importance to the livelihoods of everyone in the British fishing industry, both ashore and afloat."[4]

It didn't take long for the first confrontations to take place. On November 14, the day after the deadline, a pair of Icelandic gunboats, the *Aegir* and the *Tyr*, warned a group of British trawlers that they were fishing illegally. On the next day, the *Thor* cut the warps of two trawlers, the *Primella* and the *Boston Marauder*.[5] The British government had ordered the Royal Navy to take a wait-and-see approach, with the hope that ocean-going tugs could serve as a sufficient deterrent. But during subsequent days the gunboats continued their warp cutting, leaving

British skippers frustrated by their lack of naval protection. As in 1972–73, they began radioing one another to discuss what they could do to force the government's hand. Interestingly, the Icelandic government was monitoring the radio messages back and forth between the skippers. The skippers agreed to announce an ultimatum: either the government would provide naval protection by November 24, or the trawlers would head home. The ultimatum even caught union leaders off balance. Jack Lilley, the president of the Hull Trawler Officers' Guild, said that the skippers should "have let the Guild make the move [decision] for them." David Cairns of the TGWU pointed out that the deckhands had been ordered to "play it cool" and argued that the skippers should have "let the government make a decision."[6]

The government's hopes that ocean going tugs could protect the trawlers were dashed a day later, when on November 20, the trawler *Benella*'s warps were cut by the *Tyr*. The warp cutting, as was evidenced in the 1972–73 cod war, could be very dangerous. Tom Nielsen, the secretary of the Hull Trawler Officers' Guild explained the dire dangers involved: "The whip back from a sliced steel hawser [warp], two to three inches thick, can chop a man in half or behead him." The tension on the warps was "intense": "Trawling is like pushing your front door through the village pond with the fish caught through the letter box."[7] Skipper John Tripp of the *Ross Resolution* agreed, and he noted that warp cutting was also costly in terms of money and time lost fishing. As Tripp made clear, "Replacing the gear could take up to eight to ten hours, especially in freezing conditions." He emphasized that winter weather would make the situation even more perilous. Mate Eddie Bankworth of the *Ross Altair* hoped that the navy would support the trawlers and "fly the flag." Yet he tried to keep his apprehensions about the cod war to himself. He said that he and his wife "just treat it as a joke and laugh it off. The only time it will affect her is when all this puts me out of work."[8]

The British skippers currently fishing off the shores of Iceland were determined to abide by their ultimatum, and members of the government's working group recognized that this open revolt was endangering the government's negotiating position. Thus, on November 24, officials from the Ministry of Defence and the Foreign Office announced: "HM Government has decided to provide naval protection to enable the

British trawlers to continue fishing in international waters off Iceland in the face of efforts by Icelandic coastguard vessels to stop them." Immediately, British aircraft made a sortie over the fishing grounds, and by November 29, three British frigates, the *Leopard*, the *Falmouth*, and the *Brighton*, had joined the trawlers.[9]

The skippers and their crews had therefore been successful in pressuring the government to act. Throughout the rest of November and into December, naval frigates and tugs did their best to protect the British trawlers from the gunboats. British naval authorities established designated fishing zones to make security easier, and they positioned themselves close to groups of trawlers within those zones. This tactic enabled the naval vessels to better protect trawlers from marauding gunboats. Such tight maneuvering could result in collisions, but the navy was determined to do its best to thwart the gunboats.

Iceland, however, decided to take advantage of the situation, and by early December the gunboats began targeting the protection vessels. The escalation began on December 6, after a clash between the *Thor* and a tug, the *Euroman*, which damaged the gunboat's port side. The *Thor*'s captain warned that if the tug got any closer it would open fire. In response, the captain of a nearby frigate, the *Brighton*, said that he "had authority to open fire in self defense" to protect the *Euroman*.[10]

The strain on the trawler skippers created problems of identification of gunboats. Trawler skippers became jumpy about anything that resembled an enemy. They were constantly monitoring the radar and radio signals and scanning the sea with their binoculars. At times they overreacted, mistaking British ships for Icelandic gunboats. In one incident a skipper asked the *Brighton* for help because his trawler was being tracked by a "big bandit." The *Brighton* replied, "It would appear the gunboat tracking you is, in fact, ourselves." The embarrassed skipper responded, "You bloody well look like a gunboat." The *Brighton* retorted, "We try awfully hard not to."

While the skippers did not like fishing in designated zones, they reluctantly accepted it as a protection strategy. Skipper Albert Watson spoke for many when he said, "We don't like fishing in the boxes but that's the only way we can operate safely at present."[11] Still, they needed more room, so on December 22, the navy agreed to let them form two new zones.

Nonetheless, a fishing liaison officer, Skipper Eric Thundercliffe, warned, "Anyone who goes toddling off on his own does at his own risk."[12]

Sparring between the Britain and Iceland continued through December, as did near misses, which is no surprise, given that the distance between the two sides was sometimes a matter of a few feet. Eventually, on December 28, a collision took place. As the British frigate *Andromeda* tried to steer into a tight space between the *Tyr* and a group of trawlers, the *Tyr* "slowed and turned towards" [the frigate]. The gunboat hit the *Andromeda* on the "starboard side amidships, demolishing guard rails and deck netting and carrying away [an] accommodation ladder." The captain of the *Tyr*, Guðmunder Kjærnsted, added insult to injury, calling the British naval commanders "overgrown schoolboys" and "dockyard seamen."[13] On January 7, 1976, the *Andromeda* was hit again, this time by the *Thor*, which "struck the *Andromeda*'s port quarter." Two days later, the *Thor* hit the frigate *Leander*'s starboard bow, leaving a "rippled" scar but also damaging the gunboat's own "stern, [and] flight deck supports."[14]

For both sides, aircraft were key in identifying the movement of vessels, whether gunboats or trawlers and their escorts. The British launched small wasp planes from the frigates and used them to track gunboats and send alerts to the protection boats. Icelandic aircraft were also involved in reconnaissance identifying the position of trawlers and frigates and sending that information to the gunboats. Close maneuvering in the air sometimes resulted in near collisions. On January 14, for example, an Icelandic coast guard plane had an "airmiss" with the *Leander*'s wasp aircraft.[15]

The weather was always a factor in these episodes, and the Icelanders often tried to use poor conditions to their advantage. Roger Ratcliffe, a journalist who was traveling on a Hull trawler, observed that gunboats tended to attack when "visibility was poor" due to fog or snow. As long as the seas and wind remained relatively calm, the partially hidden gunboats could use their speed and maneuverability to easily penetrate naval defenses and target the trawlers. The trawlers were safe only in truly bad weather, when "gale-force winds with cruel seas heav[ed] up into colossal waves." But such conditions also made fishing impossible.[16]

In January 1976 Britain's foreign secretary, James Callaghan, met in Brussels with NATO's secretary general, Joseph Luns, to discuss the conflict. By the end of the meeting, Luns had agreed to mediate the dispute.

Both Iceland and Britain were NATO members, and the United States had an air base in Iceland. Luns had heard rumblings from Icelandic politicians that the United States was not doing enough to protect them from the British navy, and he was concerned about the cod war's potential to effect the alliance. He was worried that the Soviet Union might benefit from the continuing dispute. There were increasing calls inside Iceland to expel the Americans. As in previous cod wars, Icelanders saw British actions as insulting to the integrity to their small Atlantic nation. Many were angry that the United States was refusing to get involved and end British aggression on the high seas.[17]

By the middle of January, Luns seemed to be making diplomatic headway. As a gesture of good will, the British withdrew frigates and tugs from inside the two-hundred-mile limit. Then, on January 24, Geir Hallgrímsson, Iceland's prime minister, flew to England for talks with the British prime minister, Harold Wilson. Hallgrímsson began by presenting statistics from Icelandic fishery scientists, showing that fish stocks around the island were in dramatic decline. These scientists believed that the ICNAF's fishing quotas must be adopted and enforced. British fishery scientists countered that scientific data did not support the Icelandic position.[18] As officials from both sides continued to negotiate, the two prime ministers met privately at Chequers (the British prime minister's official residence), hoping to find a "formula which could be presented by both sides as a triumph." By the first week of February, however, they had made little progress.

In the meantime, Icelandic gunboats continued to sporadically target trawlers and cut warps.[19] This infuriated the skippers who were still fishing inside the two-hundred-mile limit but who now had no naval protection. Once again, they threatened to withdraw from the fishing grounds. According to Tom Nielson of the Hull Trawler Officers' Guild, the crews were pushing the skippers to retreat once more. As Nielson stated, the skippers "were having a difficult time with their crews," who were pressing them to take action. Gunboat harassment meant that trawlers could not fish, and crews were afraid of losing money. Making the situation that much more tense, the government negotiations were continuing, but little information was being released about the status of the talks. Finally, on January 29, the skippers declared they were leaving for home. The next day, the British government offered to compensate the crews for loss of earnings, and the trawlers returned to their positions inside the two-hundred-mile limit.[20]

The skippers and the crews had successfully called the government's bluff. As it searched for solutions with Iceland, and with its own fishermen, the British government was also contending with restless allies. Like Luns, Henry Kissinger, the American secretary of state, was worried about how the dispute might affect the NATO alliance and how the Soviet Union was poised to take advantage of the conflict. To complicate matters, on March 16, Prime Minister Wilson resigned due to ill health. The new prime minister, James Callaghan, tried to soothe American fears while staying firm about the stakes of the conflict. He spelled out the British case in a confidential telegram to British diplomats in Washington, D.C., while trying to dismantle Iceland's concerns. Callaghan explained that he understood "American concern[s] but Iceland has a capacity to make trouble out of all proportion to her size and she is not hesitating to do so." Callaghan pointed out that his government had ordered its naval forces to withdraw but that gunboats were still "intermittently harass[ing] our trawlers." Although Britain had tried to negotiate, the "Icelandic response was extremely inflexible." At issue was not just a fair settlement, but the welfare "of many thousands of [people]" engaged in the British fishing industry. Callaghan told the diplomats that he intended to strive for a settlement but warned "we have shown very considerable restraint" and "we are running out of cheeks to turn."[21]

Despite this political posturing and maneuvering, a settlement was not in the offing. Given that coastal nations across the globe were planning and instituting their own two-hundred-mile territorial limits, the Icelanders knew they could bide their time and resist an agreement. They also had a trump card: the argument that they were a small nation being bullied by a larger one. In a January 1976 meeting in Rome with U.N. and Italian officials, Iceland's state secretary, T. Thorsteinson, laid out his country's position. His government was "astounded" that its small country could be "exposed to violence from a large and strong country without redress." If the situation continued, Thorsteinson threatened, Iceland would break off diplomatic relations with Britain and withdraw from NATO. As for its two-hundred-mile limit, Iceland had "merely anticipated what would soon be general practice." Thorsteinson said, "The 200 mile limit territorial sea was going to be generally accepted before long, and so it was absurd to criticize Iceland" for extending its own limits.[22]

As both sides dug in their heels, the cod war was re-ignited. On February 5, the gunboat *Baldur* cut two warps on British trawler, *Loch Eribol*. In a confidential telegram sent the next day, Callaghan told the British ambassador to Iceland that the navy would once again protect the trawlers. As members of the government working group met to discuss future actions, three British frigates—*Juno, Diomede,* and *Lowestoft*—arrived at the fishing grounds, where they were joined by three tugs: *Lloydsman, Euroman,* and *Statesman*. Nimrod surveillance flights also resumed. Anticipating that Iceland would break off diplomatic relations, the working group began to organize a response. According to this plan, the British ambassador would leave Iceland, but a skeleton service would remain in the "'British interest section' of the French Embassy." The British expected the Icelanders to transfer their own diplomatic staff to the Norwegian embassy in London.[23]

While Britain waited for the Icelandic's government response, a cat-and-mouse game began between the gunboats and the protectors. To keep the gunboats from cutting warps, the naval frigates tried to position themselves between the trawlers and the gunboats so that the trawler crews had time to haul in their nets. But the tactic was perilous, and collisions were inevitable. At first the British frigates tried hard to avoid contact with the gunboats, although Icelandic gunboats sometimes seemed to be luring them into collisions. On February 9, for example, the *Juno* and *Diomede* each engaged in "violent maneuvering" to avoid colliding with the *Baldur* and *Tyr*, and the captain of the *Diomede* claimed that the "*Tyr* [was] actively seeking collision for PR purposes."[24] The frigates were at a distinct disadvantage during such maneuvers because their hulls were relatively thin so they could achieve maximum speed at sea. In an earlier confidential memorandum, Callaghan explained, "Our modern warships are thin-skinned and thus vulnerable to ramming, and many lives could be lost in one of these encounters." Therefore, the commanders who were protecting the trawlers had to "minimize the chance of a collision." In Callaghan's view, this was reason enough "for trying to bring matters to an early as well as a successful [diplomatic] conclusion."[25]

Recognizing this weakness, the Icelandic captains did not hesitate to take on the frigates in open waters. Collisions occurred between gunboats and frigates on February 12, 18, and 24. Just as problematic, the gunboats continued to cut warps. The *Aegir* cut the warps of the *Royal Lincolnshire* on February 19, and a crewman was slightly injured "due to backlash of warp." Another trawlerman was similarly injured on February 28, after the *Tyr* cut the warps of the *Boston Stirling*.[26] According to the skipper, the accident happened because the deckhand "clouted a corner of the deck-house as he was getting out of the way." Fortunately, the crewman suffered only a "bruise on his side," though he was left stunned. But a TGWU official, commenting on the February 19 incident, warned that there is "bound to be some miscalculation at some time. Life is at risk." The British Trawler Federation was more pointed: "The gunboat commanders have now got the blood which they have been thirsting for."[27]

The continuing harassment by gunboats ensured a drop in British fishing activity. Simultaneously, the Icelandic government increased the pressure on February 19 by breaking off diplomatic relations with Britain. Now their NATO allies were becoming restless for a negotiated solution, but the confrontations continued to escalate. Icelandic students and trade unionists began demonstrations outside the American airbase at Keflavik on February 12 and succeeded in preventing gas stations from selling to American military personnel. In response, angry American servicemen "physically thr[ew] out four Icelanders demanding entry" into a bar on the base.[28]

The trawler crews used gallows humor at sea to cope with the stress. According to a journalist, one skipper known only as "Wally" became a "safety valve"—not just for the fishermen but also for gunboat crews. Wally was always on the lookout for marauding gunboats and would warn the trawlers via radio, "Them bleeding Eskimos are on the run again." Leif Bryde, the radio operator of the *Odin* recalled hearing Wally ask, "Is there anybody out there who knows how to make Molotov cocktails? I want to make some to throw at the bastards. I don't care whether they put me away for the rest of my life but I'm going to throw some." Every evening each trawler would report its position to the accompanying frigates. On one particular night Wally asked, "Why don't we sink them bleeding bastards?" The journalist recalled, "You [could] almost hear the laughter on both sides" at the absurdity of his suggestion.[29]

The cat-and-mouse game continued its daily ritual into March. Nimrod aircraft were constantly looking for gunboats heading in the direction of the trawlers and sending that information to the frigates. The gunboats kept challenging and sometimes colliding with the frigates, working to get beyond the navy's defensive screen to the trawlers on the other side. The trawlers still sometimes lost their gear. But the Icelanders were soon to escalate the situation even further by switching from cutting warps to ramming frigates.

As the *Baldur* sailed toward a group of trawlers on March 8, the frigate *Mermaid* attempted to intervene. Both boats were going full astern and nearly collided. The captain of the *Mermaid* "apologized" and said it was "his fault." Two days later the dance began again. This time, however, the *Baldur* swung "her stern into [the] *Mermaid*." Later that day, the *Baldur* took aggressive action against the *Diomede*, "repeatedly attempting to rake her quarter along *Diomede's* sides." On March 12, the *Tyr* hit the *Juno* forward of the turret and "deliberately rammed [her] port quarter," and the *Thor* struck HMS *Mermaid* "amidships port side, crushing [a] whaler" and splitting her deck. A few hours later, the *Tyr* and *Juno* clashed, resulting in more damage to the frigate's "side and [a] buckling of bulkheads." And on March 13, the *Tyr* collided with the *Diomede*, "scraping down [her] starboard side [and] removing flight deck guard rails."[30]

The thin-skinned frigates could not take such pounding for long. In February the *Yarmouth* had already been forced to return to Britain for repairs after a clash with the *Baldur*.[31] Following the mid-March clashes, the situation calmed temporarily. But on March 27, the *Baldur* was in the thick of things again. According to British naval reports, the *Baldur* made "25 attempts to collide with *HMS Diomede*." Four of those attempts were successful, causing "damage that included 13' x 3' hole in *Diomede*'s wardroom." The frigate's captain, Robert McQueen, said it was like being cut with a "tin opener." The wardroom bar and fireplace were destroyed, but "we managed to save the photograph of Her Majesty the Queen [though] Prince Philip was lost in action."[32] The commander of the protection squadron, reported that either the captain of the *Baldur* "had taken it upon himself to behave in this fashion," or, he had "been instructed by his superiors to disable frigates by premeditated collision." In the commander's view, the latter was "more likely." He based his judgment on the fact that Icelandic authorities had refused thirty minutes before the incident took place to allow a Nimrod to fly over the area. As he noted, "it is well known that I always try to use the Nimrod to photograph collision incidents." The commander issued a severe warning to the *Baldur's* captain, declaring that if he persisted in ramming British frigates the navy would order the frigates to respond in kind.[33]

The threat, however, was an empty one; the fragile hulls of the frigates were no match for the gunboats. Indeed, after the incident, Roy Mason, the minister of defense, told his cabinet colleagues, "that a new pattern of deliberate ramming of HM Ships . . . has emerged" and ordered naval forces to refrain from actions that might put them at risk. He recognized that such an order would reduce "the effectiveness of our naval protection, and fishing may as a result be interrupted more frequently."

Mason spelled out the government's limited options. It could either continue to protect the trawlers using the methods it had already implemented, or it could take more aggressive action against the gunboats. While increasing naval aggression might seem appealing, Mason said the consequences could be dire. First, he argued, while tugs were sturdier than the frigates, they were slower than the gunboats and would not be able to retaliate. Second, increased aggression might encourage the gunboats to inflict "further damage on our thin-skinned frigates." Third, successfully ramming a gunboat could result in loss of life on both sides. Yet, Mason pointed out, doing nothing could encourage the Icelanders to continue ramming the frigates because of the "ease with which British fishing can as a result be interrupted."[34]

The working group decided to hold off from ordering the tugs to take aggressive action against the gunboats. Its members also agreed that the frigates should step back from any confrontations that might result in hull damage. The ministers had few options for action. Under pressure from their NATO allies, the British felt compelled to avoid taking actions that could be seen as inflammatory. As a result, throughout April the gunboats had far more success in harassing the trawlers and thus badly affected their ability to fish. It was becoming increasingly clear to the British cabinet, and to the general public, that the government's policy of restraint was not working.

With the loss of fishing and its attendant earnings, British trawlermen and boat owners complained about the government's passive response. In an April 27 meeting with officials from the Ministry of Fisheries, the owners and the fishermen's trade union representatives complained about the situation. The leader of the British Trawler Federation, James

Laing, derided the "apparent weakening of the Navy's" resolve in "defending the trawlers" and argued that Britain should create a new designated fishing zone in order to split the Icelandic naval forces. Union leaders pointed out steep declines in catches. Indeed, they noted that some of the fishing trips had been complete losses, and, correspondingly, the trawlermen's morale was low. Above all, the assembled owners and trade union representatives were concerned about how successful the Icelanders had become at harassing the trawlers than in previous conflicts.

The catches had indeed fallen. The *Hull Daily Mail* reported on April 14 that the port's Easter catch was the "worst in memory." Hull fish merchants lamented that only ten trawlers were expected to unload their catches in the coming week. They said that in the past ten trawlers per day had been the norm and fish prices were rising because of the dearth in supply.[35] In an April 28 statement to Shirley Williams (the secretary for Prices and Consumer Protection), Fred Peart, the fisheries minister, agreed that the fishing effort could not be sustained under these conditions. To avoid putting the government in "the position of compensating the industry for the loss of catch," he suggested giving the trawlers more flexibility as to where and when to fish.[36]

Frustrated and dejected, the working group met on April 29 to discuss how to proceed. Peart was the only member still arguing in favor of continuing naval operations. Roy Mason said that the Department of Defence wanted a negotiated settlement, "even at the expense of a climb-down in terms of cod." As he had already made clear in a memorandum to the working group, without a settlement "lasting damage" would be done "to the NATO Alliance and to our position within it." As he explained, NATO allies were concerned that Britain would "once more fail to sacrifice a few tons of cod for the sake of the Alliance." It was in the country's "wider national interest" that "Iceland remains a member of NATO and that the Keflavík base continues to be available to the Alliance." Mason pointed out that for Iceland the American presence at Keflavík had little economic importance. In any case, because of the "emotional significance" of the cod war, Icelanders would not be swayed by economic consequences.

Regarding the fishermen's complaints about the government's lack of protection, Mason suggested that Britain "not . . . reveal publicly" that the policy had changed. This would avoid giving Iceland a taste of victory while allowing the cabinet to manage the escalating political and economic costs of the conflict. As Mason explained, the protection obligations had severely threatened Britain's commitments to NATO. Maintaining a naval presence in the cod war had ensured that a total of "15 frigates [were] unavailable for any other commitments."[37]

Pressure to obtain a negotiated settlement and to avoid mounting financial costs was thus increasing. Just as important, operational reports continued to highlight daily confrontations off the Icelandic coast. Both trawlers and frigates were at risk. During the first week of May, gunboats had cut several trawler warps and rammed naval vessels. On May 7, a frustrated naval captain even requested permission to open fire on the gunboats, but his request was denied.[38] Adding to the volatility of the situation trawler crews were becoming increasingly restive. On May 3, the crew of the *Ross Kipling* reportedly refused "to work the fishing gear," forcing the skipper "to leave the fishing grounds." Other skippers threatened to follow suit if more naval protection were not forthcoming. A ministry official, Philip Derham, claimed that only "a voluble few" took this view, but in fact the situation was indeed volatile. British newspapers began reporting on the trawler crews' revolt on May 4. According to the *Guardian*, the frustration had spread to naval officers. The newspaper quoted one senior naval officer: "If playing bumper cars off Iceland was an operational requirement, we would build bumper cars."[39]

Clearly, the conflict was becoming increasingly precarious. Trawler skippers had little confidence in the navy's ability to protect them, and the loss of earnings from 'broken' trips was affecting crew morale. Owners were angry that the navy had been ordered to avoid physical confrontations with the gunboats. Peart, the cabinet's lone holdout, desperately tried to convince Prime Minister Callaghan to hold the line and maintain a naval presence in the region. In a May 5 memorandum to Callaghan, Peart explained that he had met again with the owners and trade unions representatives. As reported by the press, he confirmed that some trawler crews had refused to fish without adequate naval protection, and he insisted that the situation could be saved if protection were increased; otherwise, a "withdrawal seemed inevitable." This would mean the destruction of the distant water fleet because "fishing opportunities elsewhere are severely limited so that [owners] would have no alternative but to lay up ships." Peart urged Callaghan to show "determination" to "protect our principles and our economic interests," even at the expense of losing allies.[40]

Peart's plea was not well received. Many in the cabinet were tired of the continuing conflict, and the Foreign Office was already developing contingency plans for withdrawal. In a May 7 draft report, J. T. Masefield, a Foreign Office official, argued forcefully that Britain should leave Icelandic waters and end the cod war. Masefield explained the reasoning behind an "orderly withdrawal." First, poor fishing catches could not be maintained because the "industry and the crews are increasingly unwilling to go on fishing for a meager or negative return." Second, the financial cost of naval confrontations could not be maintained, and "only good luck has prevented loss of life at sea." Finally, British protests over the two-hundred-mile limit were becoming untenable as the United States, Canada, Norway, and other nations' "declared intention" to institute the same restrictions. Resisting such changes, Masefield said, "makes our case weaker." He concluded: "As time goes on we are spending more money and running greater risks for smaller prospective results."[41] He pointed out that current weekly landings of fish "were only a quarter of the totals for the same period last year." In May 1976, the figure was 432 tons; in May 1975, it had been 1,738 tons.[42]

Other government departments were also looking for ways to end the cod war, and opening negotiations with Iceland (with the Norwegians as go-betweens) seemed to be the best option. In discussions in Oslo, Anthony Crosland, the foreign secretary, had agreed to withdraw naval protection in hopes of a settlement. Out at sea, the naval commanders, now unable to defend themselves from ramming, tried to maintain a safe distance from the marauding gunboats. As Iceland's politicians sensed that a victory was in the offing, the gunboat captains decided to escalate their attacks on the frigates, gambling that this might finally push the British off the fishing grounds. On May 20, two frigates, the *Salisbury* and *Eastbourne* were rammed, and the British conceded defeat. The government ordered its naval forces to leave the area on May 30, and the trawlers followed. For the first time in centuries, Iceland had its surrounding seas to itself.[43]

Great Britain, especially its navy, had paid a heavy price in the war. Collisions at sea had been frequent and dramatic. Out of a total of twenty-nine frigates on duty during the war, fifteen had been involved in collisions—many more than once (see table 8.1). While a number of Icelandic gunboats patrolled the coastline, six of them were particularly active in warp cutting and in ramming trawlers and frigates (see table 8.2).

Table 8.1. Collisions of British Frigates and Icelandic Gunboats

FRIGATES	COLLISIONS
Andromeda	2
Diomede	7
Eastbourne	1
Falmouth	3
Galatea	1
Gurkha	7
Juno	5
Leander	2
Lowestoft	1
Mermaid	4
Naiad	1
Salisbury	7
Scylla	1
Tartar	4
Yarmouth	3
Total	49

Source: Summary of Patrols, June 1, 1976, Ministry of Defence, British National Archives 24/929.

Table. 8.2. Icelandic Gunboats Involved in Confrontations with British Vessels, 1975–76

NAME	WARPS CUT	COLLISIONS
Aegir	10	6
Baldur	5	10
Odin	4	9
Thor	5	14
Tyr	15	18
Ver	0	2
Total	39	59

Source: Summary of Iceland Coastguard Vessel Activities, June 1, 1976, Ministry of Defence, British National Archives 24/929.

The withdrawal of the trawlers and naval forces allowed Crosland to obtain a limited agreement from Iceland that permitted twenty-four British trawlers to fish for a year within the two-hundred-mile limit.

After the year was up, the trawlers would be barred from fishing in the area. Owners and unions saw the agreement as a devastating defeat, and many politicians shared their distress. Patrick Wall, a Conservative member of Parliament, lamented, "On the first of June 1794, the British won one of the great naval victories [against the French] known forever as the Glorious 1st June. On the 1st June, 1976, the British capitulated to Iceland, which has no navy, merely six gunboats."[44] In truth, however, the British government had few options. With their naval forces hamstrung by marauding gunboats, the only other choice would have been to fire directly at the Icelanders. The crews and skippers of the distant water fleet bore the cost of the defeat, for there was nowhere else they could go to fish. Their boats would be left to rust in the ports of Hull, Grimsby, and Fleetwood. Other British fishing ports would follow as restrictions on fishing increased around the North Sea. By the early 1980s, fishing boats were scrapped and the shipbuilding industries correspondingly collapsed. After centuries of fishing activity, the fishing ports became ghost towns with their local economies devastated.

CONCLUSION

With Iceland's victory in the 1975–76 cod war, British trawlers lost all access to the seas around the island. It was the death knell for the distant water fleet, but it was not the only catastrophe for British fishing. As Norway and the Faroe Islands began extending their territorial fishing limits, the middle and near water fleets were also threatened. The British fishing industry was on the losing end of a global shift in ideas about territorial sovereignty. In the United States, however, the extension of fishing limits saved the nation's fishing industry. With the passage of the Magnuson Fisheries Conservation Act, foreign fishing was eradicated on both the Atlantic and the Pacific coasts, and American fishermen once again had the waters to themselves.

The American success was predicated on the combined activism of fishermen and their supporters. As early as 1969, committed trade union leaders and fishermen's wives had created a potent support network. By aligning with boat owners, food processors, and women's organizations, the fishermen were able to convince state and federal elected politicians to champion the proposed limit in order to protect the fishery. With congressional allies, the battle against foreign fishing fleets became winnable. The goal of exclusion was also bolstered by anti-Communist rhetoric. By emphasizing that Soviet and Eastern Bloc fishing fleets were operating a mere three miles off the coast, the activists raised the stakes of the conflict.

In contrast, the British fishermen's heavy reliance on fishing thousands of miles away from their home ports exposed them to the vagaries of nationalistic fervor. During their disputes with Iceland over its expanding territorial limits, the British clung staunchly to arguments in favor of inclusion, but in the end they lost every single cod war. The British navy could not sustain its elaborate naval tactics to protect the fishing fleets, and the trawlermen were not prepared for Iceland's aggressive actions.

Like their American counterparts, the British fishermen looked to their political allies to save their livelihoods. But they did not have a diverse and dedicated network of activists who came together to form a potent coalition. In particular, unlike the New Englanders, they did not encourage a tradition of female support. As the terrible events of 1968 should have shown them, the fishermen's wives could have offered critical aid over the long term. After three Hull trawlers went down, local women succeeded in convincing the British government to investigate the working conditions of trawlermen, and in response the government instituted important safety measures. Yet the women's coalition died away, and during the cod wars their advice was neither sought nor wanted.

The various fishermen's unions were hopelessly split on tactics to use against Iceland. While the skippers' guild pushed for more aggressive action against Icelandic trawlers unloading fish in British ports, the deckhands' union preferred to stay on the sidelines and allow the government to fight the battle in policy realms such as the Law of the Sea conferences. While this approach did galvanize British public support, it could not counter Iceland's ferocious gunboat strategy of cutting warps and ramming British warships. Nor were the Icelanders shy about playing the Communist card. By threatening to leave NATO, cut off diplomatic relations with Great Britain, and close an American military base, the Icelanders were able to exert political muscle and force the British to stand down.

Though the results were so different, for the New England and British fishermen, the shift in territorial sovereignty had made one thing clear: centuries of maritime conflict had come to an end. New England fishermen and their ports were optimistic about their prospects for survival. But British fishermen and their ports now faced a painful and unrecognizable future.

NOTES

PREFACE

1. Clark and Strachey quoted in Edward Hallett Carr, *What Is History?* (New York: Knopf, 1961), 4, 13.

INTRODUCTION

1. Hugh Popham, *Cape of Storms: Trawling off the Coast of North Russia* (London: Hart-Davis, 1957), 121.
2. George A. Rose, *Cod: The Ecological History of the North Atlantic Fisheries* (St. Johns, NL: Breakwater Books, 2007); Sonja Fordham, *New England Groundfish: From Glory to Grief: A Portrait of America's Most Devastated Fishery* (Washington, D.C., 1996); Carl Safina, *Song for the Blue Ocean: Encounters Along the World's Coasts and Beneath the Seas* (New York: Henry Holt, 1998); Daniel Pauly and Jay MacLean, *In a Perfect Ocean: The State of Fisheries and Ecosystems in the North Atlantic Ocean* (Washington, D.C.: Island Press, 2002; Richard Ellis, *The Empty Ocean* (Washington, D.C.: Island Press, 2003); Helen Rozwadowski, *The Sea Knows No Boundaries: A Century of Marine Science under ICES* (Seattle: University of Washington Press, 2002).
3. Canadian anthropologists and sociologists tend to dominate the study of western Atlantic fishing communities. See, for instance, Linda Christiansen-Ruffman, "Atlantic Canadian Coastal Communities and the Fisheries Trade: A Feminist Critique, Revaluation, and Revisioning," *Canadian Woman Studies* 21/22, no. 4/1 (Spring/Summer 2002): 1–9; Susan Williams and Barbara Neis, "'Women and Children First': Fishery Collapse and Women in Newfoundland and Labrador," *Cultural Survival Quarterly* 20 (March 1996): 2–5; Barbara Neis, "From 'Shipped Girls' to 'Brides of State': The Transition from Familial to Social Patriarchy in the Newfoundland Fishing industry," *The Canadian Journal of Regional Science* 16 (Summer, 1993): 185–

211; Carolyn Ellis, "Community Organization and Family Structure in Two Fishing Communities," *Journal of Marriage and the Family* 46, no. 3 (August 1984): 515–26; Dona Davis, "The Family and Social Change in the Newfoundland Outport," *Culture* 3, no. 1 (1983): 19–32; James M Acheson, "Anthropology of Fishing," *American Review of Anthropology* 10 (1981): 275–316; Gerald M. Sider, "Christmas Mumming and the New Year in Outport, Newfoundland," *Past and Present* 71, no. 1 (May 1976): 102–25; Tom Philbrook, "Fisherman, Logger, Merchant, Miner: Social Change and Industrialism in Three Newfoundland Communities," *Newfoundland Social and Economic Studies No. 1* (St. Johns, Newfoundland, 1966).

4. Margaret E. Dewar, *Industry in Trouble: The Federal Government and the New England Fisheries* (Philadelphia: Temple University Press, 1983); William W. Warner, *Distant Water: The Fate of the North Atlantic Fisherman* (New York: Penguin, 1977); David Boeri and James Gibson, *"Tell it Good-Bye, Kiddo": The Decline of the New England Offshore Fishery* (Camden, ME: International Marine, 1976). Later studies have tried to capture the effect of declining fish stocks on fishers' way of life. See Richard Adams Carey, *Against the Tide: The Fate of the New England Fisherman* (Boston: Houghton Mifflin, 1999).
5. David J. Starkey, Chris Reid, and Neil Ashcroft, *England's Sea Fisheries: The Commercial Sea Fisheries of England and Wales Since 1300* (London: Chatham, 2000); Robb Robinson, *Trawling: The Rise and Fall of the British Trawl Industry* (Exeter: University of Exeter Press, 1996); Chris Reid, "The Status of Ports in England and Wales, 1920–1994," *International Journal of Maritime History* 10, no. 2 (December 1998): 219–40; Robb Robinson, "The Evolution of Some Key Elements of British Fisheries Policy," *International Journal of Maritime History* 9, no. 2 (December 1999): 129–50; James R. Coull, "The Trawling Controversy in Scotland in the Late Nineteenth and Early Twentieth Centuries," *International Journal of Maritime History* 6, no. 1 (June 1994): 107–22; Michael E. Ulyatt, *Trawlermen of Hull: The Rise and Decline of the World's Greatest Fishing Port* (Lancaster: Dalesman, 1985).
6. Jeremy Tunstall, *The Fishermen* (London: MacGibbon and Kee, 1962); G. W. Horobin, "Community and Occupation in the Hull Fishing Industry," *British Journal of Sociology* 8, no. 4 (December 1957): 343–56; Margaret Gerrish, "Following the Fish to Grimsby," *Local Population Studies* 50 (Spring 1993): 39–50; Ed Knipe, *Gamrie, An Exploration in Cultural Ecology: A Study of Maritime Adaptations in a Scottish Fishing Village* (Lanham: University Press of America, 1984).
7. Roger Mumby-Croft, "The Living Conditions onboard UK Distant-Water Trawlers," *The Northern Mariner* 9 (October 1999): 25–33; Roger Mumby-Croft, "The Working Conditions on UK Trawlers, 1950–1970," *International Journal of Maritime History* 11 (June 1999): 163–80; Paul Thompson, Tony Waily, and Trevor Lummis, *Living the Fishing* (London: Routledge and Keagan Paul, 1983); David Butcher, *Living from the Sea: Memories of Shoreside Life in the Days When Fishermen's Nets Were Often Full, But Their Pockets Empty* (Sulhamstead: Tops'l Books, 1982); David Butcher, *The Driftermen: Life in the Tough Days of Britain's Vanished Herring Fleets, Recalled by the Men Who Manned Them* (Reading: Tops'l Books, 1979); David Butcher, *The Trawlermen: Memories of the Men Who Manned Britain's Trawler Fleets through the Great Days of Sail and Steam* (Reading: Tops'l Books, 1980).
8. David McDonald, "Power Begins at the Cod End: The Newfoundland Trawlermen's

Strike, 1974–75," *Social and Economic Studies* 26 (1985): 1–159; Marguerite Martha Balawyder, "The Influence of Interest Groups on the Settlement of the Trawlermen's Strike in Petit De Grat in 1970" (master's thesis, St. Francis Xavier University, Antigonish, 1973). The only major U.S. study of fishers that includes trade union action is Arthur F. McEvoy, *The Fishermen's Problem: Ecology and Law in the California Fisheries, 1850–1980* (New York: Cambridge University Press, 1986).

9. Ian Tyrrell, *Transnational Nation: United States History in Global Perspective since 1789* (New York: Palgrave, 2007); David Thelen, "The Nation and Beyond: Transnational Perspectives on United States History," *Journal of American History* 86, no. 3 (1999); Thomas Bender, ed., *Rethinking American History in the Global Age* (Berkeley: University of California Press, 2002).

10. Theda Skocpol and Margaret Somers, "The Use of Comparative History in Macro-Social Enquiry," *Comparative Studies in Society and History* 22 (1980): 174–97.

11. Paul Gilroy, *The Black Atlantic: Modernity and Black Consciousness* (Cambridge, MA: Harvard University Press, 1993); Enrico Dal Lago, *American Slavery, Atlantic Slavery, and Beyond: The U.S. "Peculiar Institution" in International Perspective* (Boulder: Paradigm Publishers, 2013); Peter Kolchin, *A Sphinx on the American Land: The Nineteenth Century South in Comparative Perspective* (Baton Rouge: Louisiana University Press, 2003); John Thornton, *Africa and Africans in the Making of the Atlantic World, 1400–1800* (New York: Cambridge University Press, 1998); Gwendolyn Midlo Hall, *Slavery and African Ethnicities in the Americas: Restoring the Links* (Chapel Hill: University of North Carolina Press, 2005); Seymour Drescher, *From Slavery to Freedom: Comparative Studies in the Rise and Fall of Slavery* (New York: New York University Press, 1999); David Brion Davis, *Inhuman Bondage: The Rise and Fall of Slavery in the New World* (New York: Oxford University Press, 2006).

12. Marcus Rediker, *Between the Devil and the Deep Blue Sea: Merchant Seamen, Pirates and the Anglo-American Maritime World, 1700–1750* (New York: Cambridge University Press, 1987); Leon Fink, *Sweatshops at Sea: Merchant Seamen in the World's First Globalized Industry, from 1812 to the Present* (Chapel Hill: University of North Carolina Press, 2011); Shelton Stromquist, ed., *Labor's Cold War: Local Politics in a Global Context* (Urbana: University of Illinois Press, 2008); Shelton Stromquist, "Rethinking Working-Class Politics in Comparative-Transnational Contexts," in *Rethinking U.S. Labor History-Essays on the Working Class Experience, 1756–2009*, ed. Donna T. Haverty-Stacke and Daniel Walkowitz (New York: Continuum Press, 2010). For my work see, Colin J. Davis, *Waterfront Revolts: New York and London Dockworkers, 1946–61* (Urbana: University of Illinois Press, 2003).

13. Marian Binkley, "'Getting by' in Tough Times: Coping with the Fisheries Crisis," *Women's Studies International Forum* 23, no. 3 (May/June 2000): 323–32; Estelle Reddin, "Making Ends Meet: The Way of Prince Edward Island Fisherman's Wife," *Canadian Folklore* 13, no. 2 (1991): 85–98; Fran Danowski, "Fishermen's Wives: Coping with an Extraordinary Occupation" Marine Advisory Service, University of Rhode Island, *Marine Bulletin* 37 (1980): 1–78.

14. Paul Thompson, "Women in the Fishing: The Roots of Power between the Sexes," *Comparative Studies in Society and History* 27, no. 1 (January 1985): 3–32; Marian Binkley and Victor Thiessen, "Ten Days a 'Grass Widow'—Forty-Eight Hours a Wife: Sexual Division of Labor in Trawlermen's Households," *Culture* 8, no. 2 (January/

December 1988): 39–50; Marilyn Porter, "'The Tangly Bunch': Outport Women of the Avalon Peninsula," *Newfoundland Studies* 1, no. 1 (1985): 77–90. For mid-Atlantic fishing communities see Richard Dixon et al., "Fishermen's Wives: A Case Study of a Middle Atlantic Coastal Fishing Community," *Sex Roles* 10, no. 1/2 (1984): 33–53.

15. Valerie G. Hall, "Differing Gender Roles: Women in Mining and Fishing Communities in Northumberland, England, 1880–1914," *Women's Studies International Forum* 27 (2004): 521–30; Darlene Abreu-Ferreira, "Fishmongers and Shipowners: Women in Maritime Communities of Early Modern Portugal," *Sixteenth Century Journal* 31, no. 1 (Spring 2000): 7–23; Jane Nadel-Klein, "Granny Baited the Lines: Perpetual Crisis and the Changing Role of Women in Scottish Fishing Communities," *Women Studies International Forum* 23, no. 3 (2000): 363–72; Reginald Byron, "The Maritime Household in Northern Europe," *Comparative Studies in Society and History* 36, no. 2 (April 1994): 271–92; Victor Thiessen, Anthony Davis, and Svein Jentoft, "The Veiled Crew: An Exploratory Study of Wives' Reported and Desired Contributions to Coastal Enterprises in Northern Norway and Nova Scotia," *Human Organization* 51 no. 4 (Winter 1992): 342–52; Unnur Dis Skaptadottir, "Women Coping with Change in an Icelandic Fishing Community: A Case Study," *Women Studies International Forum* 23, no. 3 (2000): 311–21; Deirdre Elizabeth Mary Chalmers, "Fishermen's Wives: The Social Roles of Women in a Scottish Community" (PhD diss., Queens University, Belfast, 1988). For East Asian women, see Holly M. Hapke, "Petty Traders, Gender, and Development in a South Indian Fishery," *Economic Geography* 77, no. 3 (July 2001): 225–49.
16. The only major U.S. study of fishers that looks at fishers as the guardians of the sea is McEvoy, *Fishermen's Problem*. For connections between environmental and labor history, see Gunther Peck, "The Nature of Labor: Fault Lines and Common Ground in Environmental and Labor History," *Environmental History* 11, no. 2 (April 2006): 212–38; Chad Montrie, "Expedient Environmentalism: Opposition to Coal Surface Mining in Appalachia and the United Mine Workers of America, 1945–1975," *Environmental History* 5, no. 1 (January 2000): 75–95; Scott Dewey, "Working for the Environmental: Organized Labor and the Origins of Environmentalism in the United States, 1948–1970," *Environmental History* 3, no. 1 (January 1998): 45–63; Jonathan S. Franklin, "Working Class Themes in the New Environmental History," *Labor: Studies in Working-Class History of the Americas* 9, no. 1 (2012): 119–31.
17. Brian K. Obach, *Labor and the Environmental Movement: The Quest for Common Good* (Cambridge, MA: MIT Press, 2004); Obach, "Labor-Environmental Relations: An Analysis of the Relationship between Labor Unions and Environmentalists," *Social Science Quarterly* 83, no. 1 (2000): 82–100.

CHAPTER 1: Of Fish and Men

1. "Statement of James Ackert," Hearings before the Subcommittee on Fisheries and Wildlife Conservation, U.S. House of Representatives, 88th Cong., 1st Sess., 14, 94.
2. Albert C. Jensen and Harriet E. Murray, "The U.S. Cod Fishery in the Northwest Atlantic," *Commercial Fisheries Review* 27 (July 1965): 1.
3. Ibid., 4; Albert C. Jensen, "A Brief History of the New England Offshore Fisheries," *Fishery Leaflet* 594, U.S. and Wildlife Service, March 1967.

4. Jensen and Murray, "The U.S. Cod Fishery," 4.
5. "Report of the Working Group of Scientists on Fishery Assessment in Relation to Regulation Problems," *International Commission for the North Atlantic Fisheries*, 1962, 53–61; Jensen, "Brief History," 8.
6. Jensen, "Brief History," 6.
7. Boris O. Knake, "Operation of North Atlantic Type Otter Trawl Gear," *Fishery Leaflet 445*, U.S. and Wildlife Service, May 1958, 3–10; Robert Bruce, "North Atlantic Trawl Nets," *Fishery Leaflet 600*, U.S. and Wildlife Service, August 1967; Ellery Thompson, *The Draggerman's Haul* (Mystic, CT: Flat Hammock 2007).
8. Albert C. Jensen and John P. Wise, "Determining Age of Young Haddock from their Scales," *Fishery Bulletin 195*, U.S. Fish and Wildlife Service, 1962, 439.
9. "Reports on Researches in the ICNAF Area in 1961," *Red Book, 1962 Part II, International Commission for the Northwest Atlantic Fisheries*, 137–45; John B. Colton Jr., "Report on Studies of Fluctuations of Year-Class Strength of Haddock," in "Some Problems for Biological Fishery Survey and Techniques for Their Solution," *Special Publication No 1, International Commission for North Atlantic Fisheries*, 1958, 279; "Report of the Working Group of Scientists on Fishery Assessment in Relation to Regulation Problems," *International Commission for the North Atlantic Fisheries*, 1962, 53–61.
10. "Friday Meat Hurts New England Fishermen," *Commercial Fisheries Review* 30, no. 1 (February 1968): 2–4.
11. British Trawlers' Federation. Distant Water Section, *Fishing in Distant Waters: Report on the British Fishing Industry Distant Water Trawlers*, 1958, 7.
12. "The Deep Sea Fishing Industry—Note by Ministry of Agriculture, Fisheries and Food," March 7, 1968, Board of Trade, British National Archives, London 149/1 (hereafter cited as BT).
13. Fisheries Division II, Ministry of Agriculture and Fisheries, March 1968, BT 149/1.
14. Paul Hansen, "Cod: Its Biology and Habitat," in *Geo-Economics and Cod Fisheries*, ed. Jean Malaurie (Paris: Mouton, 1969), 288–93.
15. Ibid., 297.
16. Ibid., 298.
17. *Commercial Fisheries Review* 32 (March 1970), 48. For fishing activity of Soviet Union and other nations in the northwest Atlantic, see *Commercial Fisheries Review* 21 (January 1966), 40–43.
18. Roger Mumby-Croft, "The Working Conditions on UK Trawlers, 1950–1970," *International Journal of Maritime History* 11, no. 1 (1999): 164.
19. Ibid., 165–66.
20. Hugh Popham, *Cape of Storms: Trawling off the Coast of North Russia* (London: Hart-Davis, 1957) 141.
21. David Butcher, *The Trawlermen: Memories of the Men Who Manned Britain's Trawler Fleets through the Great Days of Sail and Steam* (Reading: Tops'l Books, 1980), 125.
22. Popham, *Cape of Storms*, 93; Jeremy Tunstall, *The Fisherman* (London: MacGibbon and Kee, 1962), 115.
23. Mumby-Croft, "Working Conditions on UK Trawlers," 167.
24. Popham, *Cape of Storms*, 53.
25. Mumby-Croft, "Working Conditions on UK Trawlers," 169.

26. Popham, *Cape of Storms*, 53.
27. Mumby-Croft, "Working Conditions on UK Trawlers," 173; Thompson, *Dragger-man's Haul*, 165–69.
28. Mumby-Croft, 172, 173.
29. Ibid., 170.
30. "Discussion with Mr. Charles I. Meek, chief executive, White Fish Authority," Committee of Inquiry into Trawler Safety, April 1, 1968, BT 149/1.
31. "The Trawling Industry-Evidence from Hull and District Council of Churches," May 1968, BT 149/79; *Fishing News*, June 14, 1968.
32. "Turnover Rates of Trawlermen, Distinguishing Skippers from other Crew, Grimsby, 1962–1967," Appendix 16, Evidence from British Trawlers' Federation, 1968, BT 149/66.
33. "Statement of Evidence to the Committee of Inquiry into Trawler Safety—The Lowestoft Trawler Owners Association," October 31, 1968, BT 149/88.
34. "Visit to Lowestoft [by Committee of Inquiry Members]," November 20, 1968, BT 149/88.
35. "Discussion with British Trawlers' Federation—Committee of Inquiry into Trawler Safety," May 2, 1968, BT 149/66.
36. Report of Walter J. Hickel, secretary of the Interior, to Richard Nixon, May 21, 1969, *Commercial Fisheries Review* 31 (July 1969): 5–6.
37. "New England Fishing Future Looks Good to Bank Officer," *Commercial Fisheries Review* (June 1970): 6.
38. Virgil J. Norton and Morton M. Miller, *An Economic Study of the Boston Large-Trawler Labor Force* (Washington, D.C.: U.S. Department of Interior, 1966), 41.
39. Ibid., 35.
40. Frank Tringale, in discussion with the author, October 6, 2017.
41. Tringale, discussion; Margaret Favazza, in discussion with the author, August 3, 2012; James R. Green and Hugh Carter Donahue, *Boston's Workers: A Labor History* (Boston: Boston Public Library, 1979), 61–66.
42. "Testimony of Manuel Lewis," Fishing Vessel Construction, Hearings before the Merchant Marine and Fisheries Subcommittee, Committee of Commerce, U.S. Senate, 88th Cong., 1st Sess., 67; "Testimony of Donald L. McKernan," "Fishing in Territorial Waters," Hearings before the Merchant Marine and Fisheries Subcommittee, Committee of Commerce, U.S. Senate, 88th Cong., 1st Sess., 88.
43. "Fishing Vessel Construction," Hearings before the Merchant Marine and Fisheries Subcommittee, Committee of Commerce, U.S. Senate, 88th Cong., 1st Sess., 90.
44. Ibid., 33.
45. "Statement of Frank P. Briggs, assistant secretary for Fish and Wildlife," "Fishing Vessel Construction," Hearings before the Merchant Marine and Fisheries Subcommittee, Committee of Commerce, U.S. Senate, 88th Cong., 1st Sess., 31 and 14. E. S. Holliman, *"Financial Assistance Policies and Administration for Fishery Industries," FAO Fisheries Studies*, no. 11 (1962).
46. "Statement of Manuel Lewis, executive secretary of Gloucester Fisheries Commission," "Fishing Vessel Construction," Hearings before the Merchant Marine and Fisheries Subcommittee, Committee of Commerce, U.S. Senate, 88th Cong., 1st Sess., 66.

47. "Statement of James Ackert," Hearings before the Merchant and Marine Fisheries Subcommittee, U.S. Senate, 88th Cong., 1st Sess., 92–94.
48. *Report of the Bureau of Commercial Fisheries for the Calendar Year 1967* (Washington, D.C.: U.S. Government Printing Office, 1969), 4.

CHAPTER 2: The Hazards of Fishing

1. Most labor histories of U.S. and British fishers are focused on general accounts or earlier periods: Lewis R. Fischer et al., eds., *The North Sea: Twelve Essays on Social History of Maritime Labor* (Stavanger, Norway: Stavanger Maritime Museum, 1992); Robb Robinson, *Trawling: The Rise and Fall of the British Trawl Fishery* (Exeter: University of Exeter Press, 1996); Chris Reid, "Capitalism and the Scots Fisherman: New Technology Investment and Risk in Scottish Herring Industry Before World War I," *International Journal of Maritime History* 10, no. 2 (December 1998): 65–90; Roger Mumby-Croft, "The Living Conditions Onboard UK Distant-Water Trawlers," *The Northern Mariner* 9, no. 4 (1999): 25–33; Paul Thompson, Tony Wailey, and Trevor Lummis, *Living the Fishing* (London: Routledge and Kegan Paul, 1983); Trevor Lummis, *Occupation and Society: The East Anglian Fishermen, 1880–1914* (New York: Cambridge University Press, 1985); Margaret Gerrish, "Following the Fish to Grimsby," *Local Population Studies* 50 (Spring 1993): 39–50; John Rule, "The Smacksmen of the North Sea: Recruitment and Exploitation in British Deep-Sea Fishing, 1850–90," *International Review of Social History* 21, no. 3 (December 1976): 383–411; George Matteson, *Draggermen: Fishing on George's Bank* (New York: Four Winds Press, 1979).
2. Raoul Andersen, ed., *North Atlantic Maritime Cultures: Anthropological Essays on Changing Adaptations* (New York: Mouton, 1979); Lewis R. Fischer, "Comparing Fisheries," *International Journal of Maritime History* 7, no. 1 (June 1995); James R. Coull, *The Fisheries of Europe: An Economic Geography* (London: Bell, 1972); James R. Croull, *The Sea Fisheries of Scotland: A Historical Geography* (Edinburgh: John Donald, 1996); Jeremy Tunstall, *The Fishermen* (London: MacGibbon and Kee, 1962); Peter B. Doeringer and David G. Terkla, *Troubled Waters: Economic Structure, Regulatory Reform, and Fisheries Trade* (Toronto: University of Toronto Press, 1995); Kim Bartlett, *The Finest Kind: The Fishermen of Gloucester* (New York: Norton, 1971); David Boeri and James Gibson, *"Tell it Good-Bye, Kiddo": The Decline of the New England Offshore Fishery* (Camden, ME: International Marine, 1976)
3. *Conditions of Work of Fishermen—International Labor Conference, Forty-Second Session, 1958* (Geneva: International Labor Office, 1957).
4. "Appendix B—Statistics on Accidents and Casualties," Board of Trade, British National Archives, London 149/9 (hereafter cited as BT).
5. Tunstall, *Fishermen*, 63; "Fatality Details Lowestoft Fishing Vessel Crews, 10 Years. 1958 to 1967 Inclusive. Exclusive of Vessel Losses," BT 149/88.
6. "Report of Court, No. S478, m.f.v. *St. Finbarr*, Merchant Shipping Act 1894," BT 149/22.
7. Hubert Cluett, interview by David Masters, "Toward an Oral History of Cape Ann," *NOBLE Digital Heritage*, 1978; Louis Douglas, interview by Linda Brayton, "Toward an Oral History of Cape Ann."

8. *Gloucester Daily Times*, May 27, 1969, 1; *Gloucester Daily Times*, January 27, 1971, 1.
9. "Appendix B-Statistics on Accidents and Casualties," BT 149/9.
10. "Fatality Details Lowestoft Fishing Vessels Crews, 10 Years, 1958 to 1967 Inclusive. Exclusive of Vessel Losses," BT 149/88; "Fatal Accidents in Hull Trawlers—1962 to 1966 Inclusive," Table II, BT 149/1.
11. "Summary of Rescue by Deckhand Barry Measures of Third Hand Ernest Locke both of m.t. 'Suffolk Kinsman,'" Awards for Gallantry, BT 238/95; "Statement of Ernest Locke," November 2, 1961, BT 238/95.
12. "Statement of Witness, Peter Garner relating to the death of John Sinclair," *Working Conditions of Fishermen—Hours of Deck Hand Learners*, Ministry of Agriculture and Fisheries, BT 209/2134.
13. *Gloucester Daily Times*, March 26, 1970, 1.
14. "Fatal Accidents in Hull Trawlers"; "Fatality Details Lowestoft Fishing Vessels Crews."
15. "Fatal Accidents in Hull Trawlers."
16. "Fatality Details Lowestoft Fishing Vessels Crews."
17. The Holland Martin Inquiry was established after the loss of three trawlers in the space of weeks in 1968. "Discussion with Rear-Admiral G. C. Leslie, O.B.E., April 8, 1968," BT 149/1.
18. *Guardian*, April 15, 1961, 12.
19. Louis Schwartz and Irving R. Tabershaw, "Dermatitis in the Fish Industry," *Fishery Leaflet* 124, May 1945, U.S. Fish and Wildlife Service.
20. For an international comparison of regulations concerning signing on for fishing trips see, *Conditions of Work of Fishermen—International Labor Conference, Forty-Second Session, 1958* (Geneva: International Labor Office, 1957), 56–59.
21. *Report of the Working Group on Discipline in the Fishing Industry, November, 1975* (London: HMSO, 1975), 30, 10–11.
22. Ibid., 10.
23. "Discussion with Transport and General Workers' Union, May 20, 1968," BT 149/2; "Report by J. Hargraves & J. Marriott, deckhands, undated," BT 149/58; *Fleetwood Chronicle*, undated, 1.
24. Tunstall, *Fishermen*, 202–3.
25. Cluett, interview.
26. Harry Eustis, interview by Linda Brayton and David Masters, "Toward an Oral History of Cape Ann."
27. *Report of the Working Group on Discipline in the Fishing Industry*, 10; Cluett, interview. Jeremy Tunstall also discovered that younger men tended to be the heavier drinkers; *Fishermen*, 136.
28. "Discussion with Royal National Mission to Deep Sea Fishermen, Committee of Inquiry into Trawler Safety," *Committee Papers and Agendas*, BT 149/2; Rev. Leslie Yelland, interview by Linda Brayton and David Masters, "Toward an Oral History of Cape Ann.
29. Tunstall, *Fishermen*, 137.
30. *Sunday Citizen*, June 5, 1966, 3. See also: R. S. F. Schilling, "Hazards of Deep-Sea Fishing," *British Journal of Industrial Medicine* 28 (1971): 27–35; R. S. F. Schilling, "Trawler

Fishing: An Extreme Occupation," *Proceedings of the Royal Society of Medicine* 59 (May 1966): 405–10.

31. "Discussion with Dr. Oliver G. Edholm, Department of Physiology, Medical Research Council, Committee of Inquiry into Trawler Safety, 17 October, 1968," BT 149/2.
32. "Discussion with Dr. R .S. W. Moore, 31 December, 1968," BT 149/3.
33. "Discussion with Transport and General Workers' Union, May 20, 1968," BT 149/2.
34. Alan Derickson, *Dangerously Sleepy: Overworked Americans and the Cult of Manly Wakefulness* (Philadelphia: University of Pennsylvania Press, 2014); Richard Wells, "The Labor of Reality TV: The Case of the 'Deadliest Catch,'" *Labor: Studies in Working Class History of the Americas* 12, no. 4 (2015): 33–49.
35. "Inter-Departmental Memo, to Jack Jones, Assistant Executive Secretary, from Peter Henderson, National Secretary," December 20, 1966, Correspondence, Modern Records Centre, University of Warwick 126/TG/818/B/121–1 (hereafter cited as MRC); "Letter to Ted Birkett, National Secretary, from S.W. Mills, Assistant District Organizer, Grimsby, November 11, 1957," MRC 126/TG/818/18 (S46/1). See also Tunstall, *Fishermen*, 150–55.
36. "Report to Ted Birkett, from J. O'Donnell, Branch Secretary, Fleetwood, December 4, 1957," MRC 126/TG/818/18 (S46/1).
37. *Financial Times*, February 8, 1971, 2; "Discussion with Transport and General Workers' Union, May 20, 1968."

CHAPTER 3: Trade Union Development

1. "The Fisherman's Union of the Atlantic," undated memorandum, box 11, folder 4, Henry Wise Papers, Historical and Special Collections, Harvard Law School Library (hereafter cited as Henry Wise Papers).
2. Joseph A. McCartin, *Labor's Great War: The Struggle for Industrial Democracy and the Origin of Modern Labor Relations, 1912–1921* (Chapel Hill: University of North Carolina Press, 1997); Colin J. Davis, *Power At Odds: The 1922 Railroad Shopmen's Strike* (Urbana: University of Illinois Press, 1997), 34–47.
3. Lizabeth Cohen, *Making a New Deal: Industrial Workers in Chicago, 1919–1939* (New York: Cambridge University Press, 1990); Joshua B. Freeman, *In Transit: The Transport Workers Union in New York City, 1933–1966* (Philadelphia: Temple University Press, 2001).
4. "Agreement, 1940, Atlantic Fishermen Union (hereafter cited as AFU) and "The Federated Boats of New England and New York, Inc.," box 11, folder 6, Henry Wise Papers.
5. "Findings of Fact and Conclusions: Federated Fishing Boats and Atlantic Fishermen's Union," December 18, 1944, box 11, folder 6, Henry Wise Papers; "Dissenting Opinion and Recommendations," John J. Murphy, January 22, 1945, box 11, folder 6, Henry Wise Papers.
6. Nelson Lichtenstein, *Labor's War at Home: The CIO in World War II* (Philadelphia: Temple University Press, 2003); Sally M. Miller and Daniel A. Cornford, *American Labor in the Era of World War II* (Westport, CT: Praeger, 1995).

7. *Boston Traveler*, April 10, 1946.
8. *Boston Post*, April 9, 1946; *Boston American*, April 8, 1946, 11.
9. *Boston Post*, April 17, 1946, 13.
10. *Boston Post*, April 23, 1946.
11. "Uniform Trawler Agreement," May 23, 1946, box 9, folder 11, Henry Wise Papers. The stipulation that captains were to be union members was clearly stated, "it is agreed that only Captains who are members of the said Union will be hired as Captains." "Letter to Commissioner William F. Burke," U.S. Conciliation Service, U.S. Department of Labor and AFU from Template Letter of Company or Corporation, Agreement of May 23, 1946, box 15, folder 8, Henry Wise Papers.
12. Melvyn Dubofsky and Foster Rhea Dulles, *Labor in America: A History* (Wheeling, IL: Harlan Davidson, 1993), 343–62; Norman Dolnick, "Packing House Workers Face the Cold War: A Memoir," *Labor History* 28, no. 4 (1997): 492–507.
13. *Boston Traveler*, February 20, 1947.
14. *Boston Herald*, February 22, 1947.
15. "Commonwealth of Massachusetts v. Patrick J. McHugh, et al.," box 13, folder 3, Henry Wise Papers; "Atlantic Fishermen Union vs. Clarence A. Barnes," District Court of the U.S., box 13, folder 3, Henry Wise Papers.
16. *Seafarers Log*, October 1960, 18.
17. *Seafarers Log*, August 1960, 18.
18. *Seafarers Log*, September 1960, 16; *Seafarers Log*, October 1960, 18.
19. *Seafarers Log*, October 1960, 18.
20. *Seafarers Log*, November 1960, 18.
21. *Seafarers Log*, November 1960, 18.
22. *Seafarers Log*, February 1961, 18.
23. *Seafarers Log*, May 1961, 18.
24. *Seafarers Log*, August 1961, 8.
25. *Seafarers Log*, June 1961, 18.
26. *Seafarers Log*, August 1961, 8.
27. *Seafarers Log*, August 1961, 8.
28. Howard W. Nickerson, interview, New Bedford Whaling Museum Research Library.
29. Ibid.
30. *Seafarers Log*, June 1961, 18; Nickerson, interview.
31. *Seafarers Log*, undated, 1963, 4.
32. *Seafarers Log*, undated, 1964, 4.
33. *Seafarers Log*, undated, 1964.
34. *Seafarers Log*, undated, 1964.
35. *Seafarers Log*, April 15, 1966, 2; *Gloucester Daily Times*, February 24, 1966, 1.
36. *Gloucester Daily Times*, April 11, 1966, 1.
37. *Seafarers Log*, September 30, 1966, 3.
38. *Seafarers Log*, October 28, 5.
39. *Seafarers Log*, November 11, 1966, 2.
40. "National Committee Reports and Volumes, 1960–61," April 9, 1965, Modern Records Centre, University of Warwick 126/TG/818/A (61195/8) (hereafter cited as MRC).

41. National Committee Report, April 20, 1960, MRC 126/TG/818/A.
42. National Committee Report, October 12, 1960, 5, MRC 126/TG/818/A.
43. National Joint Industrial Council for the Trawler Fishing Industry, Grimsby Port Committee, Minutes, March 11, 1960, 1–2, MRC 126/TG/818/c/2 (S46/3).
44. *Report of the Committee of Inquiry into the Fishing Industry*, January 1961, HMSO, Cmnd. 1266, 52.
45. National Committee Reports: February 20, 1961; August 29, 1961; and April 18, 1962, MRC 126/TG/818/A.
46. Minutes of the Fishing Section, Transport and General Workers' Union (TGWU), April 15, 1964, MRC 126/TG/818/A; National Committee Report, January 16, 1963, MRC 126/TG/818/A. The structural problem of a floating and casual workforce was evidenced as early as the early 1880s. Grimsby fishermen were difficult to organize because of the men being out fishing and only home for only a few days. Michaela Barnard, "Trade Unionism in Grimsby's Trawling Industry, 1850–1970," in *Politics and People in the North Atlantic Fisheries since 1485*, ed. David Starkey et al.(University of Hull Press, 2003), 108.
47. National Committee Reports: February 20, 1961; October 17, 1962; and June 16, 1963, MRC 126/TG/818/A.
48. National Committee Report, April 9, 1965, MRC 126/TG/818/A.
49. National Joint Industrial Council for the Trawler Fishing Industry, Minutes, January 1957–July 1963, MRC 126/TG/818/B2/ (S46/2), October 10, 1958.
50. National Joint Industrial Council for the Trawler Fishing Industry, Grimsby Port Committee, January 1952–November 1963, MRC 126/TG/818/c/2/ (S46/3), September 25, 1961; National Joint Industrial Council for the Trawler Fishing Industry, Minutes, January 1957–July 1963, MRC 126/TG/818/B2/ (S46/2), September 19, 1962. For TGWU further attempts to get owners to address the protective clothing issue, see National Joint Industrial Council for the Trawler Industry, Workpeople's Sides-Minutes, January 1957–November 1963, MRC 126/TG/818/B1/ (S46/2), Workpeople's Sides-Minutes, May 31, 1962; Workpeople's Sides-Minutes, September 18, 1962; January 30, 1963.
51. National Joint Industrial Council for the Trawler Fishing Industry, Grimsby Port Committee, January 1952–November 1963, MRC 126/TG/818/c/2/ (S46/3), January 18, 1963; MRC 126/TG/818/c/2/ (S46/3), May 17, 1963.
52. National Joint Industrial Council for the Trawler Fishing Industry, Hull Port Committee, Minutes, December 1957–October 1963, MRC 126/TG/818/C/3/(S46/3), February 14, 1963; National Joint Industrial Council for the Trawler Fishing Industry, Aberdeen Port Committee, Minutes, January 1957–May 1963, MRC 126/TG/818/C (S46/3), November 1, 1963. The Aberdeen men would eventually get a 5 percent discount for their purchases of protective clothing. National Committee Report, April 15, 1963, MRC 126/TG/818/A.
53. Minutes of the Fishing Section, TGWU, April 15, 1964, MRC 126/TG/818/A.
54. Inter-Departmental Memo from Peter Henderson to Jack Jones, December 20, 1966, MRC 126/TG/818/B/S121–1, Corre-NJIC.
55. TGWU-Fishing Section, November 1966, Revision of the Merchant Shipping Acts, 1–9, Board of Trade, British National Archives, London 149/22.

56. Ibid., 10.
57. Memorandum from A. W. Wood, Board of Trade, to J. K. L. Taylor, Ministry of Labor, October 30, 1967, LAB 10/2862, British National Archives, London.
58. *Yorkshire Post*, March 10, 1967.
59. National Joint Industrial Council for the Trawler Fishing Industry, Minutes, January 1963–May 1968, May 31, 1967 Meeting, MRC 126/TG/818/B2/LBR; National Joint Industrial Council for the Trawler Fishing Industry, Trade Union Side Minutes, 1946–1968, May 31, 1967, MRC 126/TG/818/B1/(1/2001/13).
60. National Joint Industrial Council for the Trawler Fishing Industry, Trade Union Side Minutes, 1946–1968, February 14, 1968, MRC 126/TG/818/B1/(1/2001/13).
61. Laurie Oliver (secretary of Hull Trawler Officer's Guild) to Jack Jones, April 5, 1968, MRC 126/TG/818/B/S121–1, Corre-NJIC.

CHAPTER 4: The Wives' Campaign

1. Seamen Missions had long been established in seafaring communities on both sides of the Atlantic. Initially they were founded by clergy and ship owners, John L. Duthie, "Philanthropy and Evangelicism among Aberdeen Seamen, 1814–1924," *Scottish Historical Review* 63, no. 176 (October 1984): 163–69. See also Roald Kverndal, *Seamen's Missions: Their Origin and Early Growth* (Pasadena, CA: William Carey Library, 1986). For contemporary activities of the Royal National Mission to Deep Sea Fishermen, see "Sinking Leaves Communities Mourning Their Loss," *Guardian*, December 13, 1990, 3.
2. *Hull Daily Mail*, January 25, 1968, 1.
3. *Hull Daily Mail*, January 29, 1968, 1.
4. *Daily Mail*, January 31, 1968, 1.
5. Obituary, *Guardian*, September 13, 1988, 39.
6. Yvonne Blenkinsop, interview, July 16, 2008. This interview, and others with Hull women, is archived at the Hull University Maritime Center.
7. Ibid.
8. *Daily Mail*, February 3, 1968, 5.
9. Mary Denness, interview, July 15, 2008.
10. Ibid.
11. Denness, interview.
12. Ibid.
13. Blenkinsop, interview.
14. Denness, interview.
15. Ibid.
16. *Daily Mail*, February 3, 1968, 1.
17. *Daily Mail*, February 23, 1968, 8.
18. Blenkinsop, interview. It was considered superstitious for fishermen's wives to say goodbye to their husbands.
19. Telegram from Jack Jones, Transport and General Workers' Union (TGWU), to Prime Minister Harold Wilson, January 31, 1968, Ministry of Agriculture and Fisheries, British National Archives 209–2791 (hereafter cited as MAF); telegram from Wilson to Jones, February 1, 1968, MAF 209–2791.

20. *Daily Mail*, February 6, 1968, 1.
21. Denness, interview.
22. Ibid.
23. *Daily Mail*, February 5, 1968, 5.
24. Denness, interview.
25. *Daily Mail*, February 6, 1968, 1.
26. "Opening Remarks for Minister, Meeting With Trawlerman and Wives, February 6," MAF 209–2791; Memorandum of Meeting from David Andrews, private secretary to the Prime Minister, to David F. Williamson, February 5, 1968, MAF 209–2791.
27. "Trawler Losses: Note of a Meeting on 6th February," 1968, MAF 209–2791.
28. Ibid.
29. "Trawler Losses."
30. *Daily Mail*, February 7, 1968, 8
31. *Hull Daily Mail*, February 8, 1968, 5; Denness, interview.
32. *Hull Daily Mail*, February 15, 1968.
33. *Hull Daily Mail*, February 16, 1968, 8.
34. *Hull Daily Mail*, February 19, 1968, 1; *Hull Daily Mail*, February 20, 1968, 5.
35. *Hull Daily Mail*, February 21, 1968, 1.
36. Denness, interview; Blenkinsop, interview.
37. *Hull Daily Mail*, February 21, 1968, 1; *Hull Daily Mail*, February 22, 1968, 1.
38. *Hull Daily Mail*, February 22, 1968, 9.
39. *Hull Daily Mail*, February 24, 1968, 5.
40. Ibid.
41. Blenkinsop, interview.
42. *Hull Daily Mail*, February 24, 1968, 5.
43. Denness, interview.
44. Blenkinsop, interview; Denness, interview.
45. *Daily Mail*, March 9, 1968, 5.
46. Denness, interview.

CHAPTER 5: The Cod Wars

1. Benno Wasserman, "The Cod War," *Contemporary Review* 225 (July 1974): 11–12.
2. David Anderson, *Modern Law of the Sea: Selected Essays* (Boston: Matinus Nijhoff, 2008), 8–9; Gudni Thorlacius Jóhannesson, "How 'Cod War' Came: The Origins of the Anglo-Icelandic Fisheries Dispute, 1958–61," *Historical Research* 77 (November 2004): 545–46.
3. Richard A. Barnes, "The Law of the Sea, 1850–2010," in *A History of the North Atlantic Fisheries, Volume 2: From the 1850s to the Early Twenty-First Century*, ed. David J. Starkey and Ingo Heidbrink (Bremen: Hauschild 2012), 187–93.
4. The British had argued that a six-mile limit could be acceptable but this was dismissed by the Icelandic delegation. Even NATO officials got involved in mediating the dispute but to no avail. Jóhannesson, "How 'Cod War' Came," 550–65.
5. "Confidential Memorandum to Reykjavik from Foreign Office, April 23, 1958," Foreign Office, British National Archives 371/134959 (hereafter cited as FO).
6. Wasserman, "Cod War," 7–13.

7. "Instructions to Skippers of British Fishing Vessels, June 3, 1958," Ministry of Agriculture and Fisheries, British National Archives 209/432 (hereafter cited as MAF).
8. Icelandic Coast Guards taken aboard HMS *Eastbourne*—Summary of Case, R. H. Ellingworth, September 30, 1958, FO 371/134991. The *Thor*'s crew was eventually landed in Iceland.
9. Confidential memo from Paul Gilchrist to Foreign Office, September 3, 1958, FO 371/134982; Confidential memo from Gilchrist to Foreign Office, September 4, 1958, FO 371/134982.
10. "HM Royal Navy Report to Admiralty, September 11, 1958," FO 371/134991; "HM Royal Navy Report to Admiralty," September 10, 1958, FO 371/134991.
11. Restricted message to Admiralty from HMS *Diana*, September 26, 1958, FO 371/134991.
12. Ibid.
13. "Message to Icelandic Government from Ambassador Gilchrist, October 1, 1958," FO 371/134991.
14. "Telegram to Foreign Office from Gilchrist, November 1, 1958," FO 371/134994.
15. Report of Kipper of *S.T. Hackness*, November 24, 1958, FO 371/135001; Report of Skipper of *S.T. St. Just*, November 24, 1958, FO 371/135001.
16. Report of Kipper of *S.T. Hackness*, November 24, 1958, FO 371/135001; Hackness Incident—Narrative and Transcript from tape recorder, December 1, 1958, FO 371/135001.
17. "Text of Additional Information by Captain of the *Thor*, December 5, 1958," FO 371/13502; "Letter to Icelandic Prime Minister from Ambassador Gilchrist, December 4, 1958," FO 371/13502; "Telegram to FO from Ambassador Gilchrist, December 3, 1958," FO 371/13502.
18. Jóhannesson, "How 'Cod War' Came," 570.
19. Ibid., 573.
20. Guðmundur Guðmundsson, "The Cod and the Cold War," *Scandinavian Journal of History* 31 (June 2006): 99–102; Robb Robinson, *Trawling: The Rise and Fall of the British Trawl Industry* (Exeter: University of Exeter Press, 1996) , 230–35.
21. "Parliamentary question and answer to Parliamentary Secretary to the Admiralty, Mr. Orr-Ewing, March 3, 1959," FO 371/143128.
22. Jóhannesson, "How 'Cod War' Came," 573. Arthur H. Dean, "The Second Geneva Law of the Sea: The Fight for Freedom of the Seas," *The American Journal of International Law* 54, no. 4 (October 1960), 777–82.
23. Letter from Captain W. Dennis Welch, secretary of Grimsby Trawler Officers' Guild, to Peter Henderson, national secretary, fishery section of Transport and General Workers' Union (TGWU), January 15, 1960, Modern Records Centre, University of Warwick 126/TG/818/19 (S46/1) (hereafter cited as MRC); letter from Henderson to G.H. Harker, secretary of Grimsby Steam Vessels Engineers' & Firemen's Union, January 18, 1960, MRC 126/TG/818/19 (S46/1).
24. Letter to R. Head, regional secretary of Grimsby TGWU, November 3, 1960, MRC 126/TG/818/B/121–1.
25. "Circular to Fishing Port Officers from Peter Henderson, September 29, 1960," MRC 126/TG/818/19 (S46/1).
26. National Committee Reports, Fishery Section, TGWU, April 20, 1960, MRC 126/

TG/818/A (61195/8); National Committee Reports, October 12, 1960, MRC 126/TG/818/A (61195/8).

27. Peter Henderson to Edward Birkett, October 27, 1960, MRC 126/TG/818/19 (S46/1).
28. Circular from Henderson to Port Officers, November 14, 1960, MRC 126/TG/818/19 (S46/1).
29. Meeting with representatives of the Fishing Industry, October 10, 1960, MAF 255/432.
30. Meeting with representatives of the Fishing Industry, October 10, 1960, MAF 255/432; Meeting with representatives of the work peoples' side, October 25, 1960, MAF 255/432.
31. Henderson to Birkett, October 27, 1960.
32. Letter from Robert Head, regional secretary of Hull TGWU, to Henderson, November 2, 1960, MSS 126/TG/818/19 (S46/1).
33. Guðmundsson, "Cod and the Cold War," 101; Hannes Jónsson, *Friends in Conflict: The Anglo-Icelandic Cod Wars and the Law of the Sea* (Connecticut: Shoe String Press, 1982).
34. Guðmundsson, "Cod and the Cold War," 101.
35. "Extraordinary meeting with Peter Henderson in Hospital, Basil Engholm, February 24, 1961," MAF 255/432.
36. "Meeting with Trawler Officers' Representatives, February 24, 1961," MAF 255/432.
37. "Circular to Fishing Port Officers from Henderson, March 2, 1961," MRC 126/TG/818/19/(S46–1); Henderson to Jan Sigurdsson, March 22, 1961, MRC 126/TG/818/19/(S46–1). Henderson was responding to Sigurdsson's message that the "harmful and irritating dispute between our two countries has been brought to an end and now belongs to history . . . and it would be desirable if a closer and better connection could be established between the trade union movements of both countries in the future." Sigurdsson to Henderson, March 13, 1961, MRC 126/TG/818/19/(S46–1).
38. National Committee Reports, May 26, 1961, 1, MRC 126/TG/818/A(61195/8); National Committee Reports, August 29, 1961, 2, MRC 126/TG/818/A(61195/8).
39. National Committee Reports, September 10, 1962, MRC 126/TG/818/A(61195/8).
40. National Committee Reports, June 16, 1963, MRC 126/TG/818/A(61195/8); National Committee Reports, January 19, 1966, MRC 126/TG/818/A(61195/8).
41. "Draft—Iceland-Assessment of Economic Damage, February 21, 1972," Icelandic Fishery Dispute, 1971, MAF 209/3054.
42. Ibid.
43. "Draft—Iceland-Assessment."
44. "Owners' Instructions to Skippers: Fishing at Iceland from September 1, 1972," MAF 209/3108.
45. Ibid.
46. "Owners' Instructions to Skippers."
47. "Incidents off Iceland Involving UK Trawlers, September 1, 1972 Onwards," MAF 209/3110.
48. Ibid.
49. Testimony of Skipper T. Watson, October 3, 1972, Icelandic Fisheries Dispute, Record of Incidents, MAF 209/3105.

50. "Gunboat Incidents," MAF 209/3105.
51. Statement by Skipper A. Buschini of M/T Robert Hewett, undated, MAF 209/3105; "Gunboat Incidents," MAF 209/3105.
52. "Additional Notes of Remarks by Skippers A. H. Vickers & A. Buschini," undated, MAF 209/3105.
53. "Vickers & A. Buschini," ibid.
54. "M/T Aldershot-Collision with Icelandic Patrol Vessel 'Aegir' 10.18.72-Statement made by Skipper Edward I. Collins, November 11, 1972," MAF 209/3105.
55. Icelandic Embassy to prime minister, October 18, 1972, MAF 209/3105.
56. "Incidents off Iceland involving UK Trawlers, September 1, 1972 Onwards," MAF 209/3110.
57. "Iceland Incident-*Brucella* March 16, 1973," MAF 209/3107; Letter from the British Embassy, Iceland, to Icelandic Ministry of Foreign Affairs, March 7, 1973, MAF 209/3107.
58. "Report on Collision Between S.T. Arsenal and the M.VC. Aldershot, by Skipper of Aldershot," MAF 209/3105; Statement made by Skipper J. Loades of S/T Arsenal, MAF 209/3107.
59. Report of meeting between Skipper Blackburn and J. Rhydderch, district inspector of fisheries, April 3, 1973, MAF 209/3107.
60. "Iceland Incident: St. Leger, M. G. Jennings, Fishery Officer, April 10, 1973," MAF 209/3108.
61. *Hull Daily Mail,* March 23, 1973, 1.
62. "Restricted Report from HMS *Leopard,*" July 2, 1973, MAF 209/1308.
63. Report from William E. Brown, defence commander of *Lloydsman,* to Mr. Jeffrey, chief inspector of fisheries, August 8, 1973, MAF 209–3109.
64. "Record of Incidents During Trawler Support Exercise, September 10, 1973," MAF 209–3109.
65. Telex report from HMS *Lynx,* September 1973, MAF 209–3109.
66. Flash Telex from Iceland Embassy in London, August 30, 1973, MAF 209–3109; Report from Ministry of Agriculture and Fisheries official P. G. Jeffrey, September 10, 1973, MAF 209–3109.
67. *Hull Daily Mail,* August 31, 1973, 1; *Hull Daily Mail,* September 1, 1973, 1.
68. *Hull Daily Mail,* September 3, 1973, 1; *Hull Daily Mail,* September 8, 1973, 1.
69. *Hull Daily Mail,* October 2, 1973, 1.
70. *Hull Daily Mail,* October 2, 1973, 1; *Hull Daily Mail,* October 3, 1973, 1.

CHAPTER 6: New England Fishermen and Foreign Competition

1. John N. Morris, *Alone at Sea: Gloucester in the Age of the Dorymen, 1623–1939* (Jaffrey, NH: David R. Godine, 2014).
2. W. Jeffrey Bolster, *The Mortal Sea: Fishing the Atlantic in the Age of Sail* (Cambridge, MA: Belknap, 2012), 238–48.
3. Helen M. Razwadowski, *The Sea Knows No Boundaries: A Century of Marine Science under ICES* (Seattle: University of Washington Press, 2002), 9–41.
4. Emory D. Anderson, "The History of Fisheries Management and Scientific Advice—

the ICNAF/NAFO History from the End of World War II to the Present," *Journal of Northwest Atlantic Fishery Science* 23 (1998): 77–80; David Cushing, "The Atlantic Fishery Commissions," *Marine Policy* 1, no. 3 (1977): 231.

5. Rozwadowski, *Sea Knows No Boundaries*, 166–67; Anderson, "History of Fisheries Management," 76.
6. *Report of the Thirteenth Annual Meeting of the International Commission for the Northwest Atlantic Fisheries, June 3–7, 1963* (Halifax, N.S., Canada, 1963), 3.
7. *Report of the Bureau of Commercial Fisheries for the Calendar Year 1962* (Washington, D.C.: U.S. Government Printing Office, 1964), 10.
8. Loyal G. Bouchard, "Overall View of Soviet Fisheries in 1963, with Emphasis on Activities off U.S. Coasts," *Commercial Fisheries Review* (November 1964): 15–18; *Report of the Bureau of Commercial Fisheries for the Calendar Year 1967* (Washington, D.C.: U.S. Government Printing Office, 1969), 19–24; *Commercial Fisheries Review* (January 1966): 40–41; *Commercial Fisheries Review* (February 1966): 25–26; *Commercial Fisheries Review* (March 1966); *Commercial Fisheries Review* (May 1966): 83–84; *Commercial Fisheries Review* (May 1967): 10–25 ; *Commercial Fisheries Review* (January 1968). For drop-in fish landings, see "Food and Fish Situation," *Annual Review*, U.S. Bureau of Commercial Fisheries (May 1968, May 1969), 22–37 and (June 1970), 21.
9. Loyal G. Bouchard, "Overall View of Soviet Fisheries in 1963, with Emphasis on Activities off U.S. Coasts," *Commercial Fisheries Review, Supplement* (November 1964): 15.
10. Commander Adrian L. Lonsdale, U.S. Coast Guard, "'No Contest' on the Fishing Grounds," *Commercial Fisheries Review* (October 1968): 41–42.
11. Bouchard, "Overall View of Soviet Fisheries," 16–17.
12. Lonsdale, "'No Contest,'" 41; *Commercial Fisheries Review* (November 1967): 45–46.
13. "Foreign Fishing off U.S. Coasts in November 1967," *Commercial Fisheries Review* (January 1968): 38.
14. *Report of the Bureau of Fisheries for the Calendar Year 1964* (Washington, D.C.: U.S. Government Printing Office, 1966), 14–15.
15. *Report of the Bureau of Fisheries for the Calendar Year 1963* (Washington, D.C.: U.S. Government Printing Office, 1965), 8.
16. *Report of the Bureau of Fisheries for the Calendar Year 1964*, 122.
17. *Report of the Bureau of Fisheries for the Calendar Year 1965* (Washington, D.C.: U.S. Government Printing Office, 1967), 52.
18. *Report of the Bureau of Fisheries for the Calendar Yea 1966* (Washington, D.C.: U.S. Government Printing Office, 1968), 64.
19. *Seafarers Log*, January 1961, 18.
20. "Northwest Atlantic Fishing Effort," *Commercial Fisheries Review* (May 1966): 84.
21. "18th Annual ICNAF Meeting," *Commercial Fisheries Review* (September 1966): 37.
22. "Foreign Fishing Off U.S. Coasts in August, (1967)," *Commercial Fisheries Review* (October 1967): 16.
23. "Foreign Fishing off U.S. in June (1968)," *Commercial Fisheries Review* (July 1968): 18–19.
24. "Georges Bank Survey Shows More Cod, Fewer Haddock," *Commercial Fisheries*

Review (March 1968): 3; "1967 New England Landings Show Ups and Downs," *Commercial Fisheries Review* (June 1968): 7.

25. "U.S. Fishermen Caught 4.1 Billion Pounds in 1968," *Commercial Fisheries Review* (April 1969): 2; Lonsdale, "'No Contest,'" 40.
26. "Foreign Fishing Off U.S. in June, 1969," *Commercial Fisheries Review* (August–September 1969): 16; "Foreign Fishing Off U.S. Coast, September 1969," *Commercial Fisheries Review* (November 1969): 16; "Foreign Fishing Off U.S., October 1969," *Commercial Fisheries Review* (December 1969): 21.
27. "Review of Possible Conservation Actions for the ICNAF Area," *ICNAF Annual Proceedings for the Year 1964-65* (Dartmouth, N.S., Canada, 1965), 6.
28. "Opening of the Meeting," *ICNAF Annual Proceedings for the Year 1970–71* (Dartmouth, N.S., Canada, 1972), 19.
29. "Statement of James Ackert," "Fishing Vessel Construction," and "Fishing Vessel Subsidies," Hearings before the Subcommittee on Fisheries and Wildlife Conservation, Committee on Merchant Marine and Fisheries, U.S. House of Representatives, 88th Cong., 1st Sess., 62–63.
30. Elliot Carlson, "A Trawler's Voyage Points up U.S. Fishermen's Problems," *Commercial Fisheries Review* (November 1969): 26.
31. "Testimony of Manuel Lewis and Keith Hasting," Hearings on Fishing in Territorial Waters, Subcommittee of Merchant Marine and Fisheries Subcommittee, Committee of Commerce, U.S. Senate, 88th Cong., 1st Sess., 98, 41.
32. "Testimony of Howard Nickerson," "Fishing Vessel Construction," Hearings before the Merchant Marine and Fisheries Subcommittee, Committee of Commerce, U.S. Senate, 88th Cong., 1st Sess., 90.
33. Ibid.
34. "Commercial Fishing has World Role, says Interior undersecretary Black," *Commercial Fisheries Review* (November 1967): 30; "BCF Director Urges Resurgence of U.S. Fisheries," *Commercial Fisheries Review* (December 1967): 4–5; *Report of the Bureau of Commercial Fisheries for the Calendar Year 1967*, 5.
35. Lonsdale, "'No Contest,'" 44.
36. *ICNAF Annual Proceedings for the Year 1971–72* (Dartmouth, N.S., Canada, 1972), 19.
37. *ICNAF Annual Report for the Year 1973–74* (Dartmouth, N.S., Canada, 1974), 62.
38. "Testimony of Gerry Lovasco, vice president of United Fishermen's Wives Organization, Gloucester," Hearings before the Subcommittee on Energy, Natural Resources, and the Environment of the Committee on Commerce, U.S. Senate, 91st Cong., 2nd Sess., 195; "Statement of United Fishermen's Wives Organization, New Bedford," Hearing before Subcommittee on Oceans and Atmosphere of the Committee of Commerce, U.S. Senate, 93rd Cong., 2nd Sess., 923.

CHAPTER 7: Fishermen's Wives and Territorial Expansion

1. Fran Danowski, "Fishermen's Wives: Coping with an Extraordinary Occupation" Marine Advisory Service, University of Rhode Island, *Marine Bulletin* 37 (1980); Valerie G. Hall, "Differing Gender Roles: Women in Mining and Fishing Communities in Northumberland, England, 1880–1914," *Women's Studies International Forum*

27 (2004): 521–30; Reginald Byron, "The Maritime Household in Northern Europe," *Comparative Studies in Society and History* 36, no. 2 (April 1994): 271–92; Ellen Antler, "Women's Work in Newfoundland Fishing Families," *Atlantis* 2, no. 2 (Spring 1977): 106–13; Marian Binkley and Victor Thiessen, "'Ten Days a 'Grass Widow'—Forty Eight Hours a Wife': Sexual Division of Labor in Trawlermen's Households," *Culture* 8 (January/December 1988): 39–50; Richard Dixon et al., "Fisherman's Wives: A Case Study of a Middle Atlantic Fishing Community," *Sex Roles* 10, no. 1 (1984): 33–52.

2. Sarah L. Henderson and Alana S. Jeydel, *Participation and Protest: Women and Politics in a Global World* (New York: Oxford University Press, 2007); see also Sonia E. Alvarez, *Engendering Democracy in Brazil: Women's Movements in Transition Politics* (Princeton: Princeton University Press, 1990).
3. Suzanne Staggenborg, "The 'Meso' in Social Movement Research," in *Social Movements: Identity, Culture, and the State,* ed. David Meyer, Nancy Whittier & Belinda Robnett (New York: Oxford University Press, 2002). As Staggenborg states, "connections among activists from different movements are an important feature of meso organization that can lead to awareness of political opportunities, resources, and the growth of a movement" (130).
4. The term "political entrepreneurs" is borrowed from Charles Tilly, *Social Movements, 1768–2004* (Boulder: Paradigm, 2004), 13.
5. *Seafarers Log,* May 1969, 19.
6. For Parson quote, undated newspaper clipping from *Gloucester Daily Times,* Gloucester Fishermen's Wives Association Papers, box 2, folder 9, Schlesinger Library, Radcliffe College, Harvard University (hereafter Gloucester Fishermen's Wives Association Papers); Commercial Fishermen's Wives Association of Brookings, Oregon, undated first newsletter, box 2, folder 9, Gloucester Fisherman's Wives Association Papers.
7. *Boston Globe,* July 23, 1986, 46.
8. *Yankee Magazine,* March 1978.
9. Gerri Lovasco, in discussion with the author, August 2, 2012.
10. *Pisces,* October 1969, Gloucester Fishermen's Wives Association Papers.
11. *Pisces-2,* Gloucester Fishermen's Wives Association Papers.
12. *Pisces,* undated, box 22, folder 6, Gloucester Fishermen's Wives Association Papers.
13. "Fisheries Legislation, 1969–70," Hearing before the Subcommittee on Energy, Natural Resources, and the Environment of the Committee on Commerce, 91 Cong., 1st and 2nd Sess. (1970), 143.
14. Ibid., 155–56.
15. Lovasco, discussion.
16. "Fisheries Legislation, 1969–70," 195.
17. Ibid., 196; Lovasco, discussion.
18. United Fishermen's Wives Organization of Gloucester, 1971, box 2, folder 9, Gloucester Fishermen's Wives Association Papers.
19. *Gloucester Daily Times,* undated.
20. *Gloucester Daily Times,* undated.
21. *Cape Ann Summer Sun,* August 22, 1997.
22. *Whole Life Times,* September and October 1980, 19.

23. *North Shore*, February 28, 1981.
24. Grace Favazza, in discussion with the author, August 3, 2012. Transcript in possession of author.
25. Margaret Favazza, in discussion with the author, August 3, 2012; Rosalie Laiachino, in discussion with the author, August 3, 2012.
26. Margaret Favazza, discussion.
27. Grace Favazza, discussion; Margaret Favazza, discussion
28. "Transcript of Interview, Program 13, NBC, March 31, 1978," Gloucester Fishermen's Wives Association Papers.
29. *Yankee Magazine*, March 31, 1978.
30. *Gloucester Daily Times*, June 7, 1978; *Gloucester Daily Times*, October 21, 1978.
31. *NEMAS-106*, November–December 1979.
32. *Gloucester Daily Times*, undated.
33. Laiachino, discussion.
34. "Transcript of Interview, Program 13, NBC, March 31, 1978," Gloucester Fishermen's Wives Association Papers.
35. *Gloucester Daily Times*, undated.
36. *Boston Globe*, July 23, 1986.
37. Lovasco, discussion.
38. "Commercial Fisheries," Hearings before the Subcommittee on Fisheries and Wildlife Conservation, 92nd Cong., 1st Sess., 553. In all, from February to late May 1971, fourteen incidents of damaged lobster gear had been reported.
39. "Statement of Joseph S. Graziano, president of Prelude Corporation," "Commercial Fisheries," Hearings before the Subcommittee on Fisheries and Wildlife Conservation, 92nd Cong., 1st Sess. (May 20, 1971), 555.
40. "Statement of Frank M. Clark, representative of Pennsylvania," Subcommittee on Coast Guard of the Committee of Merchant Marine and Fisheries, U.S. House of Representatives, 92nd Cong., 2nd Sess. (October 6, 1972), 145.
41. "Statement of Joseph S. Graziano, president of Prelude Corporation," Subcommittee on Coast Guard of the Committee of Merchant Marine and Fisheries, U.S. House of Representatives, 92nd Cong., 2nd Sess. (October 6, 1972), 160.
42. "Testimony of Russell T. Norris" and "Statement of Robert H. Steel," Subcommittee on Coast Guard of the Committee of Merchant Marine and Fisheries, U.S. House of Representatives, 92nd Cong., 2nd Sess. (October 6, 1972), 171–75.
43. "Testimony of Howard Nickerson, Seafood Dealers Association of New Bedford," "Testimony of Jacob Dykstra, president of Point Judith Fishermen's Cooperative," and "Testimony of Hugh O'Rourke, executive secretary of Boston Fisheries Association," Subcommittee on Coast Guard of the Committee of Merchant Marine and Fisheries, U.S. House of Representatives, 92nd Cong., 2nd Sess. (October 6, 1972), 177, 230, and 237, respectively.
44. *Hearings before the Senate Subcommittee on Oceans and Atmosphere*, 93 Cong., 1st Sess., 65–69.
45. "Statement of Ted Stevens, senator," Hearings before the Senate Subcommittee on Oceans and Atmosphere, 93 Cong., 2nd Sess. (April 26, 1974), 812.
46. "Statement of Senator John O. Pastore," Hearings before the Senate Subcommittee on Oceans and Atmosphere, 93 Cong., 2nd Sess. (May 13, 1974), 833; "Statement of

Senator Edward Kennedy," Hearings before the Senate Subcommittee on Oceans and Atmosphere, May 14, 1974, 93 Cong., 2nd Sess. (May 14, 1974), 869.

47. "Testimony of Austin Skinner, New Bedford Fishermen's Union," Hearings before the Senate Subcommittee on Oceans and Atmosphere, 93 Cong., 2nd Sess., 916–17; "Statement by United Fisherman's Wives Organization," Hearings before the Senate Subcommittee on Oceans and Atmosphere, 93 Cong., 2nd Sess., 922–23.
48. "Transcript of Interview, Program 13, NBC, March 31, 1978," box 4, part 3 of 4, Gloucester Fishermen's Wives Association Papers.
49. *Gloucester Daily Times*, August 14, 1974, 5; Salvatore J. Favazza, executive secretary of Fisheries Commission, City of Gloucester, to Bernard E. Delay, assistant secretary for employment standards, Department of Labor, August 30, 1974, box 2, part 1 of 4, Gloucester Fishermen's Wives Association Papers; Michael Harrington, representative, to Bernard E. DeLury, June 18, 1974, box 2, part 1 of 4, Gloucester Fishermen's Wives Association Papers.
50. Sarah Weckel Hays, "The Effects of the 200 Mile United States Fishing Zone," *Louisiana Law Review* 37 (Spring 1977), 37.
51. "Testimony of Jacob Dykstra, president, Point Judith Fishermen's Cooperative Association," Hearings before the House Committee on Merchant Marine and Fisheries, 93 Cong., 2nd Sess., *Legislative History*, 47.
52. "Testimony of Patrick Harrington, New Bedford Fishermen's Union," Hearings before the House Committee on Merchant Marine and Fisheries, 93 Cong., 2nd Sess., *Legislative History*, 516.
53. "Testimony of Howard Nickerson, on behalf of ICNAF advisors," Hearings before the House Committee on Merchant Marine and Fisheries, 93 Cong., 2nd Sess., *Legislative History*, 556; "Testimony of Greg Mayhey and skipper of *Ion*, Boston, Massachusetts," Hearings before the House Committee on Merchant Marine and Fisheries, 93 Cong., 2nd Sess., *Legislative History*, 568.
54. Sarah Weckel Hays, "The Effects of the 200-Mile United States Fishing Zone," *Louisiana Law Review* 37, no. 4 (Spring 1977): 858.
55. *Gloucester Daily Times*, February 10, 1979, 4. The president of Avon, Marion Mann, declined Novello's invitation to join her for a fish dinner. Marion Mann to Lena Novello, February 2, 1976, Gloucester Fishermen's Wives Association Papers.

CHAPTER 8: The Final Cod War

1. For British attitudes on territorial limits, see Robb Robinson, "The Evolution of Some Key Elements of British Fisheries Policy," *International Journal of Maritime History* 9, no. 2 (December 1997): 129–50.
2. *News From Iceland*, September, 1975, 1.
3. Memorandum from Robert Lowson, August 19, 1975, Ministry of Agriculture and Fisheries, British National Archives 209/3175 (hereafter cited as MAF).
4. "Strictly Confidential—Owners' Instructions to Skippers: Fishing at Iceland from 13 November 1975," MAF 209/3175.
5. Record of Incidents, Iceland, November/December 1975, Ministry of Defence, British National Archives 24/927 (hereafter cited as DEFE).
6. *Hull Daily Mail*, November 19, 1975, 1.

7. *Hull Daily Mail*, November 20, 1975, 1.
8. *Hull Daily Mail*, November 20, 1975, 12.
9. *Hull Daily Mail*, November 25, 1975, 1.
10. Record of Incidents, Iceland, November/December 1975, DEFE 24/927.
11. *Hull Daily Mail*, December 4, 1975, 5.
12. *Hull Daily Mail*, December 22, 1975, 1.
13. Record of Incidents, Iceland, November/December 1975, DEFE 24/927; Record of Incidents, Iceland, January 1976, DEFE 24/927; *Hull Daily Mail*, December 31, 1975, 1. Captain Guðmunder Kjærnsted was described by trawler skippers as the "Mad Axman" for his aggressive tactics.
14. Record of Incidents, Iceland, November/December 1975, DEFE 24/927; Record of Incidents, Iceland, January 1976, DEFE 24/927.
15. Record of Incidents, January 1976, DEFE, 24/929.
16. *Hull Daily Mail*, January 2, 1976, 18.
17. Guðmundur Guðmundsson, "The Cod and the Cold War," *Scandinavian Journal of History* 31 (June 2006): 110.
18. "Note on Scientific Disagreement," January 25, 1976, Foreign and Commonwealth Office 73/414 (hereafter cited as FCO); "The State of the Icelandic Cod Stocks," January 25, 1976, FCO 73/414; "International Commission for the Northwest Atlantic Fisheries," January 25, 1976, FCO 73/414.
19. Confidential memorandum from Patrick Hugh, private secretary to Prime Minister Wilson, to Ewen Ferguson, January 24, 1976, FCO 73/414.
20. *Hull Daily Mail*, January 29, 1976, 1; *Hull Daily Mail*, January 30, 1976, 1.
21. Confidential telegram from James Callaghan, foreign secretary, to British Embassy, February 3, 1976, DEFE 24/1666.
22. Confidential telegram from Millard to British Embassies, January 19, 1976, DEFE 24/1665.
23. Confidential telegram to British Embassies in Reykjavík, New York, Dublin, Stockholm, and Brussels, February 6, 1976, DEFE 24/1666; "Loose Minutes, Government Subgroup-Icelandic Fisheries Dispute, February 6, 1976," DEFE 24/1666.
24. Record of Incidents, January–May 1976, DEFE 24/929.
25. Memorandum from James Callaghan to Harold Wilson, undated, DEFE 24/1665.
26. Record of Incidents, January–May 1976, DEFE 24/929.
27. *Hull Daily Mail*, February 19, 1976, 1; *Hull Daily Mail*, February 28, 1976, 1.
28. Confidential telegram from British Embassy personnel to Ministry of Defence, February 27, 1976, DEFE 24/1666. The Icelandic government also tried to lease U.S. warships but Henry Kissinger "flatly refused Iceland's request." Guðmundsson, "Cod and the Cold War," 110.
29. *Hull Daily Mail*, March 26, 1976, 1.
30. Record of Incidents, January–May 1976, DEFE 24/929.
31. Record of Incidents, January–May 1976, DEFE 24/929.
32. Record of Incidents, January–May 1976, DEFE 24/929; *Hull Daily Mail*, March 30, 1976, 1.
33. Record of Incidents, January–May 1976, DEFE 24/929; Coded telegram report from British Commander, Board of Trade, March 27, 1976, DEFE 24/928.

34. "Undated Memorandum, Roy Mason, Secretary of Defence, Iceland-Rules of Engagement and Move of Designated Fishing Area," DEFE, 24/1667.
35. *Hull Daily Mail,* April 14, 1976, 1.
36. Robert Lowson, "Iceland: Meeting with the Industry, April 27, 1976," April 30, MAF 209/3176, "Report to Shirley Williams, MP, Shadow Secretary for Prices and Consumer Protection, April 28, 1976," MAF 209/3176.
37. Brief for Secretary of State for Defence, Ministerial Group on Fisheries, April 29, 1976, DEFE 24/1667.
38. Record of Incidents, January–May 1976, DEFE 24/929.
39. Iceland, Philip J. Derham, May 3, 1976, MAF 209/3176; *Guardian,* May 4, 1976. See also *Times,* May 4, 1976; *Daily Express,* May 4, 1976; *Daily Telegraph,* May 4, 1976.
40. "Confidential Letter to James Callaghan, Prime Minister, from Fred Peart, Secretary State of Agriculture and Fisheries, May 5, 1976," MAF 209/3176.
41. "Ending the Dispute with Iceland by Orderly Withdrawal, J. T. Masefield, May 7, 1976," FCO 49/667.
42. *Hull Daily Mail,* May 28, 1976, 1.
43. Record of Incidents, January–May 1976, DEFE 24/929.
44. *Hull Daily Mail,* June 2, 1976, 1.

INDEX